Holt Literature and Language Arts

Universal Access
Holt Interactive Reader

Isabel L. Beck, Ph.D., Program Consultant

HOLT, RINEHART AND WINSTON

ISBN 978-0-55-401538-5
ISBN 0-55-401538-2

13 14 15 1689 16 15 14
4500473633

Contents

To the Student ix

A Walk Through the Book x

CHAPTER 1 Setting and Plot xii
Literary and Academic Vocabulary for Chapter 1 1

Preparing To Read: All Summer in a Day 2
Literary Skills Focus: Setting 2
Reading Skills Focus: Sequencing 2
Vocabulary Development 3

Ray Bradbury   Interactive Selection: All Summer in a Day 4
Applying Your Skills 11

Preparing To Read: Wartime Mistakes,
Peacetime Apologies 12
Informational Text Focus: Taking Notes 12
Vocabulary Development 12

Nancy Day   Interactive Selection: Wartime Mistakes,
Peacetimes Apologies 13

Preparing To Read: What a Character:
Iwao Takamoto and His Toons 16
Informational Text Focus: Outlining and Summarizing
Informational Materials 16
Vocabulary Development 16

The World Almanac   Interactive Selection: What a Character:
Iwao Takamoto and His Toons 17
Applying Your Skills 21

Skills Review: Chapter 1 22

CHAPTER 2 Character 24
Literary and Academic Vocabulary for Chapter 2 25

Preparing To Read: The King of Mazy May 26
Literary Skills Focus: Character and Motivation 26
Reading Skills Focus: Visualizing 26
Vocabulary Development 27

Jack London   Interactive Selection: The King of Mazy May 28
Skills Practice: Use a Character Concept Map 38

Applying Your Skills 39

Preparing To Read: Blanca Flor 40

Literary Skills Focus: Characterization 40

Reading Skills Focus: Visualizing 40

Vocabulary Development 41

Angel Vigil   **Interactive Selection: Blanca Flor** 42

Skills Practice: Use a Time Line 62

Applying Your Skills 63

Preparing To Read: Olympic Glory: Victories in History 64

Informational Text Focus: Compare-and-Contrast
Organizational Pattern 64

Vocabulary Development 64

The World Almanac   **Interactive Selection: Olympic Glory:
Victories in History** 65

Applying Your Skills 69

Skills Review: Chapter 2 70

CHAPTER 3   Theme 72

Literary and Academic Vocabulary for Chapter 3 73

Preparing To Read: Ta-Na-E-Ka 74

Literary Skills Focus: Theme and Character 74

Reading Skills Focus: Identifying the Theme 74

Vocabulary Development 75

Mary Whitebird   **Interactive Selection: Ta-Na-E-Ka** 76

Applying Your Skills 87

Preparing To Read: Pet Adoption Application 88

Informational Text Focus: Preparing an Application 88

Vocabulary Development 88

Interactive Selection: Pet Adoption Application 89

Skills Practice: Use a Personal Information Chart 90

Applying Your Skills 91

Skills Review: Chapter 3 92

CHAPTER -4   Forms of Fiction 94

Literary and Academic Vocabulary for Chapter 4 95

Preparing To Read: La Bamba 96

Literary Skills Focus: Forms of Fiction: Identifying the
Characteristics of the Short Story 96

	Reading Skills Focus: Story and Structure	96
	Vocabulary Development	97
Gary Soto	Interactive Selection: La Bamba	98
	Skills Practice: Use a Story Structure Chart	106
	Applying Your Skills	107
	Preparing To Read: The Gold Cadillac	108
	Literary Skills Focus: Forms of Fiction: Identifying the Characteristics of the Novella	108
	Reading Skills Focus: Making and Adjusting Predictions	108
	Vocabulary Development	109
Mildred D. Taylor	Interactive Selection: The Gold Cadillac	110
	Skills Practice: Use a Table	124
	Applying Your Skills	125
	Preparing To Read: Making It Up As We Go	126
	Informational Text Focus: Structural Features of Popular Media: Magazines	126
	Vocabulary Development	126
Jennifer Kroll	Interactive Selection: Making It Up As We Go: The History of Storytelling	127
	Preparing To Read: Iraqi Treasures Hunted	130
	Informational Text Focus: Structural Features of Popular Media: Newspapers	130
	Vocabulary Development	130
Barbara Bakowski	Interactive Selection: Iraqi Treasures Hunted	131
	Skills Practice: Use a Chart	135
	Preparing To Read: CAVE Online	136
	Informational Text Focus: Structural Features of Popular Media: Web Site	136
	Vocabulary Development	136
	Interactive Selection: CAVE Online	137
	Skills Practice: Use a Chart	140
	Applying Your Skills	141
Skills Review: Chapter 4		142

CHAPTER 5 Elements of Poetry 144

Literary and Academic Vocabulary for Chapter 5 145

        Preparing To Read: The Sneetches 146

Literary Skills Focus: Rhythm and Rhyme 146

Reading Skills Focus: Reading a Poem 146

Vocabulary Development 147

Dr. Seuss (Theodor Geisel)   Interactive Selection: The Sneetches 148

Applying Your Skills 153

Preparing To Read: John Henry 154

Literary Skills Focus: Repetition and Refrain 154

Reading Skills Focus: Questioning 155

Interactive Selection: John Henry 156

Applying Your Skills 159

Preparing To Read: Ode to Mi Gato 160

Literary Skills Focus: Figurative Language 160

Reading Skills Focus: Re-reading 160

Vocabulary Development 161

Gary Soto   Interactive Selection: Ode to Mi Gato 162

Skills Practice: Use a Comparison Table 164

Applying Your Skills 165

Skills Review: Chapter 5 166

CHAPTER 6   Biography and Autobiography 168

Literary and Academic Vocabulary for Chapter 6 169

Preparing To Read: *from* The Land I Lost 170

Literary Skills Focus: First Person and Third Person 170

Reading Skills Focus: Analyzing Author's Purpose 170

Vocabulary Development 171

Huynh Quang Nhuong   Interactive Selection: *from* The Land I Lost 172

Skills Practice: Use a Venn Diagram 180

Applying Your Skills 181

Preparing To Read: Storm 182

Literary Skills Focus: Imagery 182

Reading Skills Focus: Analyzing Author's Purpose 182

Vocabulary Development 183

Gary Paulsen   Interactive Selection: Storm 184

Skills Practice: Use an Imagery Table 190

Applying Your Skills 191

Preparing To Read: The Mysterious Mr. Lincoln 192

Literary Skills Focus: Figurative Language 192

	Reading Skills Focus: Distinguishing Between Fact and Opinion	192
	Vocabulary Development	193
Russell Freedman	Interactive Selection: The Mysterious Mr. Lincoln	194
	Skills Practice: Use a Fact and Opinion Chart	198
	Applying Your Skills	199
	Preparing To Read: What Do Fish Have to Do With Anything?	200
	Literary Skills Focus: Symbolism	200
	Reading Skills Focus: Sequencing	200
	Vocabulary Development	201
Avi	Interactive Selection: What Do Fish Have to Do With Anything?	202
	Applying Your Skills	213
	Preparing To Read: All Aboard with Thomas Garrett	214
	Informational Text Focus: Identifying the Main Idea	214
	Vocabulary Development	214
Alice P. Miller	Interactive Selection: All Aboard with Thomas Garrett	215
	Skills Practice: Use a Main Idea Chart	220
	Applying Your Skills	221
Skills Review: Chapter 6		222

CHAPTER 7 Expository Critique: Persuasive Texts and Media

	Expository Critique: Persuasive Texts and Media	224
Literary and Academic Vocabulary for Chapter 7		225
	Preparing To Read: A Surprising Secret to a Long Life: Stay in School	226
	Informational Text Focus: Persuasion	226
	Reading Skills Focus: Evaluating Evidence	226
	Vocabulary Development	226
Gina Kolata	Interactive Selection: A Surprising Secret to a Long Life: Stay in School	227
	Applying Your Skills	231
	Preparing To Read: Oprah Talks About Her South African "Dreamgirls"	232
	Informational Text Focus: Logical and Emotional Appeals	232
	Reading Skills Focus: Evaluating Evidence	232
	Vocabulary Development	232

ABC News Report   **Interactive Selection: Oprah Talks About Her South African "Dreamgirls"** 233

Applying Your Skills 237

Preparing To Read: Start the Day Right! 238

Informational Text Focus: Persuasive Techniques 238

Reading Skills Focus: Evaluating Evidence 238

Vocabulary Development 238

Interactive Selection: Start the Day Right 239

Preparing To Read: Shine-n-Grow: Hair Repair That Really Works! 241

Informational Text Focus: Fallacious Reasoning 241

Reading Skills Focus: Evaluating Evidence 241

Vocabulary Development 241

Interactive Selection: Shine-n-Grow: Hair Repair That Really Works! 242

Preparing To Read: Brain Breeze 245

Informational Text Focus: Propaganda 245

Reading Skills Focus: Analyzing an Author's Purpose 245

Vocabulary Development 245

Interactive Selection: Brain Breeze 246

Applying Your Skills 249

Skills Review: Chapter 7 250

CHAPTER 8   Literary Criticism 252

Literary and Academic Vocabulary for Chapter 8 253

Preparing To Read: The Dog of Pompeii 254

Literary Skills Focus: Credibility and Historical Fiction 254

Reading Skills Focus: Reading for Details 254

Vocabulary Development 255

Louis Untermeyer   **Interactive Selection: The Dog of Pompeii** 256

Skills Practice: Use a Character Evaluation Chart 268

Applying Your Skills 269

Skills Review: Chapter 8 270

Index of Authors and Titles 272

To the Student

A Book for You

A book is like a garden carried in the pocket.
—Chinese Proverb

The more you put into reading, the more you get out of it. This book is designed to do just that—help you interact with the selections you read by marking them up, asking your own questions, taking notes, recording your own ideas, and responding to the questions of others.

A Book Designed for Your Success

Holt Interactive Reader goes hand in hand with *Holt Literature and Language Arts*. It is designed to help you interact with the selections and master important language arts skills.

Holt Interactive Reader has three types of selections: literature, informational texts, and documents that you may encounter in your various activities. All the selections include the same basic preparation, support, and review materials. Vocabulary previews, skill descriptions, graphic organizers, review questions, and other tools help you understand and enjoy the selections. Moreover, tips and questions in the side margins ensure that you can apply and practice the skills you are learning as you read.

A Book for Your Own Thoughts and Feelings

Reading is about *you*. It is about connecting your thoughts and feelings to the thoughts and feelings of the writer. Make this book your own. The more you give of yourself to your reading, the more you will get out of it. We encourage you to write in this book. Jot down how you feel about the selection. Write down questions you have about the text. Note details you think need to be cleared up or topics that you would like to investigate further.

A Walk Through the Book

The *Holt Interactive Reader* is arranged in chapters, just like *Holt Literature and Language Arts*, the book on which this one is based. Each chapter has a theme, or basic idea. The stories, poems, articles, or documents within the chapter follow that theme. Let's look at how the arrangement of *Holt Interactive Reader* helps you enjoy a chapter as a whole and the individual selections within the chapter.

Before Reading the Chapter

Literary and Academic Vocabulary

Literary and academic vocabulary refers to the specialized language that is used to talk about books, tests, and formal writing. Each chapter begins with the literary and academic terms that you need to know to master the skills for that chapter.

Before Reading the Selection

Preparing to Read

From experience, you know that you understand something better if you have some idea of what's going to happen. So that you can get the most from the reading, this page previews the skills and vocabulary that you will see in the reading.

Literary Skills Focus

For fiction selections—stories, poems, and plays—this feature introduces the literary skill that is the focus for the selection. Examples and graphic elements help explain the literary skill.

Reading Skills Focus

Also in fiction selections, this feature highlights a reading skill you can apply to the story, poem, or play. The feature points out why this skill is important and how it can help you become a better reader.

Informational Text Focus

For informational, or nonfiction, selections, this feature introduces you to the format and characteristics of nonfiction texts. Those texts may be essays, newspaper articles, Web sites, employment regulations, application forms, or other similar documents.

Selection Vocabulary

This feature introduces you to selection vocabulary that may be unfamiliar. Each entry gives the pronunciation and definition of the word as well as a sentence in which the word is used correctly.

Word Study

Various activities reinforce what you have learned about the selection's vocabulary.

While Reading the Selection

Background gives you basic information on the selection, its author, or the time period in which the story, essay, poem, or article was written.

Side-Column Notes

Each selection has notes in the side column that guide your reading. Many notes ask you to underline or circle in the text itself. Others provide lines on which you can write your responses to questions.

A Walk Through the Book

Types of Notes

Several different types of notes throughout the selection provide practice for the skills introduced on the Preparing to Read pages. The notes help you with various strategies for understanding the text. The types of side-column notes are

- **Read and Discuss** notes ask you to pause at certain points so that you can think about basic ideas before proceeding further. Your teacher may use these notes for class discussions.
- **Literary Focus** notes practice the skill taught in the Literary Skills Focus feature on the Preparing to Read page. Key words related to the specific skill are highlighted.
- **Reading Focus** notes practice the reading skill from the Preparing to Read page.
- **Language Coach** notes reinforce the language skill found in the Preparing to Read pages of *Holt Literature and Language Arts*.
- **Vocabulary** notes examine selection vocabulary, academic vocabulary, and topics related to how words are used.

After Reading the Selection

Skills Practice

For some selections, graphic organizers reinforce the skills you have practiced throughout the selection.

Applying Your Skills

This feature helps you review the selection. It provides additional practice with selection vocabulary and literary, reading, and informational text focus skills.

After Reading the Chapter

Skills Review

On the first page of the Skills Review, you can practice using the chapter's academic vocabulary and selection vocabulary.

Language Coach

The second Skills Review page draws on the Language Coach skills in the *Holt Literature and Language Arts* Preparing to Read pages. This feature asks you to apply those skills to texts from throughout the chapter.

Writing Activity

You may have found that you need more practice writing. These short writing activities challenge you to apply what you have learned to your own ideas and experiences.

Oral Language Activity

Writing Activities alternate with Oral Language Activities. These features are designed to help you express your thoughts clearly aloud. The features are particularly helpful if you are learning English or if you need practice with Standard English.

Setting and Plot

HRW Photo by Nathan Keay, SMINK, Inc.

Literary and Academic Vocabulary for Chapter 1

achieve (UH CHEEV) *v.:* succeed in getting a good result or in doing something you want.
She hoped to achieve her goal of writing a book and getting it published.

influence (IHN FLU UHNS) *n.:* the ability or power to affect thought, behavior, or development.
Gina's favorite author had a strong influence on her desire to become a writer.

interact (IHN TUHR AKT) *v.:* talk to and deal with others.
Conflict can develop when unfriendly characters interact.

major (MAY JUHR) *adj.:* very large and important, especially compared to other things of a similar kind.
The major plot twist in the novel caught me off guard.

setting (SEH TIHNG) *n.:* where and when the action of a story takes place.
The story depended heavily on the setting, a dense jungle where only wild animals lived.

plot (PLAHT) *n.:* series of related events that make up a story.
The plot of the story focused on what happened before, during, and after the bank robbery.

conflict (KAHN FLIHKT) *n.:* struggle or problem a character faces in a story.
The narrator's main conflict involved his failing grades.

climax (KLY MAKS) *n.:* most exciting part of a story.
The climax of the story was when the tornado hit the town.

Preparing to Read

All Summer in a Day
by Ray Bradbury

LITERARY SKILLS FOCUS: SETTING

Setting is an important part of a story. The **setting** is the location and time in which the story takes place. The **plot** includes all of the events in the story. Sometimes the setting of a story greatly affects the plot, as in the story "All Summer in a Day."

Describe Setting   Written below is an example of the plot of a story. Describe the setting you imagine for such a story.

Plot: *A boy from a rural town in the South dreams of moving out of his hometown to become an actor.*

Setting: _____

READING SKILLS FOCUS: SEQUENCING

The events of the plot take place in a particular order, or **sequence**. As you read "All Summer in a Day," keep track of the sequence of the main events in a chart like this one. Add as many boxes for events as you need. Include a few key details for each event.

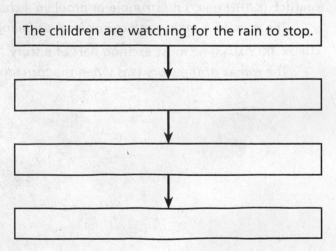

The children are watching for the rain to stop.

Reading Standard 3.3
Analyze the influence of setting on the problem and its resolution.

Vocabulary Development

All Summer in a Day

SELECTION VOCABULARY

frail (FRAYL) *adj.:* not very strong; easily broken.
   The girl was small and frail.

vital (VY TUHL) *adj.:* necessary for life; very important.
   It was vital that everyone see the sun.

consequence (KON SUH KWEHNS) *n.:* importance; result or effect.
   The students realized the consequence of their actions.

surged (SURJD) *v.:* moved forward, as if in a wave.
   The children surged toward the door, eager to escape.

savored (SAY VUHRD) *v.:* delighted in.
   The children savored the chance to play outside.

WORD STUDY

DIRECTIONS: Try to think of an antonym for each vocabulary word below. An antonym has the opposite meaning of the original word. For example, *dull* is an antonym of *sharp*. Use a dictionary if you need help.

Vocabulary Word	Antonym
consequence	1.
savored	2.
vital	3.
surged	4.
frail	5.

ALL SUMMER IN A DAY

by Ray Bradbury

> ### BACKGROUND
> Author Ray Bradbury is known for his imaginative settings. He has written hundreds of stories, set everywhere from Earth to Mars. In "All Summer in a Day," Bradbury uses a real planet—Venus—for the setting. However, he also creates an entirely fictional climate for Venus, one in which it only stops raining for two hours every seven years. It is this setting that sets up the plot of the story for readers.

A VOCABULARY

Word Study

Underline the *simile* on this page. Similes are figures of speech that compare two things that are not otherwise alike. Similes usually include the word *like* or *as*.

"Ready."

"Ready."

"Now?"

"Soon."

"Do the scientists really know? Will it happen today, will it?"

"Look, look; see for yourself!"

10   The children pressed to each other like so many roses, so many weeds, intermixed, peering out for a look at the hidden sun.

It rained.

It had been raining for seven years; thousands upon thousands of days compounded and filled from one end to the other with rain, with the drum and gush of water, with the sweet crystal fall of showers and the concussion[1] of storms so heavy they

20   were tidal waves come over the islands. **A** A thousand forests had

© Digital Art/Corbis

---

1.   **concussion** (KUHN KUH SHUHN): violent shaking or shock.

"All Summer in a Day" by Ray Bradbury. Copyright © 1954 and renewed © 1982 by Ray Bradbury. Reproduced by permission of **Don Congdon Associates, Inc.**

been crushed under the rain and grown up a thousand times to be crushed again. And this was the way life was forever on the planet Venus, and this was the schoolroom of the children of the rocket men and women who had come to a raining world to set up civilization and live out their lives. **B**

"It's stopping, it's stopping!"

"Yes, yes!"

Margot stood apart from them, from these children who could never remember a time when there wasn't rain and rain
30 and rain. They were all nine years old, and if there had been a day, seven years ago, when the sun came out for an hour and showed its face to the stunned world, they could not recall. Sometimes, at night, she heard them stir, in remembrance, and she knew they were dreaming and remembering gold or a yellow crayon or a coin large enough to buy the world with. She knew they thought they remembered a warmness, like a blushing in the face, in the body, in the arms and legs and trembling hands. But then they always awoke to the tatting drum, the endless shaking down of clear bead necklaces upon the roof, the walk,
40 the gardens, the forests, and their dreams were gone. All day yesterday they had read in class about the sun. About how like a lemon it was, and how hot. And they had written small stories or essays or poems about it. **C**

I think the sun is a flower
That blooms for just one hour.

That was Margot's poem, read in a quiet voice in the still classroom while the rain was falling outside.

"Aw, you didn't write that!" protested one of the boys.

"I did," said Margot. "*I did.*"
50 "William!" said the teacher.

But that was yesterday. **D** Now the rain was slackening[2], and the children were crushed in the great thick windows.

"Where's teacher?"

"She'll be back."

"She'd better hurry; we'll miss it!"

---

2. **slackening** (SLA KUH NIHNG): lessening; slowing.

Copyright © by Holt, Rinehart and Winston. All rights reserved.

B **LITERARY FOCUS**

What does this paragraph tell you about the **setting** of the story?

_____

_____

_____

_____

C **VOCABULARY**

Academic Vocabulary

Achieve means "succeed in getting a good result." In this paragraph, the author makes a comparison between Margot and the other children. How does he *achieve* this?

_____

_____

_____

_____

_____

_____

D **READING FOCUS**

In lines 33–50, the author gives us details out of **sequence**. What new information do we learn in these lines?

_____

_____

_____

_____

A READ AND DISCUSS

Comprehension

What are we learning about how the other children view Margot?

B LANGUAGE COACH

Recall that the words characters speak in a story are called **dialogue**. What does the dialogue in lines 65 and 67 tell you about William?

They turned on themselves like a feverish wheel, all tumbling spokes. **A**

Margot stood alone. She was a very frail girl who looked as if she had been lost in the rain for years and the rain had washed 60 out the blue from her eyes and the red from her mouth and the yellow from her hair. She was an old photograph dusted from an album, whitened away, and if she spoke at all her voice would be a ghost. Now she stood, separate, staring at the rain and the loud wet world beyond the huge glass.

"What're *you* looking at?" said William.

Margot said nothing.

"Speak when you're spoken to." He gave her a shove. But she did not move; rather she let herself be moved only by him and nothing else. **B**

70 They edged away from her; they would not look at her. She felt them go away. And this was because she would play no games with them in the echoing tunnels of the underground city. If they tagged her and ran, she stood blinking after them and did not follow. When the class sang songs about happiness and life and games, her lips barely moved. Only when they sang about the sun and the summer did her lips move as she watched the drenched windows.

And then, of course, the biggest crime of all was that she had come here only five years ago from Earth, and she remembered the sun and the way the sun was and the sky was

80 when she was four in Ohio. And they, they had been on Venus all their lives, and they had been only two years old when last the sun came out and had long since forgotten the color and heat of it and the way it really was. But Margot remembered.

"It's like a penny," she said once, eyes closed.

"No, it's not!" the children cried.

"It's like a fire," she said, "in the stove."

"You're lying; you don't remember!" cried the children.

But she remembered and stood quietly apart from all of them and watched the patterning windows. And once, a month ago, she

90 had refused to shower in the school shower rooms, had clutched her hands to her ears and over her head, screaming the water mustn't touch her head. So after that, dimly, dimly, she sensed it, she was different, and they knew her difference and kept away.

There was talk that her father and mother were taking her back to Earth next year; it seemed vital to her that they do so, though it would mean the loss of thousands of dollars to her family. **C** And so, the children hated her for all these reasons of big and little consequence. They hated her pale snow face, her waiting silence, her thinness, and her possible future. **D**

100 "Get away!" The boy gave her another push. "What're you waiting for?"

Then, for the first time, she turned and looked at him. And what she was waiting for was in her eyes.

"Well, don't wait around here!" cried the boy savagely. "You won't see nothing!"

Her lips moved.

"Nothing!" he cried. "It was all a joke, wasn't it?" He turned to the other children. "Nothing's happening today. Is it?"

They all blinked at him and then, understanding, laughed

110 and shook their heads. "Nothing, nothing!"

"Oh, but," Margot whispered, her eyes helpless. "But this is the day, the scientists predict, they say, they know, the sun . . ."

"All a joke!" said the boy, and seized her roughly. "Hey everyone, let's put her in a closet before teacher comes!"

C **VOCABULARY**

Selection Vocabulary
Look at the word *vital*. In Latin, words with the roots *vit-* and *viv-* relate to life. What other words can you think of with these roots? Do they share similar meanings?

_____

_____

_____

_____

D **READ AND DISCUSS**

Comprehension
What is the author explaining to us here?

"No," said Margot, falling back.

They surged about her, caught her up and bore her, protesting, and then pleading, and then crying, back into a tunnel, a room, a closet, where they slammed and locked the door. They stood looking at the door and saw it tremble from her
120   beating and throwing herself against it. They heard her muffled cries. Then, smiling, they turned and went out and back down the tunnel, just as the teacher arrived. **A**

"Ready, children?" She glanced at her watch.

"Yes!" said everyone.

"Are we all here?"

"Yes!"

The rain slackened still more.

They crowded to the huge door.

The rain stopped.
130   It was as if, in the midst of a film concerning an avalanche, a tornado, a hurricane, a volcanic eruption, something had, first, gone wrong with the sound apparatus, thus muffling and finally cutting off all noise, all of the blasts and repercussions and thunders, and then, second, ripped the film from the projector and inserted in its place a peaceful tropical slide which did not move or tremor. The world ground to a standstill. The silence was so immense and unbelievable that you felt your ears had been stuffed or you had lost your hearing altogether. The children put their hands to their ears.

They stood apart. The door slid back and the smell of the
140   silent, waiting world came in to them.

The sun came out.

It was the color of flaming bronze and it was very large. And the sky around it was a blazing blue tile color. And the jungle burned with sunlight as the children, released from their spell, rushed out, yelling, into the springtime. **B**

"Now, don't go too far," called the teacher after them. "You've only two hours, you know. You wouldn't want to get caught out!"

But they were running and turning their faces up to the sky and feeling the sun on their cheeks like a warm iron; they were
150   taking off their jackets and letting the sun burn their arms.

"Oh, it's better than the sun lamps, isn't it?"

"Much, much better!"

They stopped running and stood in the great jungle that covered Venus, that grew and never stopped growing, tumultuously,[3] even as you watched it. It was a nest of octopuses, clustering up great arms of fleshlike weed, wavering, flowering in this brief spring. It was the color of rubber and ash, this jungle, from the many years without sun. It was the color of stones and white cheeses and ink, and it was the color of the moon.

160   The children lay out, laughing, on the jungle mattress and heard it sigh and squeak under them, resilient[4] and alive. They ran among the trees, they slipped and fell, they pushed each other, they played hide-and-seek and tag, but most of all they squinted at the sun until tears ran down their faces; they put their hands up to that yellowness and that amazing blueness and they breathed of the fresh, fresh air and listened and listened to the silence which suspended them in a blessed sea of no sound and no motion. They looked at everything and savored everything. Then, wildly, like animals escaped from their caves, they ran and ran in shouting

170   circles. They ran for an hour and did not stop running.

And then—

In the midst of their running, one of the girls wailed.

Everyone stopped.

The girl, standing in the open, held out her hand.

"Oh, look, look," she said, trembling.

They came slowly to look at her opened palm.

In the center of it, cupped and huge, was a single raindrop.

She began to cry, looking at it.

They glanced quietly at the sky.

180   "Oh. Oh."

A few cold drops fell on their noses and their cheeks and their mouths. The sun faded behind a stir of mist. A wind blew cool around them. They turned and started to walk back toward

---

3.   **tumultuously** (TOO MUHL CHOO UHS LEE): wildly; violently.
4.   **resilient** (RIH ZIHL YUHNT): springy, quick to recover.

C LANGUAGE COACH

Look at the **dialogue** here. Who is speaking in lines 151 and 152?

_____

_____

D READ AND DISCUSS

Comprehension
What has happened here?

Word Study

How do you think the children now feel about locking Margot in the closet? Considering this, write a definition for *solemn*. Use a dictionary to check your answer.

_____

_____

_____

_____

_____

_____

B READ AND DISCUSS

Comprehension

What does this say about the students?

the underground house, their hands at their sides, their smiles vanishing away.

A boom of thunder startled them, and like leaves before a new hurricane, they tumbled upon each other and ran. Lightning struck ten miles away, five miles away, a mile, a half-mile. The sky darkened into midnight in a flash.

190   They stood in the doorway of the underground for a moment until it was raining hard. Then they closed the door and heard the gigantic sound of the rain falling in tons and avalanches, everywhere and forever.

"Will it be seven more years?"

"Yes. Seven."

Then one of them gave a little cry.

"Margot!"

"What?"

"She's still in the closet where we locked her."

200   "Margot."

They stood as if someone had driven them, like so many stakes, into the floor. They looked at each other and then looked away. They glanced out at the world that was raining now and raining and raining steadily. They could not meet each other's glances. Their faces were solemn and pale. They looked at their hands and feet, their faces down. A

"Margot."

One of the girls said, "Well . . . ?"

No one moved.

210   "Go on," whispered the girl.

They walked slowly down the hall in the sound of cold rain. They turned through the doorway to the room in the sound of the storm and thunder, lightning on their faces, blue and terrible. They walked over to the closet door slowly and stood by it.

Behind the closet door was only silence.

They unlocked the door, even more slowly, and let Margot out. B

Applying Your Skills

All Summer in a Day

VOCABULARY DEVELOPMENT

DIRECTIONS: Write words from the Word Box in the correct blanks. Not all words will be used.

Word Box

surged

consequence

frail

savored

vital

The short story "All Summer in a Day" is set on the planet Venus, where readers are told the sun comes out for only two hours every seven years. Margot feels that seeing and feeling the sun is

(1) _____. While living on Venus, she becomes very

(2) _____ and quiet. She longs for Earth, where she

(3) _____ the daily sunlight.

LITERARY SKILLS FOCUS: SETTING

DIRECTIONS: Answer these questions about how the **setting** affects the **plot** and the characters in "All Summer in a Day."

1. How does the constant rain affect the forests on Venus?

_____

2. Margot has memories of the sun from her days on Earth. How does this affect her relationship with the other children?

_____

3. How do the children feel when the rain starts again after briefly stopping?

_____

READING SKILLS FOCUS: SEQUENCING

DIRECTIONS: Put these events from the story in the correct **sequence**. Write the number of each event in the correct order on the blank line below.

1. After it begins raining again, the children head back inside.

2. The children lock Margot in the closet.

3. The children look out the window, waiting for the rain to stop.

4. The children let Margot out of the closet.

5. The children play outside while the sun is out.

_____

Reading Standard 3.3 Analyze the influence of setting on the problem and its resolution.

Wartime Mistakes, Peacetime Apologies

by Nancy Day

INFORMATIONAL TEXT FOCUS: TAKING NOTES

Taking notes while reading nonfiction selections is an excellent way to keep track of many details. To take notes, first read the entire selection once to find the main ideas, or most important points. Write each main idea on its own note card. Then, write details to support each main idea. Your note cards should look like this:

> **Main Idea**
>
> • Supporting detail
>
> • Supporting detail
>
> • Supporting detail

SELECTION VOCABULARY

prescribe (PRIH SKRYB) *v.*: define officially.

Governments often prescribe new laws during wartime.

discretion (DIHS KREHSH UHN) *n.*: authority to make decisions.

I left the decision of where we would go for dinner at her discretion.

compensation (KAHM PUHN SAY SHUHN) *n.*: payment given to make up for a loss or injury.

He received compensation for his broken leg.

rectify (REHK TUH FY) *v.*: correct.

It is difficult to rectify the mistakes of the past.

WORD STUDY

DIRECTIONS: Write words from the list above in the correct blanks below.

The article you are about to read gives an example of what can

happen when officials (1) _____ a law. Under his own

(2) _____, President Roosevelt issued Executive Order 9066

during World War II. Decades later, the Japanese Americans who were forced

into internment camps were given (3) _____ by the U.S.

government. This was done in order to (4) _____ the injustice

of Executive Order 9066.

Reading Standard 2.4
Clarify an understanding of texts by creating outlines, logical notes, summaries, or reports.

WARTIME MISTAKES, PEACETIME APOLOGIES

by Nancy Day, from *Cobblestone Magazine*

Dorothea Lange/National Archive

On March 13, 1942, Yoshiko Imamoto opened her door to face three FBI agents. They let her pack a nightgown and a Bible, then took her to jail while they "checked into a few things." Imamoto had lived in America for twenty-four years. She was a teacher and had done nothing wrong. But a month earlier, President Franklin D. Roosevelt had issued Executive Order 9066, which drastically changed the lives of Imamoto and more than 120,000 other people of Japanese ancestry living in the United States. **A**

10   When Japan bombed Pearl Harbor on December 7, 1941, Japanese Americans were caught in the middle. They felt like

A   **READING FOCUS**

To begin **taking notes,** underline the main idea of this paragraph.

"Wartime Mistakes, Peacetime Apologies" by Nancy Day from *Cobblestone: Japanese Americans,* April 1996. Copyright © 1996 by Cobblestone Publishing, 30 Grove Street, Suite C, Peterborough, NH 03458. All rights reserved. Reproduced by permission of **Carus Publishing Company.**

In the word *prisonlike*, the **suffix** *-like* is used to turn the root word *prison* into an adjective with a similar meaning. Other suffixes, like *–able* and *–ful*, are used the same way. Write a few words ending in *–like*, *–able*, or *–ful*, and compare their meanings to their root words. Are the words similar in meaning?

_____

_____

_____

_____

B **READING FOCUS**

Take notes on this new information by underlining the main idea of this paragraph.

C **READ AND DISCUSS**

Comprehension

What did we learn about Executive Order 9066?

D **VOCABULARY**

Selection Vocabulary

You now know that *lobbying* refers to the way people act to influence public officials. Its root word, *lobby*, can also be used as a noun when talking about politics. What do you think is the definition of *lobby*? Use a dictionary to check your answer.

_____

_____

Americans but looked like the enemy. Neighbors and co-workers eyed them suspiciously. Then Executive Order 9066, issued on February 19, 1942, authorized the exclusion of "any or all persons" from any areas the military chose. The word "Japanese" was never used, but the order was designed to allow the military to force Japanese Americans living near the coast to leave their homes for the duration of the war. Some were allowed to move inland, but most, like Yoshiko Imamoto, were herded into

20 prisonlike camps. **A**

After the war, Japanese Americans tried to start over. They had lost their jobs, their property, and their pride. Some used the Japanese American Evacuation Claims Act of 1948 to get compensation for property they had lost. But it was not until the late 1960s that cries for redress—compensation for all they had suffered—began to emerge. **B**

In 1976, Executive Order 9066 was officially ended by President Gerald Ford. Four years later, President Jimmy Carter signed a bill that created the Commission on Wartime Relocation

30 and Internment of Civilians (CWRIC) to investigate the relocation of Japanese Americans. The CWRIC concluded that Executive Order 9066 was "not justified by military necessity" but was the result of "race prejudice, war hysteria, and a failure of political leadership." In 1983, the commission recommended to Congress that each surviving Japanese American evacuee be given a payment of twenty thousand dollars and an apology. **C**

A bill to authorize the payments was introduced in the House of Representatives in 1983 but met resistance. Intensive lobbying[1] by Japanese Americans was met by arguments that the

40 government had acted legally and appropriately at the time. **D**

Meanwhile, three men who had long since served their jail sentences for refusing to comply with curfew[2] or relocation orders filed suit[3] to challenge the government's actions. The court

---

1. **lobbying** (LAHB EE IHNG): activity aimed at influencing public officials.
2. **curfew** (KUR FYOO): Shortly before the relocation began, the head of the Western Defense Command, Lt. Gen. John DeWitt, set a curfew. Between 8:00 P.M. and 6:00 A.M. each day, "all persons of Japanese ancestry" had to remain indoors, off the streets.
3. **filed suit**: went to court in an attempt to recover something.

President Ronald Reagan signs redress bill.

© Wally McNamee/Corbis

E **READ AND DISCUSS**

Comprehension

How does Yoshiko's story come full circle and connect to the beginning of the selection?

ruled that the government had had no legal basis for detaining Japanese Americans.

The rulings increased pressure to provide redress. In 1988, Congress approved the final version of the redress bill, which became known as the Civil Liberties Act. It was signed by President Ronald Reagan on August 10, 1988. Two years later,
50 Congress funded the payments.

In 1990, at the age of ninety-three, Yoshiko Imamoto opened her door not to FBI agents, but to a small brown envelope containing a check for twenty thousand dollars and an apology from President George Bush. It had taken almost fifty years and the actions of four presidents, but the government had made redress and apologized for its mistakes. **E**

What a Character:
Iwao Takamoto and His Toons

INFORMATIONAL TEXT FOCUS: OUTLINING AND SUMMARIZING INFORMATIONAL MATERIALS

An effective way to organize your notes is to create an **outline**. Creating an outline helps you to organize and easily review **main ideas** and their supporting **details**. Outlines place main ideas on the top levels and details on the lower levels:

I. Main Idea #1

   A. Detail that supports Main Idea #1

      1. Detail that supports Detail A

   B. Detail that supports Main Idea #1

A **summary** is a brief retelling of the main ideas and events in a text. Summaries can be especially helpful if you are doing research from more than one source. You can read your summaries to see how the two sources are similar and how they are different.

A good summary should:

- Be much shorter than the original text.

- Include only the most important points, or **main ideas**, and their **key supporting details**.

SELECTION VOCABULARY

apprentice (UH PREHN TIHS) *n.:* beginner; someone who is just starting to learn a craft or job.
Takamoto was an apprentice to Disney's animators.

instrumental (IHN STRUH MEHN TUHL) *adj.:* helpful in making something happen.
Takamoto was instrumental in Hanna-Barbera's success.

legacy (LEHG UH SEE) *n.:* anything handed down or left for others.
Takamoto's legacy for cartoon fans includes many memorable characters.

WORD STUDY

DIRECTIONS: Write words from the vocabulary list above in the correct blanks to complete the passage.

Iwao Takamoto's first job was as a(n) (1) _____ at

Disney. His work with comical characters was (2) _____ in

the development of popular animation. These characters live on as Takamoto's

(3) _____, influencing other animators.

Reading Standard 2.4
Clarify an understanding of texts by creating outlines, logical notes, summaries, or reports.

WHAT A CHARACTER: IWAO TAKAMOTO AND HIS TOONS

by The World Almanac

© CBS/Photofest, © Everett Collection, Inc.

Animated cartoons—or Toons, as many call them today—aren't just for children any more. Books, magazines, and Web sites are devoted to cartoon trivia, and famous cartoon characters are everywhere in popular culture: on T-shirts, lunch boxes, toys, bedsheets, pajamas, fast foods, and practically any other kind of product you can name. Most of us know certain cartoon characters, but what do we know about the real people behind the Toons—the writers, producers, directors, and, perhaps most importantly, the artists who bring these beloved characters to life?

10 Here's the story of one of those artists, a name from the cartoon world everyone should know: Iwao Takamoto, the animator.

A Journey Begins in Manzanar Ⓐ

You'd never think that a Japanese internment camp near Los Angeles in the early 1940s and a cartoon canine by the name of Scooby-Doo could possibly have any connection to each other, but they do. Ⓑ The connection is animator Iwao Takamoto. His name may not be a household word, but many of his creations are. Takamoto's journey from an internment camp to the world of animation makes for a unique story of creative success.

Ⓐ **READING FOCUS**

Do you think this heading is **a main idea** or a **supporting detail**? Explain your answer.

_____

_____

_____

_____

_____

_____

Ⓑ **VOCABULARY**

Word Study

Internment means "confinement during wartime." Look up *intern* in the dictionary, and write its definition on the following lines.

_____

_____

_____

_____

A **READ AND DISCUSS**

Comprehension

What does the author mean that sometimes good comes from bad situations?

B **READING FOCUS**

Read the section "An Animated Life." On the lines below, create a brief **outline** in which you state the **main idea** of this section and two **supporting details**.

_____

_____

_____

_____

_____

_____

_____

_____

_____

20   Takamoto, a Japanese American, was born in Los Angeles in 1925. By age 15, he had graduated ahead of his high school class. His promising future was put on hold when the Japanese bombed Pearl Harbor in 1941. He and his family were forced into Manzanar Internment Camp, in the desert outside Los Angeles.

Japan had been declared an enemy of war by the United States. Thousands of Japanese and Japanese Americans were shuttled into camps, supposedly for their and the country's protection. But out of bad situations, good sometimes comes, and this was true for Takamoto. **A** While in Manzanar, the teenage

30   Takamoto met some former Hollywood art directors who were interned with him. The men saw his sketches of scenes in the camp and encouraged him to draw. They gave him valuable informal training in illustration.

An Animated Life **B**

In order to escape the camp, Takamoto agreed to become a laborer, picking fruit in Idaho. But it was his drawing talent that freed him in the end. Just two months before the end of World War II, Takamoto contacted Disney Studios and landed an interview. He was not even fully aware of what Disney was or how large it was. Asked to bring his portfolio, he went to a corner store and bought sketchpads and pencils. He had no portfolio of

40   work to show; he had been doing farm labor.

Over a weekend he filled two sketchpads with images, everything he liked to draw "from knights to cowboys." He got a job at Disney Studios on the spot. He became an apprentice, training under famous animators of the day during a Golden Age of animation.

At Disney, Takamoto had the chance to work on cartoon shorts and longer films. In the 1950s, he worked on popular Disney animated films such as *Cinderella, Peter Pan, Lady and the Tramp,* and *Sleeping Beauty.* He learned his craft at Disney but

50   eventually realized that he could go no further there. In 1961, he took what he learned to Hanna-Barbera Studios, a company that

Takamoto at Disney

C **LANGUAGE COACH**

A **pun** (or a play on words) suggests more than one meaning for a word or phrase. Circle the pun in this paragraph. Explain how the author plays with words through this pun.

_____

_____

_____

_____

_____

_____

was energizing TV cartoons with such creations as *Huckleberry Hound*, *Top Cat*, *The Yogi Bear Show*, and *The Flintstones*.

For the next 40 years, Takamoto created art and design for Hanna-Barbera shows, taking a hand in virtually everything they produced, including licensed products and theme park rides. He brought many classic characters to life, including Secret Squirrel and Atom Ant. Later, he was instrumental in *Josie and the Pussy Cats* and other successful cartoon series.

Crazy Canine Characters

60   Takamoto's legacy includes characters of all kinds. But, no bones about it, his four-legged creations are his most memorable. There is Astro, the family dog on *The Jetsons;* the perpetually wheezing pooch Muttley of *The Wacky Races;* and the unforgettable Scooby-Doo of *Scooby-Doo, Where Are You?* a big dog who solves mysteries despite being afraid of practically everything. **C**

By design, the animator made Scooby's appearance all wrong, which was more than all right with his audiences. Takamoto called Scooby-Doo a Great Dane, but most of the
70   details of the cartoon dog's appearance were in fact the *opposite* of that breed's characteristics. "There was a lady that bred Great Danes," he said. "She showed me some pictures and talked about the important points of a Great Dane, like a straight back, straight legs, small chin and such. I decided to go the opposite and give him a hump back, bowed legs, big chin and such. Even his color was wrong."

© Moses Sparks

A READ AND DISCUSS

Comprehension

How did Takamoto approach the creation of cartoons, including Scooby Doo?

B READING FOCUS

On the lines below, write a brief **summary** of the section titled "Crazy Canine Characters."

_____

_____

_____

_____

C READING FOCUS

What is the **main idea** of this article?

_____

_____

_____

_____

_____

D READ AND DISCUSS

Comprehension

How do the author's words "[the] Japanese internment camp seemed to place his future in doubt, but it ended up putting him on the road to lasting success" sum up Takamoto's life as it was presented here?

Takamoto had a sense of humor and a talent for turning what we see, hear, and know into something new. The name Scooby-Doo, for instance, came from a playful refrain[1] in the Frank Sinatra song "Strangers in the Night." Sinatra sings the phrase "scooby-dooby-do" as if it means something. Even nonsense inspired Takamoto. **A B**

Creative Recognition

For Scooby-Doo and other beloved and distinctive creations, Takamoto won the Windsor McKay Lifetime Achievement Award by the International Animated Film Association in 1996. The Japanese American National Museum honored him in 2001, and the Animation Guild gave him their Golden Award in 2005.

Scooby was a breed apart, as was his creator. Takamoto died in 2007 at age 81, but his admirers are still drawing lessons from his spirited ways. Imprisonment in a Japanese internment camp seemed to place his future in doubt, but it ended up putting him on the road to a lasting success. He went from a world of grim and limited reality to a world of fantasy and unlimited imagination in a few short years. His death was a contradiction, too. He died of heart failure, but those who knew him say that, above all, he was full of heart. And that heart lives on in his beloved creations. **C D**

---

1. **refrain** (RIH FRAYN): a phrase or verse repeated during a song.

Applying Your Skills

Wartime Mistakes, Peacetime Apologies *and* What a Character

VOCABULARY DEVELOPMENT

DIRECTIONS: The words listed below are synonyms of vocabulary words. A synonym is a word with a similar meaning to another word. Next to each word below, write the correct synonym from the Word Box. Not all words will be used.

Word Box

discretion	apprentice
prescribe	instrumental
rectify	legacy
compensation	

1. choice _____

2. fix _____

3. helpful _____

4. define _____

INFORMATIONAL TEXT FOCUS: TAKING NOTES, OUTLINING, AND SUMMARIZING INFORMATIONAL MATERIALS

DIRECTIONS: Re-read "Wartime Mistakes, Peacetime Apologies" and "What a Character" and review the **notes** you took on the **main ideas** and **supporting details** of each article. Then make an **outline** for each of these articles. Finally, use your outline to write a **summary** of one of the articles on the following lines.

_____

_____

_____

_____

_____

_____

_____

_____

_____

_____

_____

Reading Standard 2.4
Clarify an understanding of texts by creating outlines, logical notes, summaries, or reports.

Skills Review

Chapter 1

VOCABULARY REVIEW

DIRECTIONS: Match the Chapter 1 academic and selection vocabulary words in the left column with their synonyms, or words with similar meanings, in the right column. Write the letter of each word on the correct blank.

_____ 1. major		**a.** payment
_____ 2. discretion		**b.** define
_____ 3. interact		**c.** affect
_____ 4. rectify		**d.** mingle
_____ 5. compensation		**e.** weak
_____ 6. apprentice		**f.** correct
_____ 7. achieve		**g.** succeed
_____ 8. frail		**h.** heritage
_____ 9. influence		**i.** important
_____ 10. prescribe		**j.** necessary
_____ 11. legacy		**k.** beginner
_____ 12. vital		**l.** choice

Skills Review

Chapter 1

LANGUAGE COACH

Remember that a **pun** is a play on words that suggests more than one meaning for a word or phrase. Puns are often clever or humorous.

DIRECTIONS: Work with a partner and circle three puns in the passage below. Discuss with your partner why you think each is a pun. As you read, look for words or phrases that have to do with one another, and think about the different meanings those words and phrases might have.

Two army men were talking one day. Major Minor said to General Surgery, "General, did you know that I used to be a farmer? I grew almost every kind of vegetable you could imagine!"

"That explains why you were so green when we started working together," said the general. "Did you have any cows?"

"I did, but I sold them all to a friend of mine," replied the major. "I charged him so much that I milked him for all he was worth! I had gotten tired of looking at cows all the time. I wanted something different."

"Did you need the money?" asked the general.

Said the major, "I needed the change."

WRITING ACTIVITY

DIRECTIONS: Suppose that the author of "All Summer in a Day" had chosen Earth as the **setting** of the story. Could the plot have been the same? Write a paragraph explaining why or why not.

_____

_____

_____

_____

_____

_____

_____

2

Character

Found-Object Faces/© Jim Shores

Literary and Academic Vocabulary for Chapter 2

adapt (UH DAPT) *v.:* change ideas or behavior to fit a new situation.

After he moved from California to Alaska, he had to adapt to the freezing weather.

circumstance (SUR KUHM STANS) *n.:* event or condition that affects a person.

Because of her financial circumstance, she could not buy a new car.

obvious (AHB VEE UHS) *adj.:* easy to notice or understand.

A character's personality is sometimes obvious from his or her actions.

qualities (KWAHL UH TEEZ) *n.:* traits; distinguishing characteristics.

The character's qualities included a good sense of humor and a kind manner.

resolution (REHZ UH LOO SHUHN) *n.:* outcome.

In the resolution of the story, the main characters solved their differences and became friends.

The King of Mazy May

by Jack London

LITERARY SKILLS FOCUS: CHARACTER AND MOTIVATION

Why do characters act the way they do in a story? When we ask this question, we are talking about the characters' **motivation**—the reasons for their actions. In "The King of Mazy May," some of the characters' motivation is to get rich. This leads them to try to cheat and steal from other people. The main **character**'s qualities and motivation influence his or her choices and actions. In this way, the character's motivation can become an important part of the plot.

Adventure stories usually have one or more **external conflicts**. This is a conflict between the main character and nature or other characters. In a conflict between characters, the main character, or protagonist, struggles against another character, or antagonist. In "The King of Mazy May," Walt is the protagonist. As you read, think about the effect of Walt's qualities and motivation on the conflict's **resolution**, or outcome.

READING SKILLS FOCUS: VISUALIZING

When you imagine pictures of a story's setting, characters, and action, you are **visualizing**. This can make a story more exciting and easier to understand. As you read "The King of Mazy May," write details about Walt's actions in a concept map like the one below. Add as many ovals as you need.

Reading Standard 3.2
Analyze the effect of the qualities of the character (e.g., courage or cowardice, ambition or laziness) on the plot and the resolution of the conflict.

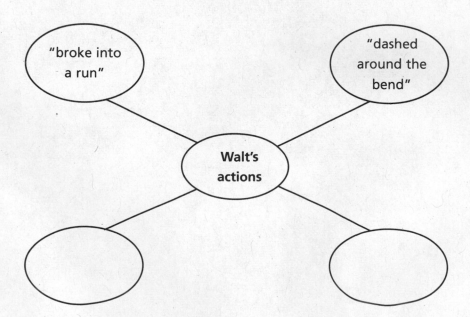

"broke into a run"

"dashed around the bend"

Walt's actions

Vocabulary Development

The King of Mazy May

SELECTION VOCABULARY

adjoining (UH JOY NIHNG) *adj.*: next to.
>   *His claim was the one adjoining Walt's.*

claim (KLAYM) *n.*: piece of land a prospector takes as his or her own.
>   *Walt had to help the old man protect his claim.*

stampede (STAM PEED) *n.*: sudden rush.
>   *A stampede of people arrived in search of gold.*

endured (EHN DURD) *v.*: withstood or held out.
>   *The dogs endured months of freezing weather.*

WORD STUDY

DIRECTIONS: Analogies are comparisons. For each number below, figure out how the first two words are compared and how they are related. Fill in the blank with a vocabulary word that has the same relationship to the remaining word. Here's how you read the analogy in the example: "big is to small as tall is to short." Big and small are opposite sizes. Tall and short are also opposite sizes.

EXAMPLE: big : small :: tall : short

1. won : lost :: _____ : surrendered

2. slice : cake :: _____ : land

3. far : near :: unconnected : _____

THE KING OF MAZY MAY

by Jack London

BACKGROUND

In 1896, gold was discovered in the Klondike region of the Yukon Territory in Canada. People who had been living in the area for years quickly "staked claims" (put stakes in a piece of land and registered it under their name). Many of these long-time residents became quite wealthy, gaining the nickname "Klondike Kings." However, the "Kings" also had to struggle with newcomers, who often tried to "jump," or steal, claims.

A **LITERARY FOCUS**

London begins telling us about the **character** Walt in the first two paragraphs. By learning what he has *not* experienced, what do we learn about Walt?

_____

_____

_____

_____

_____

_____

_____

_____

Walt Masters is not a very large boy, but there is manliness in his make-up, and he himself, although he does not know a great deal that most boys know, knows much that other boys do not know.

He has never seen a train of cars or an elevator in his

© Julian Winslow/Corbis

10 life, and for that matter, he has never once looked upon a corn-field, a plow, a cow, or even a chicken. He has never had a pair of shoes on his feet, or gone to a picnic or a party, or talked to a girl. But he has seen the sun at midnight, watched the ice-jams on one of the mightiest of rivers, and played beneath the northern lights, the one white child in thousands of square miles of frozen wilderness. **A**

Walt has walked all the fourteen years of his life in sun-tanned, moose-hide moccasins, and he can go to the Indian camps and "talk big" with the men, and trade calico and beads

20 with them for their precious furs. He can make bread without baking-powder, yeast or hops, shoot a moose at three hundred

yards, and drive the wild wolf-dogs fifty miles a day on the packed trail.

Last of all, he has a good heart and is not afraid of the darkness and loneliness, of man or beast or thing. His father is a good man, strong and brave, and Walt is growing up like him.

Walt was born a thousand miles or so down the Yukon, in a trading-post below the Ramparts. After his mother died, his father and he came on up the river, step by step, from camp to camp, till now they are settled down on the Mazy May Creek in the Klondike country. Last year they and several others had spent much toil and time on the Mazy May, and endured great hardships; the creek, in turn, was just beginning to show up its richness and to reward them for their heavy labor. **B** But with the news of their discoveries, strange men began to come and go through the short days and long nights, and many unjust things they did to the men who had worked so long upon the creek. **C**

Si Hartman had gone away on a moose-hunt, to return and find new stakes driven and his claim jumped. **D** George Lukens and his brother had lost their claims in a like manner, having delayed too long on the way to Dawson to record them. In short, it was an old story, and quite a number of the earnest, industrious prospectors had suffered similar losses.

But Walt Masters's father had recorded his claim at the start, so Walt had nothing to fear, now that his father had gone on a short trip up the White River prospecting for quartz. Walt was well able to stay by himself in the cabin, cook his three meals a day, and look after things. Not only did he look after his father's claim, but he had agreed to keep an eye on the adjoining one of Loren Hall, who had started for Dawson to record it.

Loren Hall was an old man, and he had no dogs, so he had to travel very slowly. After he had been gone some time, word came up the river that he had broken through the ice at Rosebud Creek, and frozen his feet so badly that he would not be able to travel for a couple of weeks. Then Walt Masters received the news that old Loren was nearly all right again, and about to move on afoot for Dawson, as fast as a weakened man could.

30

40

50

B VOCABULARY

Selection Vocabulary

Endured means "withstood or held out." The author doesn't give many details about the hardships that Walt and his father endured. What do you think these hardships were? Use details in this paragraph to help you.

_____

_____

_____

_____

C READ AND DISCUSS

Comprehension

What is the author setting up for us? **Follow-up:** What seems to be the problem?

D LANGUAGE COACH

Claim is a word with **multiple** or many **meanings**. Which meaning of *claim* is used here? Use a dictionary to help you.

_____

_____

_____

Academic Vocabulary

Obvious means "easy to notice or understand." What is obvious about Walt's personality from his actions in this paragraph?

_____

_____

_____

_____

_____

_____

_____

B   **LITERARY FOCUS**

How does the author use the Irishman's own words to explain his **motivation**?

_____

_____

_____

_____

_____

_____

_____

_____

Walt was worried, however; the claim was liable to be jumped at any moment because of this delay, and a fresh
60   stampede had started in on the Mazy May. He did not like the looks of the newcomers, and one day, when five of them came by with crack dog-teams and the lightest of camping outfits, he could see that they were prepared to make speed, and resolved to keep an eye on them. So he locked up the cabin and followed them, being at the same time careful to remain hidden.

He had not watched them long before he was sure that they were professional stampeders, bent on jumping all the claims in sight. Walt crept along the snow at the rim of the creek and saw them change many stakes, destroy old ones, and set up new ones.

70   In the afternoon, with Walt always trailing on their heels, they came back down on the creek, unharnessed their dogs, and went into camp within two claims of his cabin. When he saw them make preparations to cook, he hurried home to get something to eat himself, and then hurried back. He crept so close that he could hear them talking quite plainly, and by pushing the underbrush aside he could catch occasional glimpses of them. They had finished eating and were smoking around the fire. **A**

"The creek is all right, boys," a large, black-bearded man, evidently the leader, said, "and I think the best thing we can do
80   is to pull out tonight. The dogs can follow the trail; besides, it's going to be moonlight. What say you?"

"But it's going to be beastly cold," objected one of the party. "It's forty below zero now."

"An' sure, can't ye keep warm by jumpin' on the sleds an' runnin' after the dogs?" cried an Irishman. "An' who wouldn'? The creek as rich as a United States mint! Faith, it's an ilegant chanst to be gettin' a run fer yer money! An' if ye don't run, it's mebbe you'll not get the money at all, at all." **B**

"That's it," said the leader. "If we can get to Dawson and
90   record, we're rich men; and there is no telling who's been sneaking along in our tracks, watching us, and perhaps now off to give the alarm. The thing for us to do is to rest the dogs a bit, and then hit the trail as hard as we can. What do you say?"

Evidently the men had agreed with their leader, for Walt Masters could hear nothing but the rattle of the tin dishes which were being washed. Peering out cautiously, he could see the leader studying a piece of paper. Walt knew what it was at a glance—a list of all the unrecorded claims on Mazy May. Any man could get these lists by applying to the gold commissioner at Dawson.

100 "Thirty-two," the leader said lifting his face to the men. "Thirty-two isn't recorded, and this is thirty-three. Come on; let's take a look at it. I saw somebody working on it when we came up this morning."

Three of the men went with him, leaving one man to remain in camp. Walt crept carefully after them till they came to Loren Hall's shaft. One of the men went down and built a fire on the bottom to thaw out the frozen gravel, while the others built another fire on the dump and melted water in a couple of gold-pans. This they poured into a piece of canvas stretched between

110 two logs, used by Loren Hall in which to wash his gold.

In a short time a couple of buckets of dirt were sent up by the man in the shaft, and Walt could see the others grouped anxiously about their leader as he proceeded to wash it. When this was finished, they stared at the broad streak of black sand and yellow gold-grains on the bottom of the pan, and one of them called excitedly for the man who had remained in camp to come. Loren Hall had struck it rich, and his claim was not yet recorded. It was plain that they were going to jump it. **C D**

Walt lay in the snow, thinking rapidly. He was only a

120 boy, but in the face of the threatened injustice against old lame Loren Hall he felt that he must do something. He waited and watched, with his mind made up, till he saw the men begin to square up new stakes. Then he crawled away till out of hearing, and broke into a run for the camp of the stampeders. Walt's father had taken their own dogs with him prospecting, and the boy knew how impossible it was for him to undertake the seventy miles to Dawson without the aid of dogs.

Gaining the camp, he picked out, with an experienced eye, the easiest running sled and started to harness up the

In this paragraph, the author tells you how the men test Loren Hall's claim for gold. Underline the words that help you **visualize** this.

Comprehension
What is happening with Walt here? **Follow-up**: Why doesn't Loren record his claim like Walt's dad did?

Comprehension

How does Walt's plan connect to what we've been saying about Walt's character?

Word Study

What could happen to Walt if only one sled runner is touching the ground? Based on your answer, which word is most likely a synonym for *perilously—dangerously* or *safely*?

_____

_____

_____

_____

130 stampeders' dogs. There were three teams of six each, and from these he chose ten of the best. Realizing how necessary it was to have a good head-dog, he strove to discover a leader amongst them; but he had little time in which to do it, for he could hear the voices of the returning men. By the time the team was in shape and everything ready, the claim-jumpers came into sight in an open place not more than a hundred yards from the trail, which ran down the bed of the creek. They cried out to him, but he gave no heed, grabbing up one of their fur sleeping-robes which lay loosely in the snow, and leaping

140 upon the sled. **A**

"Mush! Hi! Mush on!" he cried to the animals, snapping the keen-lashed whip among them.

The dogs sprang against the yoke-straps, and the sled jerked under way so suddenly as to almost throw him off. Then it curved into the creek, poising perilously on one runner. **B** He was almost breathless with suspense, when it finally righted with a bound and sprang ahead again. The creek bank was high and he could not see, although he could hear the cries of the men and knew they were running to cut him off. He did not dare to think

150 what would happen if they caught him; he only clung to the sled, his heart beating wildly, and watched the snow-rim of the bank above him.

Suddenly, over this snow-rim came the flying body of the Irishman, who had leaped straight for the sled in a desperate attempt to capture it; but he was an instant too late. Striking on the very rear of it, he was thrown from his feet, backward, into the snow. Yet, with the quickness of a cat, he had clutched the end of the sled with one hand, turned over, and was dragging behind on his breast, swearing at the boy and threatening

160 all kinds of terrible things if he did not stop the dogs; but Walt cracked him sharply across the knuckles with the butt of the dog-whip till he let go.

It was eight miles from Walt's claim to the Yukon—eight very crooked miles, for the creek wound back and forth like a snake, "tying knots in itself," as George Lukens said. And

© Colin Hawkins/Getty Images

because it was so crooked, the dogs could not get up their best speed, while the sled ground heavily on its side against the curves, now to the right, now to the left.

170 Travelers who had come up and down the Mazy May on foot, with packs on their backs, had declined to go around all the bends, and instead had made short cuts across the narrow necks of creek bottom. Two of his pursuers had gone back to harness the remaining dogs, but the others took advantage of these short cuts, running on foot, and before he knew it they had almost overtaken him. **C**

"Halt!" they cried after him. "Stop, or we'll shoot!"

But Walt only yelled the harder at the dogs, and dashed round the bend with a couple of revolver bullets singing after him. At the next bend they had drawn up closer still, and the

180 bullets struck uncomfortably near to him; but at this point the Mazy May straightened out and ran for half a mile as the crow flies. Here the dogs stretched out in their long wolf-swing, and the stampeders, quickly winded, slowed down and waited for their own sled to come up.

Looking over his shoulder, Walt reasoned that they had not given up the chase for good, and that they would soon be after him again. So he wrapped the fur robe about him to shut out the stinging air, and lay flat on the empty sled, encouraging the dogs, as he well knew how.

C (LITERARY FOCUS)

What two **external conflicts** does Walt face here?

_____

_____

_____

_____

_____

_____

A **READING FOCUS**

Circle the words that help you to **visualize** the Yukon River in this paragraph.

B **LITERARY FOCUS**

What **external conflict** does Walt face in this paragraph? What does he do to deal with this conflict?

_____

_____

_____

_____

C **VOCABULARY**

Word Study

The word *toiled* may be unfamiliar to you. However, you can probably guess its meaning from its context, or the words around it. By looking at the first three sentences in this paragraph, what do you think *toiled* means?

_____

_____

190   At last, twisting abruptly between two river islands, he came upon the mighty Yukon sweeping grandly to the north. He could not see from bank to bank, and in the quick-falling twilight it loomed a great white sea of frozen stillness. There was not a sound, save the breathing of the dogs, and the churn of the steel-shod sled. **A**

No snow had fallen for several weeks, and the traffic had packed the main-river trail till it was hard and glassy as glare ice. Over this the sled flew along, and the dogs kept the trail fairly well, although Walt quickly discovered that he had made a
200   mistake in choosing the leader. As they were driven in single file, without reins, he had to guide them by his voice, and it was evident the head-dog had never learned the meaning of "gee" and "haw." He hugged the inside of the curves too closely, often forcing his comrades behind him into the soft snow, while several times he thus capsized the sled.

There was no wind, but the speed at which he traveled created a bitter blast, and with the thermometer down to forty below, this bit through fur and flesh to the very bones. Aware that if he remained constantly upon the sled he would freeze to
210   death, and knowing the practice of Arctic travelers, Walt shortened up one of the lashing-thongs, and whenever he felt chilled, seized hold of it, jumped off, and ran behind till warmth was restored. Then he would climb on and rest till the process had to be repeated. **B**

Looking back he could see the sled of his pursuers, drawn by eight dogs, rising and falling over the ice hummocks[1] like a boat in a seaway. The Irishman and the black-bearded leader were with it, taking turn in running and riding.

Night fell, and in the blackness of the first hour or so,
220   Walt toiled desperately with his dogs. **C** On account of the poor lead-dog, they were constantly floundering off the beaten track into the soft snow, and the sled was as often riding on its side or top as it was in the proper way. This work and strain tried

---

1. **ice hummocks** (YS HUH MUHKS): small hills made of ice.

his strength sorely. Had he not been in such haste he could have avoided much of it, but he feared the stampeders would creep up in the darkness and overtake him. However, he could hear them occasionally yelling to their dogs, and knew from the sounds that they were coming up very slowly.

230   When the moon rose he was off Sixty Mile, and Dawson was only fifty miles away. He was almost exhausted, and breathed a sigh of relief as he climbed on the sled again. Looking back, he saw his enemies had crawled up within four hundred yards. At this space they remained, a black speck of motion on the white river-breast. Strive as they would, they could not shorten this distance, and strive as he would he could not increase it.

    He had now discovered the proper lead-dog, and he knew he could easily run away from them if he could only change the bad leader for the good one. But this was impossible, for a

240   moment's delay, at the speed they were running, would bring the men behind upon him.

    When he got off the mouth of Rosebud Creek, just as he was topping a rise, the ping of a bullet on the ice beside him, and the report of a gun, told him that they were this time shooting at him with a rifle. And from then on, as he cleared the summit of each ice-jam, he stretched flat on the leaping sled till the rifle-shot from the rear warned him that he was safe till the next ice-jam.

    Now it is very hard to lie on a moving sled, jumping and

250   plunging and yawing[2] like a boat before the wind, and to shoot through the deceiving moonlight at an object four hundred yards away on another moving sled performing equally wild antics. So it is not to be wondered at that the black-bearded leader did not hit him. **D**

    After several hours of this, during which, perhaps, a score of bullets had struck about him, their ammunition began to give out and their fire slackened. They took greater care, and only

---

2. **yawing** (YAW ɪHNG): turning from a straight course; swerving.

Visualize the scene described in this paragraph. Why can't the black-bearded leader shoot his rifle accurately?

_____

_____

_____

_____

_____

_____

_____

Plump is another example of a word with **multiple meanings**. It is used as an adverb here and means "directly." Write a sentence using *plump* as an adjective.

_____

_____

_____

_____

_____

What is the **resolution** of Walt's conflict?

_____

_____

_____

_____

_____

_____

_____

_____

_____

_____

_____

_____

_____

whipped a shot at him at the most favorable opportunities. He was also beginning to leave them behind, the distance slowly increasing to six hundred yards.

Lifting clear on the crest of a great jam off Indian River, Walt Masters met his first accident. A bullet sang past his ears, and struck the bad lead-dog.

The poor brute plunged in a heap, with the rest of the team on top of him.

Like a flash, Walt was by the leader. Cutting the traces with his hunting knife, he dragged the dying animal to one side and straightened out the team.

He glanced back. The other sled was coming up like an express-train. With half the dogs still over their traces, he cried, "Mush on!" and leaped upon the sled just as the pursuing team dashed abreast of him.

The Irishman was just preparing to spring for him,—they were so sure they had him that they did not shoot,—when Walt turned fiercely upon them with his whip.

He struck at their faces, and men must save their faces with their hands. So there was no shooting just then. Before they could recover from the hot rain of blows, Walt reached out from his sled, catching their wheel-dog by the fore legs in mid-spring, and throwing him heavily. This brought the whole team into a snarl, capsizing the sled and tangling his enemies up beautifully.

Away Walt flew, the runners of his sled fairly screaming as they bounded over the frozen surface. And what had seemed an accident proved to be a blessing in disguise. The proper lead-dog was now to the fore, and he stretched low to the trail and whined with joy as he jerked his comrades along. By the time he reached Ainslie's Creek, seventeen miles from Dawson, Walt had left his pursuers, a tiny speck, far behind. At Monte Cristo Island he could no longer see them. And at Swede Creek, just as daylight was silvering the pines, he ran plump into the camp of old Loren Hall. A B

© Karen Su/Corbis

C READ AND DISCUSS

Comprehension

How does Jack London end the selection? **Follow-up:** What does "the King of Mazy May" refer to?

Almost as quick as it takes to tell it, Loren had his sleeping-furs rolled up, and had joined Walt on the sled. They permitted the dogs to travel more slowly, as there was no sign of the chase in the rear, and just as they pulled up at the gold commissioner's office in Dawson, Walt, who had kept his eyes open to the last, fell asleep.

300   And because of what Walt Masters did on this night, the men of the Yukon have become very proud of him, and always speak of him now as the King of Mazy May. C

The King of Mazy May

USE A CHARACTER CONCEPT MAP

DIRECTIONS: Choose a character in "The King of Mazy May" other than Walt, such as Loren Hall or the Irishman. Complete the concept map below by filling in the ovals with details from the story that tell about this **character** and the character's **motivation**.

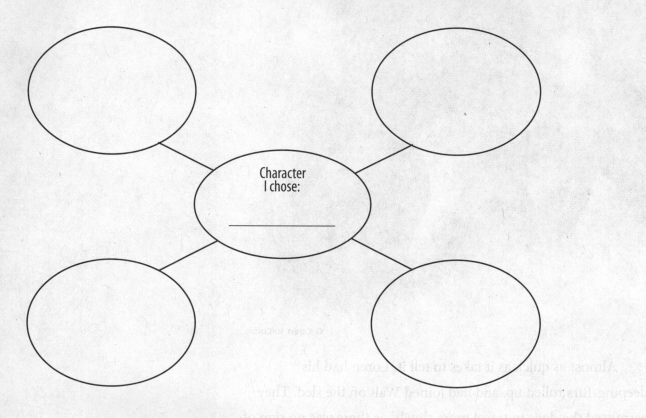

Character I chose:
_____

Applying Your Skills

The King of Mazy May

VOCABULARY DEVELOPMENT

DIRECTIONS: Write words from the Word Box in the correct blanks to complete the passage.

Word Box

- endured
- claim
- stampede
- adjoining

Once gold was found in Canada's Yukon Territory in 1896, there was a(n) (1) _____ of people hoping to strike it rich. The newcomers (2) _____ the harsh weather of the region while they searched for gold. In the story "The King of Mazy May," the main character, Walt, looks after his father's (3) _____. He also keeps an eye on the (4) _____ land, owned by Loren Hall.

LITERARY SKILLS FOCUS: CHARACTER AND MOTIVATION

DIRECTIONS: Give details about each type of **external conflict** that Walt faces.

Type of Conflict	Details
Nature	
Other Characters	

READING SKILLS FOCUS: VISUALIZING

DIRECTIONS: List details from the story that help you **visualize** Walt's actions.

_____

_____

_____

Reading Standard 3.2 Analyze the effect of the qualities of the character (e.g., courage or cowardice, ambition or laziness) on the plot and the resolution of the conflict.

Blanca Flor

by Angel Vigil

LITERARY SKILLS FOCUS: CHARACTERIZATION

The way writers show characters' qualities is called **characterization**. The characters' appearance, speech, actions, thoughts, and feelings are all part of characterization. So are the ways other characters respond to them.

In plays, dialogue—conversation between characters—tells us about the characters' thoughts and feelings. Stage directions—notes in parentheses or brackets that aren't read aloud in a performance—provide more information about characters' actions and reactions. In *Blanca Flor*, a narrator also tells us about the characters and events. The narrator speaks about events but is not a character in the story. However they are shown, characters' qualities can be an important part of a play's or story's plot.

READING SKILLS FOCUS: VISUALIZING

It is a lot harder to imagine what is happening in a play when you are reading it instead of seeing it on stage. In order to **visualize**, or picture what is happening in your mind, pay close attention to dialogue, stage directions, and all of the narrator's descriptions. Use these "clues" to picture everything from the characters' appearances to the setting.

Use the Skill   As you read *Blanca Flor*, complete a chart like the one below, listing the different ways the setting and characters are described. The descriptions you find will not be very specific, so you may have to add to these using your imagination and what you know about the play's characters and actions. Use this chart to help you visualize the play.

Setting	river, middle of the forest, ...
Juanito	
Blanca Flor	young woman, brushes Juanito's hair, ...

Vocabulary Development

Blanca Flor

SELECTION VOCABULARY

valiant (VAL yuhnt) *adj.:* determined; brave.

Juanito made a valiant effort to help Blanca Flor.

barren (BAR uhn) *adj.:* not producing crops or fruit.

Don Ricardo had a barren field.

flourish (FLUR ihsh) *n.:* sweeping movement.

Don Ricardo left with a flourish.

apprehensively (AP rih HEHN sihv lee) *adv.:* fearfully; uneasily.

Blanca Flor looked around apprehensively.

WORD STUDY

DIRECTIONS: Write words from the vocabulary list in the correct blanks to complete the passage. One word will not be used.

In Angel Vigil's play *Blanca Flor*, the main conflict involves Juanito, Blanca Flor, and Don Ricardo. In order to free Blanca Flor, Juanito must complete a series of tasks for Don Ricardo, such as making a(n)

(1) _____ field produce wheat. Although Juanito seems

(2) _____ when faced with his first task, the situation quickly appears impossible. Later in the play there is a chase scene that will have both the reader and Juanito looking (3) _____ over their shoulders.

BLANCA FLOR

by Angel Vigil

BACKGROUND

Angel Vigil based his play *Blanca Flor* on a European tale and Hispanic folktales. Folktales are part of most cultures around the word. The stories are passed down through generations, both by word of mouth and in writing. Fairy tales, legends, fables, and myths are all considered types of folktales.

A READING FOCUS

How well can you **visualize** the characters from these brief descriptions? Why is it not necessary that the writer include a description of The Narrator?

_____

_____

_____

_____

_____

_____

Adapted from "Blanca Flor/White Flower" from *¡Teatro! Hispanic Plays for Young People* by Angel Vigil. Copyright © 1996 by Teacher Ideas Press. Reproduced by permission of Greenwood Publishing Group, Inc., Westport, CT.

Characters

(in order of appearance)

The Narrator

Juanito, a young man

The Duende, a gnome-like, mischievous creature who lives in the forest

Blanca Flor, a young woman

Don[1] **Ricardo,** an evil man

Don Ramon, the father of Juanito

10 **Doña**[2] **Arlette,** the mother of Juanito

Two Doves, actors in costume

Scene 1.
IN THE FOREST.

The Narrator. *Blanca Flor,* "White Flower." There never was a story with such a beautiful name as this story of Blanca Flor. At the beginning of our story, a young man named Juanito has left home to seek his fortune in the world. With the blessing of his parents to aid and protect him, he has begun what will be a fantastic adventure. At the beginning of his journey, he wanders

---

1. **Don** (DOHN): Spanish for "Sir" or "Mr."
2. **Doña** (DOH NYAH): Spanish for "Lady" or "Madam."

into a forest and stops by a stream to rest and eat some of the tortillas his mother had packed for his journey.

20 [JUANITO *enters and walks around the stage as if looking for a comfortable place to rest. He finally decides upon a spot and sits down. He takes out a tortilla from his traveling bag and he begins to talk to himself.*]

Juanito. Whew! I'm hot. This river looks like a good spot to rest for a while. I'm so tired. Maybe this journey wasn't such a good idea. Right now I could be home with *la familia* eating a good supper that *mamacita* cooked for us. **B** But no, I'm out in the world seeking my fortune. So far I haven't found very much, and all I have to show for my efforts are two worn-out feet and a

30 tired body . . . oh, and don't forget (*holding up a dried tortilla*) a dried-out tortilla . . . **C** (*He quickly looks around as if startled.*) What was that? (*He listens intently and hears a sound again.*) There it is again. I know I heard something . . .

[*As* JUANITO *is talking,* THE DUENDE *enters, sneaking up behind him.*]

Juanito. Must be my imagination. I've been out in the woods too long. You know, if you're alone too long, your mind starts to play tricks on you. Just look at me. I'm talking to my tortilla and hearing things . . .

40 **The Duende** (*in a crackly voice*). Hello.
Juanito. Yikes! Who said that! (*He turns around quickly and is startled to see* THE DUENDE *behind him.*) Who are you?
The Duende (*with a mischievous twinkle in his eye*). Hello.
Juanito. Hello . . . who, who are you? And where did you come from?

[THE DUENDE *grabs the tortilla out of* JUANITO'S *hand and begins to eat it. During the rest of the scene* THE DUENDE *continues to eat tortillas.*] **D**

B LANGUAGE COACH

Many English words have come from the Spanish language. Knowing this, what do you think the Spanish words *la familia* and *mamacita* mean?

_____

_____

C LITERARY FOCUS

In this speech, Juanito tells us a little bit about himself. How does this information help **characterize** Juanito?

_____

_____

_____

_____

_____

_____

D LITERARY FOCUS

Sometimes stage directions can help **characterize** characters in plays. What do these stage directions tell you about the Duende that you would otherwise not know?

_____

_____

_____

A READ AND DISCUSS

Comprehension

Why do you think the author has Juanito talk directly to the audience here?

Juanito. Hey, that's my tortilla.

50 **The Duende** (*in a playful manner*). Thank you very much. Thank you very much.

Juanito (*to the audience*). He must be a forest Duende. I've heard of them. They're spirits who live in the wood and play tricks on humans. I better go along with him or he might hurt me. (*He offers* THE DUENDE *another tortilla.* THE DUENDE *takes the tortilla and begins to eat it, too.*) I hope he's not too hungry. If he eats all my tortillas, I won't have any left, and it'll be days before I get food again. I'll have to eat wild berries like an animal. (*He reaches for the tortilla and* THE DUENDE *hits his hand.*) Ouch,

60 that hurt!

The Duende. Looking for work, eh?

Juanito. Now I know he's a Duende. He can read minds. **A**

The Duende. No work here. Lost in the forest. No work here.

Juanito. I know that. We're in the middle of the forest. But I know there'll be work in the next town.

The Duende. Maybe work right here. Maybe.

Juanito. Really. Where?

[THE DUENDE *points to a path in the forest.* JUANITO *stands up and looks down the path.*]

70 **Juanito.** There's nothing down that path. I've been down that path and there is nothing there.

The Duende. Look again. Look again. Be careful. Be careful. (*He begins to walk off, carrying the bag of tortillas with him.*)

Juanito. Hey, don't leave yet. What type of work? And where? Who do I see? Hey, don't leave yet!

The Duende (THE DUENDE *stops and turns*). Be careful. Danger. Danger. (*He exits.*)

Juanito. Hey! That's my bag of tortillas. Oh, this is great. This is really going to sound good when I get back home. My tortillas?

80 . . . Oh, they were stolen by a forest Duende. Not to worry . . . (*He yells in the direction of the departed* DUENDE.) And I'm not lost! . . . This is great. Lost and hungry and no work. I guess I'm

never going to find my fortune in the world. But what did he mean about work . . . and be careful . . . and danger. I've been down that path and there was nothing there . . . I don't think there was anything there. Oh well, there is only one way to find out. It certainly can't get much worse than things are now, and maybe there is work there.

[JUANITO *exits, in the direction of the path* THE DUENDE
90   *indicated.*] **B**

B (READ AND DISCUSS)

Comprehension
What have we learned
so far?

Scene 2.
FARTHER IN THE FOREST.

The Narrator. In spite of the Duende's warning, Juanito continued on the path of danger. As he came into a clearing, he came to a house and saw a young woman coming out of it.

[JUANITO *enters,* BLANCA FLOR *enters from the opposite side of the stage and stops, remaining at the opposite side of the stage.*]

Juanito. Where did this house come from? I was here just yesterday and there was no house here. I must really be lost and turned around. (*He sees the young woman and waves to her.*)
100   Hey! Come here. Over here!

[BLANCA FLOR *runs to* JUANITO.]

Blanca Flor (*with fear in her voice*). How did you find this place? You must leave right away. The owner of this place is gone, but he will return soon. He leaves to do his work in the world, but he will return unexpectedly. If he finds you here, you'll never be able to leave. You must leave right away.
Juanito. Why? I haven't done anything.
Blanca Flor. Please, just leave. And hurry!
Juanito. Who are you? And why are you here?
110   **Blanca Flor.** I am Blanca Flor. My parents died long ago, and I am kept by this man to pay off their debts to him. I have to

Exhaustion means "extreme fatigue." Think of a synonym for *exhaustion*. A synonym is a word that has a similar meaning to another word.

_____

_____

B **LITERARY FOCUS**

What do these stage directions tell you about Don Ricardo's mood? How do these stage directions help with the **characterization** of Don Ricardo?

_____

_____

_____

_____

_____

_____

work day and night on his farm until I can be free. But he is mean, and he has kept prisoner others who have tried to free me. He makes them work until they die from exhaustion. A

Juanito. Who would be so mean?

Blanca Flor. His name is Don Ricardo.

[DON RICARDO *enters, suddenly and with great force.*] B

Don Ricardo (*addressing* JUANITO). Why are you here! Didn't she tell you to leave!

120 **Blanca Flor** (*scared*). Don't hurt him. He is lost in the forest and got here by mistake. He was just leaving.

Don Ricardo. Let him answer for himself. Then I will decide what to do with him.

Juanito (*gathering all his courage*). Yes, she did tell me to leave. But . . . but I am in the world seeking my fortune and I am looking for work. Is there any work for me to do here?

Don Ricardo. Seeking your fortune! They always say that, don't they, Blanca Flor. Well, I will give you the same chance I have given others. For each of three days, I will give you a job. If in

130   three days you have completed the jobs, then you may leave.
       If not, then you will work here with me until you are dead. What
       do you say, fortune-seeker?

       Blanca Flor (*pulling* JUANITO *aside*). Do not say yes. You will
       never leave here alive. Run and try to escape.

       Juanito. But what about you? You are more trapped than
       anybody.

       Blanca Flor. That is not your worry. Just run and try to escape.

       Juanito (*suddenly turning back to* DON RICARDO). I will do the
       work you ask.

140   **Don Ricardo** (*laughing*). Blanca Flor, it is always your fault
       they stay. They all think they will be able to set you free. Well,
       let's give this one his "fair" chance. (*To* JUANITO) Here is your
       first job. See that lake over there? Take this thimble (*he gives a
       thimble to* JUANITO) and use it to carry all the water in the lake
       to that field over there. **C**

       Juanito. You want me to move a lake with a thimble?!

       Don Ricardo. You wanted work, fortune-seeker. Well, this is
       your job. Have it finished by morning or your fate will be the
       same as all the others who tried to save poor Blanca Flor. (*He
150   exits*.) **D**

       Juanito. What type of man is he? I have heard legends of evil
       men who keep people captive, and in my travels I heard many
       stories of young men seeking their fortunes who were never seen
       again, but I always thought they were just stories.

       Blanca Flor. You have had the misfortune to get lost in a terrible
       part of the forest. Didn't anyone warn you to stay away from here?

       Juanito. Yes . . . one person did. But I thought he was a forest
       Duende, and I didn't really believe him.

       Blanca Flor. It was a forest Duende. In this part of the forest
160   there are many creatures with magic. But my keeper, his magic
       is stronger than any of ours.

       Juanito. Ours? . . . What do you mean, ours? Are you part of the
       magic of this forest?

C READ AND DISCUSS

Comprehension

Why is Don Ricardo laughing?
Follow up: Does this action
make his character more
complex, or complicated?
Why or why not?

D VOCABULARY

Academic Vocabulary

What clues does the dialogue
among Juanito, Blanca
Flor, and Don Ricardo give
us about their personality
qualities, or traits?

_____

_____

_____

_____

_____

_____

_____

B READING FOCUS

Re-read Scene 2. What additional stage directions would you add to help the reader better **visualize** the action in the scene?

_____

_____

_____

_____

_____

C LITERARY FOCUS

Compare and contrast the role of The Narrator and the role of stage directions in the play. How do they provide both similar and different information to the reader? How do they help you better understand the **characterization** of the characters?

_____

_____

_____

_____

_____

_____

Blanca Flor. Do not ask so many questions. The day is passing by, and soon it will be morning.

Juanito. Morning. I'm supposed to have moved the lake by then. I know this job is impossible, but while God is in his heaven there is a way. I will do this job. And when I am done, I will help you escape from here.

170 [JUANITO _and_ BLANCA FLOR _exit._] **A** **B**

Scene 3.
THE NEXT MORNING.

JUANITO _and_ BLANCA FLOR _enter. As_ THE NARRATOR _speaks,_ JUANITO _and_ BLANCA FLOR _act out the scene as it is described._

The Narrator. Juanito took the thimble and started to carry the water from the lake. He worked as hard as he could, but soon he began to realize that the job really was an impossible one, and he knew he was doomed. He sat down and began to cry because his luck had abandoned him and because his parents' blessings offered no protection in that evil place. Blanca Flor watched Juanito's valiant effort to move the water. As she watched him 180 crying, her heart was touched, and she decided to use her powers to help him. She knew that it was very dangerous to use her powers to help Juanito and to cross Don Ricardo, but she felt it was finally time to end her own torment. As Juanito cried, Blanca Flor took out her brush and began to brush his hair. She cradled Juanito in her arms and her soothing comfort soon put him to sleep . . . **C**

[_As soon as_ JUANITO _is asleep,_ BLANCA FLOR _gently puts his head down and leaves, taking the thimble with her._]

The Narrator. When Juanito awoke, he frantically looked for the 190 thimble and, not finding it, ran to the lake. When he reached the lake, he stood at its banks in amazement. All the water was gone. He looked over to the other part of the field, and there stood a lake where before there was nothing. He turned to look for Blanca Flor, but instead there was Don Ricardo.

[DON RICARDO *enters.*]

Don Ricardo (*in full force and very angry*). This must be the work of Blanca Flor, or else you have more power than I thought. I know Blanca Flor is too scared to ever use her powers against me, so as a test of your powers, tomorrow your next job
200   will not be so easy. See that barren ground over on the side of the mountain? You are to clear that ground, plant seeds, grow wheat, harvest it, grind it, cook it, and have bread for me to eat before I return. You still have your life now, but I better have bread tomorrow. (*He exits, with a flourish.*) **D** **E**

[JUANITO *exits.*]

Scene 4.
THE NEXT MORNING.

As THE NARRATOR *speaks,* JUANITO *and* BLANCA FLOR *enter and act out the scene as it is described.*

The Narrator. Immediately upon waking the next morning, Juanito tried to move the rocks in the field, but they were
210   impossible to move because of their great size. Once again, Juanito knew that his efforts were useless. He went over to the new lake and fell down in exhaustion. As he lay in the grass by the lake, Blanca Flor came to him once more and began to brush his hair. Soon, Juanito was asleep.

[BLANCA FLOR *exits.*]

The Narrator. As before, when he awoke, Juanito dashed to the field to make one last attempt to do his work. When he got there, he again stopped in amazement. The field was clear of rocks, and the land had been planted and harvested. As he
220   turned around, there stood Blanca Flor.

D **VOCABULARY**

Selection Vocabulary
Although *flourish* is used as a noun here, it can also be used as a verb, meaning "to make bold gestures." Try writing a sentence using the verb form of *flourish*.

_____

_____

_____

E **LITERARY FOCUS**

What does Don Ricardo's *dialogue* here tell us about his relationship with Blanca Flor? How does this information help **characterize** Don Ricardo?

_____

_____

_____

_____

_____

A READING FOCUS

Visualize these directions in parentheses. How do these directions help an audience understand what Juanito is feeling?

_____

_____

_____

B READ AND DISCUSS

Comprehension

What has happened during the last two days?

[BLANCA FLOR *enters.*]

Blanca Flor (*she hands a loaf of bread to* JUANITO). Give this to Don Ricardo.

Juanito. How did you do this?

[DON RICARDO *enters, quickly.*]

Don Ricardo. What do you have?

Juanito (*shaking with fear*). **A** Just . . . just this loaf of bread. (*Giving the bread to* DON RICARDO) Here is the bread you asked for.

230 **Don Ricardo** (*very angry*). This is the work of Blanca Flor. This will not happen again. Tomorrow, your third job will be your final job, and even the powers of Blanca Flor will not help you this time!

(*He exits.*)

Blanca Flor. Believe me, the third job will be impossible to do. It will be too difficult even for my powers. We must run from here if there is to be any chance of escaping his anger. He will kill you because I have helped you. Tonight I will come for you. Be ready to leave quickly as soon as I call for you.

240 [JUANITO *and* BLANCA FLOR *exit.*] **B**

Scene 5.
LATER THAT NIGHT.

On one side of the stage, JUANITO *sits waiting. On the other side,* BLANCA FLOR *is in her room grabbing her traveling bag. As she leaves her room, she turns and mimes spitting three times as* THE NARRATOR *describes the action.*

The Narrator. Late that night, as Juanito waited for her, Blanca Flor packed her belongings into a bag. Before she left the house, she went to the fireplace and spat three times into it.

[BLANCA FLOR *joins* JUANITO.]

Blanca Flor (*quietly calling*). Juanito . . . Juanito.

250 **Juanito.** Blanca Flor, is it time?

Blanca Flor. Yes. We must leave quickly, before he finds out
I am gone, or it will be too late.

Juanito. Won't he know you are gone as soon as he calls for you?

Blanca Flor. Not right away. I've used my powers to fool him.
But it won't last long. Let's go! **C**

[JUANITO *and* BLANCA FLOR *exit.*]

The Narrator. When Don Ricardo heard the noise of Juanito
and Blanca Flor leaving, he called out . . .

Don Ricardo (*from offstage*). Blanca Flor, are you there?

260 **The Narrator.** The spit she had left in the fireplace answered.

Blanca Flor (*from offstage*). Yes, I am here.

The Narrator. Later, Don Ricardo called out again.

Don Ricardo (*from offstage*). Blanca Flor, are you there?

The Narrator. For a second time, the spit she had left in the
fireplace answered.

Blanca Flor (*from offstage*). Yes, I am here.

The Narrator. Still later, Don Ricardo called out again, a
third time.

Don Ricardo (*from offstage*). Blanca Flor, are you there?

270 **The Narrator.** By this time, the fire had evaporated Blanca Flor's
spit, and there was no answer. Don Ricardo knew that Blanca
Flor was gone, and that she had run away with Juanito. He
saddled his horse and galloped up the path to catch them before
they escaped from his land. **D**

Scene 6.
IN THE FOREST.

JUANITO *and* BLANCA FLOR *enter, running and out of breath.*

Juanito. Blanca Flor, we can rest now. We are free.

Blanca Flor. No, Juanito, we will not be free until we are beyond

C  READING FOCUS

At this point in the play, has the way you originally **visualized** Blanca Flor changed? Explain.

_____

_____

_____

D  READ AND DISCUSS

Comprehension
What is this part about?

A READING FOCUS

Given what you already know about Juanito and Blanca Flor, **visualize** what you think will happen in their upcoming journey across Don Ricardo's land. Describe your visualization.

the borders of Don Ricardo's land. As long as we are on his land, his powers will work on us. **A**

280 **Juanito.** How much farther?

Blanca Flor. Remember the river where you met the Duende? That river is the border. Across it we are free.

Juanito. That river is still really far. Let's rest here for a while.

Blanca Flor. No, he is already after us. We must keep going. I can hear the hooves of his horse.

Juanito (*he looks around desperately*). Where? How can that be?

Blanca Flor. He is really close. Juanito, come stand by me. Quickly!

Juanito (*still looking around*). I don't hear anything.

290 **Blanca Flor** (*grabbing him and pulling him to her*). Juanito! Now!

[*As THE NARRATOR describes the action, JUANITO and BLANCA FLOR act out the scene. BLANCA FLOR does not actually throw a brush. She mimes throwing the brush and the action.*]

The Narrator. Blanca Flor looked behind them and saw that Don Ricardo was getting closer. She reached into her bag, took her brush, and threw it behind her. The brush turned into a church by the side of the road. She then cast a spell on Juanito and turned him into a little old bell ringer. She turned herself
300 into a statue outside the church.

[DON RICARDO *enters, as if riding a horse.*]

Don Ricardo (*addressing the bell ringer* [JUANITO]). Bell ringer, have you seen two young people come this way recently? They would have been in a great hurry and out of breath.

Juanito (*in an old man's voice*). No . . . I don't think so. But maybe last week, two young boys came by. They stopped to pray in the church . . . Or was it two girls. I don't know. I am just an old bell ringer. Not many people actually come by this way at all. You're the first in a long time.

310 **Don Ricardo.** Bell ringer, if you are lying to me you will be sorry. (*He goes over to the statue* [BLANCA FLOR], *who is standing very still, as a statue. He examines the statue very closely and then addresses the bell ringer* [JUANITO].) Bell ringer, what saint is this a statue of? The face looks very familiar.

Juanito. I am an old bell ringer. I don't remember the names of all the saints. But I do know that the statue is very old and has been here a long time. Maybe Saint Theresa or Saint Bernadette.

Don Ricardo. Bell ringer, if you are lying, I will be back! (*He exits.*)

Juanito. Adiós, Señor!

320 [BLANCA FLOR *breaks her pose as a statue and goes to* JUANITO.]

Blanca Flor. Juanito, Juanito. The spell is over.

Juanito. What happened? I did hear the angry hooves of a horse being ridden hard.

Blanca Flor. We are safe for a while. But he will not give up, and we are not free yet.

[JUANITO *and* BLANCA FLOR *exit.*] **B**

Scene 7.
FARTHER INTO THE FOREST.

The Narrator. Blanca Flor and Juanito desperately continued their escape. As they finally stopped for a rest, they had their
330 closest call yet.

[BLANCA FLOR *and* JUANITO *enter.*]

Juanito. Blanca Flor, please, let's rest just for a minute.

Blanca Flor. OK. We can rest here. I have not heard the hooves of his horse for a while now.

Juanito. What will he do if he catches us?

Blanca Flor. He will take us back. I will be watched more closely than ever, and you will—

B READ AND DISCUSS

Comprehension
What did you just find out, and what does this say about Blanca Flor?

A **READING FOCUS**

Do the details given here
by The Narrator help you
visualize the action? Explain
your answer.

_____

_____

_____

_____

Juanito (*sadly*). I know. Was there ever a time when you were free? Do you even remember your parents?

340 **Blanca Flor.** Yes. I have the most beautiful memories of my mother, our house, and our animals. Every day, my father would saddle the horses and together we would—

Juanito. Blanca Flor . . . I hear something.

Blanca Flor (*alarmed*). He's close. Very close.

[*As* THE NARRATOR *describes the action,* JUANITO *and* BLANCA FLOR *act out the scene.* BLANCA FLOR *does not actually throw a comb. She mimes throwing the comb and the action.*]

The Narrator. Blanca Flor quickly opened her bag and threw
350 her comb behind her. Immediately the comb turned into a field of corn. This time she turned Juanito into a scarecrow, and she turned herself into a stalk of corn beside him. **A**

[DON RICARDO *enters, as if riding a horse.*]

Don Ricardo. Where did they go? I still think that the bell ringer knew more than he was saying. They were just here. I could hear their scared little voices. Juanito will pay for this, and Blanca Flor will never have the chance to escape again . . . Now where did they go? Perhaps they are in this field of corn. It is strange to see a stalk of corn grow so close to a scarecrow. But

360　this is a day for strange things. (*He exits.*)

Blanca Flor. Juanito, it is over again. Let's go. The river is not far. We are almost free.

[JUANITO *breaks his pose as a scarecrow and stretches and rubs his legs as* BLANCA FLOR *looks around apprehensively.*]

Juanito. Blanca Flor, that was close. We have to hurry now. The river is just through these trees. We can make it now for sure if we hurry.

The Narrator. But they spoke too soon. Don Ricardo had gotten suspicious about the field of corn and returned to it. When he

370　saw Juanito and Blanca Flor he raced to catch them.

[DON RICARDO *enters suddenly and sees them.*]

Don Ricardo. There you are. I knew something was wrong with that field of corn. Now you are mine.

[*As* THE NARRATOR *describes the action,* JUANITO *and* BLANCA FLOR *act out the scene.* BLANCA FLOR *does not actually throw a mirror. She mimes throwing the mirror and the action.*] **B**

The Narrator. When Blanca Flor saw Don Ricardo, she reached into her bag and took out a mirror, the final object in the bag.

380　She threw the mirror into the middle of the road. Instantly, the mirror became a large lake, its waters so smooth and still that it looked like a mirror as it reflected the sky and clouds. When Don Ricardo got to the lake, all he saw was two ducks, a male and a female, swimming peacefully in the middle of the lake. Suddenly, the ducks lifted off the lake and flew away. As

B **VOCABULARY**

Word Study

Even if you do not know the meaning of the word *mime*, you can guess at least part of its definition from context clues, or words surrounding an unfamiliar word that give hints to its meaning. Underline these context clues.

A READING FOCUS

Try to **visualize** the effect you think Don Ricardo's curse will have on Juanito and Blanca Flor. Describe your visualization.

_____

_____

_____

_____

_____

_____

_____

_____

_____

_____

_____

_____

they flew away, Don Ricardo knew that the ducks were Juanito and Blanca Flor, and that they were beyond his grasp. As they disappeared, he shouted one last curse.

[JUANITO *and* BLANCA FLOR *exit.*]

390   **Don Ricardo.** You may have escaped, Blanca Flor, but you will never have his love. I place a curse on both of you. The first person to embrace him will cause him to forget you forever! (*He exits.*) **A** **B**

Scene 8.
NEAR JUANITO'S HOME.

BLANCA FLOR *and* JUANITO *enter.*

The Narrator. Disguised as ducks, Blanca Flor and Juanito flew safely away from that evil land and escaped from Don Ricardo. They finally arrived at Juanito's home, and using Blanca Flor's magical powers, they returned to their human selves.

Juanito. Blanca Flor, we are close to my home. Soon we will be
400   finally safe forever. I will introduce you to my family, and we will begin our new life together . . . Blanca Flor, why do you look so sad? We have escaped the evil Don Ricardo, and soon we will be happy forever.

Blanca Flor. We have not escaped. His final curse will forever be over us.

Juanito. Remember, that curse will work only in his own land. You yourself told me that once we were beyond the borders of his land, his powers would have no hold on us.

Blanca Flor. His powers are very great, Juanito.

410   **Juanito.** Blanca Flor, you have never explained to me the source of your own powers. Are your powers also gone?

Blanca Flor. The powers have always been in the women of my family. That is why Don Ricardo would not let me leave. He was afraid that I would use my powers against him. I have never been away from that land, so I do not know about my powers in this new land.

Juanito. You will have no need for your powers here. Soon we will be with my family. Wait outside while I go and tell my family that I have returned from seeking my fortune, safe at last. Then I will tell them that the fortune I found was you.

Blanca Flor. Juanito, remember the curse.

Juanito. I am not afraid of any curse. Not with you here with me. All my dreams have come true. Come, let's go meet my family.

[JUANITO *and* BLANCA FLOR *exit.*]

Scene 9.
AT JUANITO'S HOME.

DON RAMON *and* DOÑA ARLETTE *are sitting at home passing the time with idle talk.*

The Narrator. Juanito's parents had waited patiently for their son to return from seeking his fortune in the world. They did not know that his return home was only the beginning of another chapter of his great adventure.

Don Arlette. Do you ever think we will hear from Juanito? It has been months since he left to seek his fortune in the world.

Don Ramon. We will hear word soon. I remember when I left home to seek my fortune in the world. Eventually, I found that the best thing to do was return home and make my fortune right here, with my *familia* at my side. Soon he will discover the same thing and you will have your son back.

Doña Arlette. It is easier for a father to know those things. A mother will never stop worrying about her children. **C**

Don Ramon. I worry about the children just as much as you do. But there is no stopping children who want to grow up. He has our blessing and permission to go, and that will be what brings him back safe to us. Soon. You just wait.

How does the author use dialogue to **characterize** Juanito's parents?

_____

_____

_____

_____

_____

A **LANGUAGE COACH**

Even though you are reading this play in English, some Spanish words, such as *mi 'jito*, are included. How do these words add to or take away from your ability to visualize the play?

_____

_____

_____

_____

B **READ AND DISCUSS**

Comprehension

What does the conversation between Juanito and his mother tell you about Don Ricardo's curse?

[JUANITO *enters. His parents are overjoyed to see him.*]

Juanito. Mama! Papa! I am home.

Doña Arlette. ¡Mi 'jito![3]

Don Ramon. Juanito!

450 [*Overjoyed with seeing* JUANITO, *his parents rush and embrace him.*]

Doña Arlette. God has answered my prayers. Mi 'jito has returned home safe. **A**

Don Ramon. Juanito, come sit close to us and tell us all about your adventures in the world. What great adventures did you have?

Juanito. I had the greatest adventures. For the longest time I was unlucky and unable to find work but finally I . . . I . . .

Doña Arlette. What is it? Are you OK? Do you need some food?

Juanito. No, I'm OK. It's just that I was going to say something

460 and I forgot what I was going to say.

Don Ramon. Don't worry. If it is truly important, it'll come back.

Juanito. No, I've definitely forgotten what I was going to say. Oh well, it probably wasn't important anyway.

Doña Arlette. Did you meet someone special? Did you bring a young woman back for us to meet?

Juanito. No, I didn't have those kind of adventures. Pretty much nothing happened, and then I finally decided that it was just best to come home. **B**

470 **Don Ramon** (*to* DOÑA ARLETTE). See what I told you? That is exactly what I said would happen.

Doña Arlette. Now that you are home, it is time to settle down and start your own family. You know our neighbor Don Emilio has a younger daughter who would make a very good wife. Perhaps we should go visit her family this Sunday.

---

3. **mi 'jito** (MEE HEE TOH): contraction of *mi hijito*, Spanish for "my little son."

Juanito. You know, that would probably be a good idea. I must admit that I was hoping I would find love on my adventures, but I have come home with no memories of love at all. Perhaps it is best to make my fortune right here, close to home.

480 **Don Ramon** (*to* DOÑA ARLETTE). See? That is exactly what I said would happen.

[*All exit.*] **C**

Scene 10.
MONTHS LATER AT JUANITO'S HOME.

The Narrator. Blanca Flor had seen the embrace and knew that the evil curse had been fulfilled. Brokenhearted, she traveled to a nearby village and lived there in hopes that one day the curse could be broken. The people of the village soon got to know Blanca Flor and came to respect her for the good person she was. One day, Blanca Flor heard news that a celebration was being held in honor of Juanito's return home. She immediately

490 knew that this might be her one chance to break the curse. From the times when she had brushed Juanito's hair, she had kept a lock of his hair. She took one strand of his hair and made it into a dove. She then took one strand of her own hair and turned it into another dove. She took these two doves to Juanito's celebration as a present.

[JUANITO *and* DON RAMON *are sitting talking.*]

Don Ramon. Juanito, what was the most fantastic thing that happened on your adventures?

Juanito. Really, Father, nothing much at all happened.

500 Sometimes I begin to have a memory of something, but it never becomes really clear. At night I have these dreams, but when I awake in the morning I cannot remember them. It must be some dream I keep trying to remember . . . or forget.

Don Ramon. I remember when I went into the world to seek my fortune. I was a young man like you . . .

VOCABULARY

Word Study

Which synonyms could you use if you wanted to replace *good* in this paragraph with a stronger adjective?

_____

_____

_____

READING FOCUS

Re-read these stage directions. What do you **visualize** happening to Juanito as the Doves sing?

_____

_____

_____

[DOÑA ARLETTE *enters.*]

Doña Arlette. Juanito, there's a young woman here with a present for you.

Juanito. Who is it?

510 **Doña Arlette.** I don't really know her. She is the new young woman who just recently came to the village. The women of the church say she is constantly doing good works for the church and that she is a very good person. **A** She has brought you a present to help celebrate your coming home safe.

Juanito. Sure. Let her come in.

[BLANCA FLOR *enters with the* TWO DOVES. *The* DOVES *are actors in costume.*]

Blanca Flor (*speaking to* JUANITO). Thank you for giving me the honor of presenting these doves as gifts to you.

520 **Juanito.** No. No. The honor is mine. Thank you. They are very beautiful.

Blanca Flor. They are special doves. They are singing doves.

Doña Arlette. I have never heard of singing doves before. Where did you get them?

Blanca Flor. They came from a special place. A place where all things have a magic power. There are no other doves like these in the world.

Don Ramon. Juanito, what a gift! Let's hear them sing!

Doña Arlette. Yes, let's hear them sing.

530 **Blanca Flor** (*to* JUANITO). May they sing to you?

Juanito. Yes, of course. Let's hear their song.

[*Everyone sits to listen to the* DOVES' *song. As the* DOVES *begin to chant, their words begin to have a powerful effect on* JUANITO. *His memory of* BLANCA FLOR *returns to him.*] **B**

Doves. Once there was a faraway land

A land of both good and evil powers.

A river flowed at the edge like a steady hand

60   Blanca Flor

And it was guarded by a Duende for all the hours.

Of all the beautiful things the land did hold

540   The most beautiful with the purest power

Was a young maiden, true and bold

Named Blanca Flor, the White Flower.

Juanito. I remember! The doves' song has made me remember.
(*Going to* BLANCA FLOR) Blanca Flor, your love has broken the
curse. Now I remember all that was struggling to come out.
Mama, Papa, here is Blanca Flor, the love I found when I was
seeking my fortune.

[JUANITO *and* BLANCA FLOR *embrace.*]

Don Ramon. This is going to be a really good story!

550   [*All exit, with* JUANITO *stopping to give* BLANCA FLOR *a
big hug.*] **D**

C READING FOCUS

What words in the doves' song help you **visualize** what has already happened in the play?

_____

_____

_____

D READ AND DISCUSS

Comprehension

What was Blanca Flor's plan?
Follow Up: How has it worked out?

Skills Practice

Blanca Flor

USE A TIMELINE

DIRECTIONS: Fill in the timeline below to track the main action in *Blanca Flor*. Be sure to include any events that are important to the entire plot, such as when Juanito meets Blanca Flor and Don Ricardo. Add extra lines to the timeline as necessary. The first event has been filled in for you.

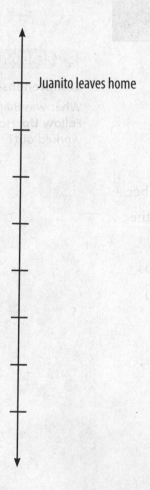

Juanito leaves home

Applying Your Skills

Blanca Flor

VOCABULARY DEVELOPMENT

DIRECTIONS: Put a check next to the sentences in which the *italicized* word is a synonym (word with a similar meaning) for the vocabulary word in parentheses.

1. (apprehensively) Sam looked around *anxiously* as he entered the dark alley.

2. (barren) The farmer's large orchard was incredibly *productive*.

3. (flourish) With a *sweep* of his hand, my friend indicated that I was worried about nothing.

4. (valiant) The knight was too *scared* to enter the castle alone.

LITERARY SKILLS FOCUS: CHARACTERIZATION

DIRECTIONS: Choose one character from *Blanca Flor*. Think about how the writer **characterizes** that person using dialogue, stage directions, and the narrator's words. Then write a short description of the character based on these details from the play.

_____

_____

_____

_____

_____

READING SKILLS FOCUS: VISUALIZING

DIRECTIONS: In the box below, sketch how you **visualized** the last scene in the play, when Blanca Flor gives Juanito the doves. Then label your drawing with the clues that helped you visualize the scene.

Reading Standard 3.2 Analyze the effect of the qualities of the character (e.g., courage or cowardice, ambition or laziness) on the plot and the resolution of the conflict.

Olympic Glory: Victories in History

from The World Almanac

INFORMATIONAL TEXT FOCUS: COMPARE-AND-CONTRAST ORGANIZATIONAL PATTERN

Authors often compare and contrast ideas to show their readers the similarities and differences between two or more people, places, or things. For example, a Great Dane and Chihuahua are both dogs (**comparing**), but a Great Dane is much larger (**contrasting**). "Olympic Glory: Victories in History" uses the **compare-and-contrast organizational pattern** to compare and contrast the modern Olympics with the Olympics held in ancient Greece.

Use the Skill As you read, use a **Venn diagram** like this one to compare and contrast the ancient and modern Olympics. In the area where the ovals overlap, write the similarities between the two Olympics. In areas that do not overlap, write the differences.

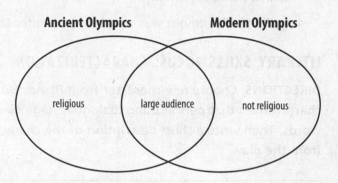

Ancient Olympics — religious | large audience | Modern Olympics — not religious

SELECTION VOCABULARY

victorious (VIHK TAWR EE UHS) *adj.:* having won.
> *Sara Hughes was victorious in the 2002 Winter Olympics.*

contemporary (KUHN TEHM PUH REHR EE) *adj.:* relating to the present time; modern.
> *Contemporary Olympics fans can watch the Games on television.*

amateurs (AM UH CHURZ) *n.:* people who participate in sports or other activities for fun rather than money; not professionals.
> *Ancient Olympians earned money and prizes, so they weren't amateurs.*

WORD STUDY

DIRECTIONS: Practice identifying context clues, or hints about a word's meaning, from the words surrounding it. Read each of the following sentences and underline the context clue(s) for each boldfaced word.

1. The race car drivers I talked to were **amateurs**, but they hope to turn professional one day so they can earn money.

2. The **contemporary** movie had many similarities to the original version from the 1940s.

3. Sara was **victorious** in her tennis match and celebrated by going out to dinner with friends.

Reading Standard 2.2
Analyze text that uses the compare-and-contrast organizational pattern.

OLYMPIC GLORY: VICTORIES IN HISTORY

from The World Almanac

In Greece in 1896, a shepherd named Spyridon Louis ran a footrace from Marathon to Athens, becoming the first "marathon" champion of the modern Olympics. He ran the race in borrowed shoes. In the Olympic Games today and in the future, you

© Erich Lessing/Art Resource, NY

10 will be hard-pressed to find athletes who have trouble finding footwear. Makers of specialized athletic shoes can't wait to give free expensive shoes to Olympians, hoping to give their brands important public exposure.

Still, present-day Olympic athletes will be like Louis in some important ways. Victorious runners will be asked how it feels to triumph, and they will sound like he did: "That hour was something unimaginable, and it still appears in my memory like a dream," Louis said 40 years after his moment of glory. "Everybody was calling out my name and throwing their hats
20 in the air." Now, as then, crowds will gather. Flags will unfurl. Athletes will triumph. Some elements of the Games change with time; others are eternal. Ⓐ

Exported from Greece

The very first Games were part of a Greek religious festival honoring Zeus, the "father" of Greek gods and goddesses. "They were a celebration of Hellenic culture,"[1] says David Potter, professor

---

1. **Hellenic** (HEH LEH NIHK) **culture:** culture of the ancient Greeks during the period 776 B.C. to 323 B.C. Hellen was a mythological king believed to be the ancestor of all true Greeks.

Ⓐ READ AND DISCUSS

Comprehension
The author begins this article by mentioning that even the modern Olympics have changed through time. What is the author's point here? **Follow-up:** What features of the Olympics remain the same across time?

A READING FOCUS

How does the author **contrast**, or show differences between, the ancient and modern Olympic Games in this paragraph?

_____

_____

_____

_____

_____

B READING FOCUS

In the first two paragraphs on this page, how does the author **compare**, or show similarities between, the ancient and modern Olympic Games?

_____

_____

_____

_____

_____

C READ AND DISCUSS

Comprehension

What has changed since the ancient Grecian games?

of Greek and Latin at the University of Michigan. Today, those gods and goddesses are ancient myth, and the Games include athletes from all around the world, not just the Greek city-states of ancient times. **A**

30　　The ancient Olympics were held every four years in Olympia from 776 B.C. through A.D. 393—over one thousand years! The Games were revived in 1896 as international competitions. Today's Olympics are run by international committees, rather than by Greek officials, and athletes gather in different host cities each time, not just in Olympia. But in both times, says Potter, "The point in part [was and] is for people to come and represent who they are and where they're from."

Games for All Seasons

The ancient Games were summertime events. In the modern world, however, there are Winter Games as well. Like 40　the ancient Games, the modern Summer and Winter Olympics are each held every four years, with the two alternating on even-numbered years. **B**

When the Olympics began in 776 B.C., they consisted of one footrace—covering a distance of 600 feet. In contrast, twenty-eight summer sports were set for the year 2008, and seven sports were scheduled for the 2010 Winter Games. "The range of sports has expanded enormously," says Potter. "The Olympians established a very small canon[2] of sports initially. Now it appears to be an Olympian sport in itself to see what can 50　be added each time."

Ancient Olympians battled the Mediterranean heat, so to toughen up, they practiced in the sun. At the events, according to historians, they wore little or no clothing. Such a dress code would be shocking to modern sensibilities, and a blow to manufacturers of sportswear and accessories—who, like shoemakers, make certain to place their products in the public eye during the Olympic Games. **C**

2.　**canon** (KA NUHN): accepted body of rules, principles, or other norms. Here, the word refers to sports approved for the ancient Olympics.

© Pete Saloutos/Corbis

D **LANGUAGE COACH**

Many English words come from ancient Latin. For example, the root of *contemporary* comes from the Latin word *tempos*, meaning "time." Use a dictionary to find the meaning of *tempo*, then explain how its Latin root is related to its definition.

_____

_____

_____

_____

_____

_____

Timeless Traditions

What has stayed the same in the Olympic Games between ancient and contemporary times? **D** The motivation of the

60 athletes is one enduring value. The hope of victory and the chance for fame propel an athlete's future, and there is "enormous economic benefit" for winning, says Potter. (In fact, the Greek word *athlete* means "one who competes for a prize.") In 516 B.C., Milo of Kroton wrestled his way into history, becoming the most famous Olympian of ancient times and the subject of legends. In 2002, Sarah Hughes figure-skated her way to a Gold Medal. One was a man from an ancient world; the other a woman from our time. But both stand in a long line of athletes who established Olympian fame and then fortune. Although contemporary

70 athletes may not become the subjects of legends that last for centuries, they can end up temporarily "immortalized" on cereal boxes, magazine and TV ads, billboards, and product labels.

Amateurs and Other Myths

"A myth was promulgated[3] that these guys were amateurs," says Potter of the original Olympians. "But these guys were professionals. The people who go to the Games want to see the best possible performance." Now, as in ancient times, people expect to witness the highest levels of athletic achievement at the

_____

3. **promulgated** (PRAH MUHL GAYT IHD): spread; made known.

A VOCABULARY

Selection Vocabulary

What is the author saying about the role of *amateurs* in today's Olympics?

_____

_____

_____

_____

B READ AND DISCUSS

Comprehension

What is the author letting us know here about Olympic athletes?

C READ AND DISCUSS

Comprehension

What does this paragraph tell us about the Olympic torch?

D READING FOCUS

The author waits until the final paragraph to describe the "main constant," the major thing the ancient and modern Olympics have in common. Why do you think she saves this **comparison** for the end?

_____

_____

_____

_____

80
Olympics. The athletes may not be "professionals" in the strict sense of the term—people of outstanding qualifications and experience hired and paid to perform—but they are true professionals in their level of achievement and commitment to their sport. **A**

Another myth is that female Olympians like Hughes are something new. But ancient Olympia had a festival to honor Hera, the wife of Zeus, and in that festival unmarried girls ran footrace competitions. So women, too, have been holding the Olympic torch from the start. **B**

Carrying a Torch for the Olympics

90
Actually, though, no one has held the torch from the "start" of the Olympics in ancient times—just since 1928, when the symbol of the Olympic torch was introduced. Most people think that the Olympic torch must have been part of the Games since ancient times, since the Greeks used torches in many of their religious festivals. Although a fire in honor of the god Prometheus was kept burning throughout the ancient Olympic games, there was no opening ceremony involving an Olympic torch. The Olympic torch ceremony—like the Olympic symbol of five interconnected rings—is actually a modern touch, a bit of dramatic staging. **C**

100
The main constant in the Olympics, says Potter, is the sense that the Games stand apart in time. "That weekend, for that weekend, the world would stop," he says. "You wanted to be there." Judging by the interest in today's Olympics, that old feeling remains. It's just that the audience has widened from those hundreds or thousands in attendance at the ancient Greek Olympic Games to the many millions of fascinated TV and Internet viewers around the world today. **D**

© Pete Saloutos/Corbis

Applying Your Skills

Olympic Glory: Victories in History

VOCABULARY DEVELOPMENT

DIRECTIONS: Write the vocabulary words from the Word Box on the correct blanks to complete the paragraph.

Word Box

victorious

contemporary

amateurs

The author of "Olympic Glory" gives readers a close look at the differences and similarities between the ancient Olympic Games and (1) _____ Olympic Games. Unlike the paid professional athletes who participated in the first Games, today's athletes are (2) _____. Whether or not they are paid for their participation in the Games, (3) _____ participants will certainly consider their achievement one of the most important moments of their lives.

INFORMATIONAL TEXT FOCUS: COMPARE-AND-CONTRAST ORGANIZATIONAL PATTERN

DIRECTIONS: Use some of the words and phrases below to write three sentences in which you compare and contrast two people, places, or things. An example has been provided.

in contrast	similarly	however
also	while	compared to

Example: In contrast *to the Olympic Games of ancient times, which were run by Greek officials, today's Games are run by officials from around the world.*

1. _____

   _____

2. _____

   _____

3. _____

   _____

Reading Standard 2.2
Analyze text that uses the compare-and-contrast organizational pattern.

Skills Review

Chapter 2

VOCABULARY REVIEW

DIRECTIONS: The sentences in the table below include Chapter 2 academic and selection vocabulary words. Some of the words are used correctly and some are not. If a word is used correctly, put a check mark in the "Correct" column. If a word is used incorrectly, explain why and suggest a replacement in the "Incorrect" column.

	Correct	Incorrect
There was a *stampede* of people in the theater, so it was very quiet.		
The *victorious* player was upset over how close his team came to winning.		
Contemporary novels typically use much different language from that in novels written 200 years ago.		
The basketball players were paid large amount for playing the game today because they are *amateurs*.		
The judge took the person's *circumstance* into consideration when announcing how much jail time he would need to serve.		
Since the ground was too muddy to dig in, the prospector let the cows graze on the *claim*.		
He could see right through her story because her lie was *obvious*.		
I asked for an *adjoining* cubicle because I wanted to be as far away as possible from my co-workers.		

Chapter 2

LANGUAGE COACH

Words with **multiple meanings** can mean more than one thing. *Bark,* for example, might mean "the sound a dog makes," or it could mean "the outer part of a tree."

DIRECTIONS: Each word below has multiple meanings. For each word, write two sentences that show two different meanings of the word.

1. left

_____

_____

2. bat

_____

_____

3. foot

_____

_____

4. clear

_____

_____

5. rock

_____

_____

ORAL LANGUAGE ACTIVITY

With a partner, conduct an interview with Walt Masters from "The King of Mazy May." One partner will pretend to be Walt, and the other will be the interviewer. As the interviewer, ask questions related to what happened in the story. As Walt, use the characterization clues the author gives you throughout the story to answer questions the way Walt probably would answer them. Take turns playing the interviewer and Walt.

Theme

It Takes the Village by Sami Bentil/courtesy of Sami Bentil.

Literary and Academic Vocabulary for Chapter 3

attitude (AT UH TOOD) *n.:* opinions and feelings you usually have about someone or something.

The character's attitude toward hockey became more positive as he learned more about the sport.

communicate (KUH MYOO NUH KAYT) *v.:* express your thoughts or feelings clearly, so that other people understand them.

Writers communicate lessons about life through their stories.

conveyed (KUHN VAYD) *v.:* made known.

The writer conveyed her strong feelings about democracy in her poem.

illustrate (IHL UH STRAYT) *v.:* explain or make something clear by giving examples.

Use details from a story to illustrate your idea of its theme.

theme (THEEM) *n.:* idea about life that a story's characters, events, and images suggest.

In the short story, the importance of family was a theme that ran throughout the conversations between the mother and son.

Preparing to Read

Ta-Na-E-Ka

by Mary Whitebird

LITERARY SKILLS FOCUS: THEME AND CHARACTER

Writers often try to share a message through their stories. This message, or **theme,** usually tells us something about people or life in general. One way writers develop a story's theme is through **characters**. What the characters say and do, how they change, and what they learn can all help express parts of the story's theme. In the beginning of this story, Mary, the main character, is worried about the difficult ritual she is about to face. As you read, think about Mary's changing attitudes. These may provide an important clue to help you discover the story's theme.

READING SKILLS FOCUS: IDENTIFYING THE THEME

Writers do not usually state the theme in their stories. In most stories, readers must guess the theme. As you read, look for clues that will help you **identify the theme**. Examine what the characters say, the main events and conflicts, how characters change, and what they learn.

Use a Chart to Find Theme   One helpful strategy for finding the theme is to take notes on a chart as you read. Fill in the rest of the chart with information about "Ta-Na-E-Ka."

"Ta-Na-E-Ka"	Notes for Finding the Theme
Comments by Characters	Mrs. Richardson says, "All of us have rituals of one kind or another."
Main Events and Conflicts	Mary does not want to participate in Ta-Na-E-Ka.
How Characters Change	
What Characters Learned	

Reading Standard 3.6
Identify and analyze features of themes conveyed through characters, actions, and images.

Vocabulary Development

Ta-Na-E-Ka

SELECTION VOCABULARY

loftiest (LAWF TEE UHST) *adj.:* noblest; highest.

> Grandfather described endurance as the loftiest virtue.

shrewdest (SHROOD UHST) *adj.:* sharpest; most clever.

> Only the shrewdest could survive Ta-Na-E-Ka.

grimaced (GRIHM IST) *v.:* twisted the face to express pain, anger, or disgust.

> Roger grimaced at the thought of eating grasshoppers.

gorging (GAWRJ ING) *v.:* filling up; stuffing.

> During his Ta-Na-E-Ka the boy dreamed of gorging himself on hamburgers.

audacity (AW DAS UH TEE) *n.:* boldness; daring.

> Mary's parents were shocked at her audacity.

WORD STUDY

DIRECTIONS: Match each vocabulary word in the left column with the example it best matches in the second column.

_____ 1. loftiest   **a.** the best student in a class

_____ 2. shrewdest   **b.** the courage to stand up for your beliefs

_____ 3. gorging   **c.** the highest goal to reach

_____ 4. audacity   **d.** a bear eating excessively before hibernating

TA-NA-E-KA

by Mary Whitebird

A LITERARY FOCUS

The narrator and main **character** is a Kaw Indian. Do you think her family's Native American traditions might factor into the story's **theme?** Explain.

_____

_____

_____

_____

B READ AND DISCUSS

Comprehension

What is the narrator's attitude toward her approaching birthday? How does the information about Amos Deer Leg and the idea of tradition relate to Mary's birthday?

C READ AND DISCUSS

Comprehension

How does "Eleven" connect to Ta-Na-E-Ka?

As my birthday drew closer, I had awful nightmares about it. I was reaching the age at which all Kaw Indians had to participate in Ta-Na-E-Ka. Well, not all Kaws. Many of the younger families on the reservation were beginning to give up the old customs. But my grandfather, Amos Deer Leg, was devoted to tradition. He still wore handmade beaded moccasins instead of shoes and kept his iron-gray hair in tight braids. He could speak English, but he spoke it only with white men. With his family he used a Sioux dialect.[1] **A**

10   Grandfather was one of the last living Indians (he died in 1953, when he was eighty-one) who actually fought against the U.S. Cavalry. Not only did he fight, he was wounded in a skirmish at Rose Creek—a famous encounter in which the celebrated Kaw chief Flat Nose lost his life. At the time, my grandfather was only eleven years old. **B**

    Eleven was a magic word among the Kaws. It was the time of Ta-Na-E-Ka, the "flowering of adulthood." It was the age, my grandfather informed us hundreds of times, "when a boy could prove himself to be a warrior and a girl took the first steps to

20 womanhood." **C**

    "I don't want to be a warrior," my cousin, Roger Deer Leg, confided to me. "I'm going to become an accountant."

---

1. **Sioux** (SOO) **dialect:** one of the languages spoken by the Plains Indians, including the Kaw.

"Ta-Na-E'-Ka" by Mary Whitebird from *Scholastic Voice,* December 13, 1973. Copyright © 1973 by **Scholastic Inc.** Reproduced by permission of the publisher.

© Alison Wright/Corbis

"None of the other tribes make girls go through the endurance ritual," I complained to my mother. **D**

"It won't be as bad as you think, Mary," my mother said, ignoring my protests. "Once you've gone through it, you'll certainly never forget it. You'll be proud."

I even complained to my teacher, Mrs. Richardson, feeling that, as a white woman, she would side with me.

30   She didn't. "All of us have rituals of one kind or another," Mrs. Richardson said. "And look at it this way: How many girls have the opportunity to compete on equal terms with boys? Don't look down on your heritage."

Heritage, indeed! I had no intention of living on a reservation for the rest of my life. I was a good student. I loved school. My fantasies were about knights in armor and fair ladies in flowing gowns being saved from dragons. It never once occurred to me that being an Indian was exciting. **E**

D VOCABULARY

Academic Vocabulary

Describe the narrator's *attitude*, or thoughts and feelings, toward Ta-Na-E-Ka.

E READING FOCUS

Remember that examining what a character learns can help you **identify the theme**. What conflict does Mary describe here?

Comprehension

How does women's liberation connect to Kaw history and traditions? **Follow-up:** What does Mary think of this?

B **VOCABULARY**

Selection Vocabulary

The narrator's grandfather feels that Ta-Na-E-Ka is an important tradition to be proud of. Considering this, what do you think *loftiest* means? Check your answer against a dictionary definition.

_____

_____

_____

C **READING FOCUS**

Underline words or phrases in this paragraph that might help you **identify the theme** of the story.

40   But I've always thought that the Kaw were the originators of the women's liberation movement. No other Indian tribe—and I've spent half a lifetime researching the subject—treated women more "equally" than the Kaw. Unlike most of the subtribes of the Sioux Nation, the Kaw allowed men and women to eat together. And hundreds of years before we were "acculturated,"[2] a Kaw woman had the right to refuse a prospective husband even if her father arranged the match.

The wisest women (generally wisdom was equated with age) often sat in tribal councils. Furthermore, most Kaw legends revolve around "Good Woman," a kind of supersquaw, a Joan

50   of Arc[3] of the high plains. Good Woman led Kaw warriors into battle after battle, from which they always seemed to emerge victorious.

And girls as well as boys were required to undergo Ta-Na-E-Ka.

The actual ceremony varied from tribe to tribe, but since the Indians' life on the plains was dedicated to survival, Ta-Na-E-Ka was a test of survival. A

"Endurance is the loftiest virtue of the Indian," my grandfather explained. B "To survive, we must endure. When I was a

60   boy, Ta-Na-E-Ka was more than the mere symbol it is now. We were painted white with the juice of a sacred herb and sent naked into the wilderness without so much as a knife. We couldn't return until the white had worn off. It wouldn't wash off. It took almost eighteen days, and during that time we had to stay alive, trapping food, eating insects and roots and berries, and watching out for enemies. And we did have enemies—both the white soldiers and the Omaha warriors, who were always trying to capture Kaw boys and girls undergoing their endurance test. It was an exciting time." C

70   "What happened if you couldn't make it?" Roger asked. He was born only three days after I was, and we were being

2. **acculturated** (UH KUHL CHUHR AYT ID) *v.* used as *adj.*: adapted to a new or different culture.
3. **Joan of Arc** (1412–1431): French heroine who led her country's army to victory over the English in 1429.

trained for Ta-Na-E-Ka together. I was happy to know he was frightened, too.

"Many didn't return," Grandfather said. "Only the strongest and shrewdest. **D** Mothers were not allowed to weep over those who didn't return. If a Kaw couldn't survive, he or she wasn't worth weeping over. It was our way."

"What a lot of hooey," Roger whispered. "I'd give anything to get out of it."

80   "I don't see how we have any choice," I replied.

Roger gave my arm a little squeeze. "Well, it's only five days."

Five days! Maybe it was better than being painted white and sent out naked for eighteen days. But not much better.

We were to be sent, barefoot and in bathing suits, into the woods. Even our very traditional parents put their foot down when Grandfather suggested we go naked. For five days we'd have to live off the land, keeping warm as best we could, getting food where we could. It was May, but on the northernmost reaches of the Missouri River, the days were still chilly and the nights were

90   fiercely cold. **E**

Grandfather was in charge of the month's training for Ta-Na-E-Ka. One day he caught a grasshopper and demonstrated how to pull its legs and wings off in one flick of the fingers and how to swallow it.

I felt sick, and Roger turned green. "It's a darn good thing it's 1947," I told Roger teasingly. "You'd make a terrible warrior." Roger just grimaced.

I knew one thing. This particular Kaw Indian girl wasn't going to swallow a grasshopper no matter how hungry she

100   got. And then I had an idea. Why hadn't I thought of it before? It would have saved nights of bad dreams about squooshy grasshoppers.

I headed straight for my teacher's house. "Mrs. Richardson," I said, "would you lend me five dollars?" **F**

"Five dollars!" she exclaimed. "What for?"

"You remember the ceremony I talked about?"

D VOCABULARY

Selection Vocabulary
Completing Ta-Na-E-Ka requires strength and intelligence. Considering this, what do you think *shrewdest* means? Check your answer against a dictionary definition.

_____

E READ AND DISCUSS

Comprehension
How is Ta-Na-E-Ka of Grandfather's time connected to Ta-Na-E-Ka that Roger and Mary will experience? **Follow-up:** What does Ta-Na-E-Ka show the elders about the children?

F READ AND DISCUSS

Comprehension
What do you think Mary is planning to do?

A LITERARY FOCUS

How do you think friends and family relate to the story's possible **theme?**

_____

_____

_____

_____

B VOCABULARY

Selection Vocabulary

Using what you know about how the children must survive during Ta-Na-E-Ka, guess the definition of _gorging_. Check your answer against a dictionary definition.

_____

_____

_____

_____

_____

C READ AND DISCUSS

Comprehension

How are Roger and Mary dealing with all the Ta-Na-E-Ka stories?

"Ta-Na-E-Ka. Of course. Your parents have written me and asked me to excuse you from school so you can participate in it."

"Well, I need some things for the ceremony," I replied, in a half-truth. "I don't want to ask my parents for the money."

"It's not a crime to borrow money, Mary. But how can you pay it back?"

"I'll baby-sit for you ten times."

"That's more than fair," she said, going to her purse and handing me a crisp, new five-dollar bill. I'd never had that much money at once.

"I'm happy to know the money's going to be put to a good use," Mrs. Richardson said.

A few days later the ritual began with a long speech from my grandfather about how we had reached the age of decision, how we now had to fend for ourselves and prove that we could survive the most horrendous of ordeals. All the friends and relatives who had gathered at our house for dinner made jokes about their own Ta-Na-E-Ka experiences. **A** They all advised us to fill up now, since for the next five days we'd be gorging ourselves on crickets. **B** Neither Roger nor I was very hungry. "I'll probably laugh about this when I'm an accountant," Roger said, trembling.

"Are you trembling?" I asked.

"What do you think?"

"I'm happy to know boys tremble, too," I said. **C**

At six the next morning, we kissed our parents and went off to the woods. "Which side do you want?" Roger asked. According to the rules, Roger and I would stake out "territories" in separate areas of the woods, and we weren't to communicate during the entire ordeal.

"I'll go toward the river, if it's OK with you," I said.

"Sure," Roger answered. "What difference does it make?"

To me, it made a lot of difference. There was a marina a few miles up the river, and there were boats moored there. At least, I hoped so. I figured that a boat was a better place to sleep than under a pile of leaves.

"Why do you keep holding your head?" Roger asked.

"Oh, nothing. Just nervous," I told him. Actually, I was afraid I'd lose the five-dollar bill, which I had tucked into my hair with a bobby pin. As we came to a fork in the trail, Roger shook my hand. "Good luck, Mary."

"N'ko-n'ta," I said. It was the Kaw word for "courage." **D**

150 The sun was shining and it was warm, but my bare feet began to hurt immediately. I spied one of the berry bushes Grandfather had told us about. "You're lucky," he had said. "The berries are ripe in the spring, and they are delicious and nourishing." They were orange and fat, and I popped one into my mouth.

Argh! I spat it out. It was awful and bitter, and even grass-hoppers were probably better tasting, although I never intended to find out.

I sat down to rest my feet. A rabbit hopped out from under the berry bush. He nuzzled the berry I'd spat out and ate it. He
160 picked another one and ate that, too. He liked them. He looked at me, twitching his nose. I watched a redheaded woodpecker bore into an elm tree, and I caught a glimpse of a civet cat[4] waddling through some twigs. All of a sudden I realized I was no longer frightened. Ta-Na-E-Ka might be more fun than I'd anticipated. I got up and headed toward the marina. **E**

"Not one boat," I said to myself dejectedly. But the resta-urant on the shore, Ernie's Riverside, was open. I walked in, feeling silly in my bathing suit. The man at the counter was big and tough-looking. He wore a sweat shirt with the words "Fort
170 Sheridan, 1944," and he had only three fingers on one of his hands. He asked me what I wanted.

"A hamburger and a milkshake," I said, holding the five-dollar bill in my hand so he'd know I had money.

"That's a pretty heavy breakfast, honey," he murmured.

"That's what I always have for breakfast," I lied.

---

4. **civet** (SIV ɪHT) **cat** *n.:* furry spotted skunk.

What clues in lines 146–148 might help you **identify the theme** of the story?

_____

_____

_____

_____

E READ AND DISCUSS

Comprehension
What is happening with Mary?

Word Study

In line 179, *'n* is a slang contraction for *than*. What contraction is repeated in lines 174 and 175? What words are combined to form the contraction?

"Forty-five cents," he said, bringing me the food. (Back in 1947, hamburgers were twenty-five cents and milkshakes were twenty cents.)

"Delicious," I thought. "Better 'n grasshoppers—and

180   Grandfather never once mentioned that I couldn't eat hamburgers." **A**

While I was eating, I had a grand idea. Why not sleep in the restaurant? I went to the ladies' room and made sure the window was unlocked. Then I went back outside and played along the riverbank, watching the water birds and trying to identify each one. I planned to look for a beaver dam the next day.

The restaurant closed at sunset, and I watched the three-fingered man drive away. Then I climbed in the unlocked

window. There was a night light on, so I didn't turn on any
190 lights. But there was a radio on the counter. I turned it on to a
music program. It was warm in the restaurant, and I was hungry.
I helped myself to a glass of milk and a piece of pie, intending to
keep a list of what I'd eaten so I could leave money. I also planned
to get up early, sneak out through the window, and head for the
woods before the three-fingered man returned. I turned off the
radio, wrapped myself in the man's apron, and in spite of the
hardness of the floor, fell asleep. **B**

"What the heck are you doing here, kid?"

It was the man's voice.

200 It was morning. I'd overslept. I was scared.

"Hold it, kid. I just wanna know what you're doing here.
You lost? You must be from the reservation. Your folks must be
worried sick about you. Do they have a phone?"

"Yes, yes," I answered. "But don't call them."

I was shivering. The man, who told me his name was
Ernie, made me a cup of hot chocolate while I explained about
Ta-Na-E-Ka.

"Darnedest thing I ever heard," he said, when I was
through. **C** "Lived next to the reservation all my life and this
210 is the first I've heard of Ta-Na-whatever-you-call-it." He looked
at me, all goose bumps in my bathing suit. "Pretty silly thing to
do to a kid," he muttered.

That was just what I'd been thinking for months, but when
Ernie said it, I became angry. "No, it isn't silly. It's a custom of the
Kaw. We've been doing this for hundreds of years. My mother
and my grandfather and everybody in my family went through
this ceremony. It's why the Kaw are great warriors." **D**

"OK, great warrior," Ernie chuckled, "suit yourself. And,
if you want to stick around, it's OK with me." Ernie went to the
220 broom closet and tossed me a bundle. "That's the lost-and-found
closet," he said. "Stuff people left on boats. Maybe there's
something to keep you warm."

B (READ AND DISCUSS)

Comprehension
Based on what we know
about Grandfather, what
might he think of Mary's
plan?

C (LANGUAGE COACH)

Darnedest is an example
of a **superlative** adjective—
one that compares three
or more things. *Bigger* is a
comparative adjective—it
only compares two things.
On the lines below, give two
examples of comparative and
superlative adjectives.

_____

_____

_____

D (READING FOCUS)

Characters' comments can
help us **identify the theme**.
How do Mary's comments
show us that she has
changed? How does this
relate to the theme of the
story?

_____

_____

_____

_____

_____

_____

_____

A READING FOCUS

Noting how characters change can help you **identify the theme**. How does Mary's knowledge of the Kaw show that she is changing?

_____

_____

_____

_____

_____

B READ AND DISCUSS

Comprehension

How does Mary's situation look here? How do you think Roger is getting along?

The sweater fitted loosely, but it felt good. I felt good. And I'd found a new friend. Most important, I was surviving Ta-Na-E-Ka.

My grandfather had said the experience would be filled with adventure, and I was having my fill. And Grandfather had never said we couldn't accept hospitality.

I stayed at Ernie's Riverside for the entire period. In the mornings I went into the woods and watched the animals and picked flowers for each of the tables in Ernie's. I had never felt better. I was up early enough to watch the sun rise on the Missouri, and I went to bed after it set. I ate everything I wanted—insisting that Ernie take all my money for the food. "I'll keep this in trust for you, Mary," Ernie promised, "in case you are ever desperate for five dollars." (He did, too, but that's another story.)

I was sorry when the five days were over. I'd enjoyed every minute with Ernie. He taught me how to make western omelets and to make Chili Ernie Style (still one of my favorite dishes). And I told Ernie all about the legends of the Kaw. I hadn't realized I knew so much about my people. **A**

But Ta-Na-E-Ka was over, and as I approached my house at about nine-thirty in the evening, I became nervous all over again. What if Grandfather asked me about the berries and the grasshoppers? And my feet were hardly cut. I hadn't lost a pound and my hair was combed.

"They'll be so happy to see me," I told myself hopefully, "that they won't ask too many questions." **B**

I opened the door. My grandfather was in the front room. He was wearing the ceremonial beaded deerskin shirt which had belonged to *his* grandfather. "N'g'da'ma," he said. "Welcome back."

I embraced my parents warmly, letting go only when I saw my cousin Roger sprawled on the couch. His eyes were red and swollen. He'd lost weight. His feet were an unsightly mass of blood and blisters, and he was moaning: "I made it, see. I made it. I'm a warrior. A warrior."

My grandfather looked at me strangely. I was clean, obviously well-fed, and radiantly healthy. My parents got the message.

260 My uncle and aunt gazed at me with hostility.

Finally my grandfather asked, "What did you eat to keep you so well?"

I sucked in my breath and blurted out the truth: "Hamburgers and milkshakes."

"Hamburgers!" my grandfather growled.

"Milkshakes!" Roger moaned.

"You didn't say we *had* to eat grasshoppers," I said sheepishly.

"Tell us all about your Ta-Na-E-Ka," my grandfather

270 commanded.

I told them everything, from borrowing the five dollars, to Ernie's kindness, to observing the beaver.

"That's not what I trained you for," my grandfather said sadly.

I stood up. "Grandfather, I learned that Ta-Na-E-Ka is important. I didn't think so during training. I was scared stiff of it. I handled it my way. And I learned I had nothing to be afraid of. There's no reason in 1947 to eat grasshoppers when you can eat a hamburger." **C**

280 I was inwardly shocked at my own audacity. But I liked it. "Grandfather, I'll bet you never ate one of those rotten berries yourself." **D**

Grandfather laughed! He laughed aloud! My mother and father and aunt and uncle were all dumbfounded. Grandfather never laughed. Never.

"Those berries—they are terrible," Grandfather admitted. "I could never swallow them. I found a dead deer on the first day of my Ta-Na-E-Ka—shot by a soldier, probably—and he kept my belly full for the entire period of the test!" **E**

290 Grandfather stopped laughing. "We should send you out again," he said.

I looked at Roger. "You're pretty smart, Mary," Roger groaned. "I'd never have thought of what you did."

C LITERARY FOCUS

Part of the story's **theme** is the relationship between traditional beliefs (Grandfather's) and modern practices (Mary's). How does Mary feel that she has gotten the best of both worlds?

_____

_____

_____

_____

_____

_____

D VOCABULARY

Selection Vocabulary

In this paragraph Mary takes a risk and stands up for herself. Considering this, what do you think *audacity* means? Check your answer against a dictionary definition.

_____

_____

_____

_____

E READ AND DISCUSS

Comprehension

How does Grandfather react to Mary's recounting of her Ta-Na-E-Ka?

"Accountants just have to be good at arithmetic," I said comfortingly. "I'm terrible at arithmetic."

Roger tried to smile but couldn't. My grandfather called me to him. "You should have done what your cousin did. But I think you are more alert to what is happening to our people today than we are. I think you would have passed the test under any circumstances, in any time. Somehow, you know how to exist in a world that wasn't made for Indians. I don't think you're going to have any trouble surviving."

Grandfather wasn't entirely right. But I'll tell about that another time. A

Applying Your Skills

Ta-Na-E-Ka

VOCABULARY DEVELOPMENT

DIRECTIONS: Write the correct words from the Word Box in the blanks. Some words will not be used.

Word Box

- loftiest
- shrewdest
- grimaced
- gorging
- audacity

Roger (1) _____ at the thought of the berries he had eaten during his Ta-Na-E-Ka. He felt that Mary was the (2) _____ Kaw Indian ever for thinking to stay with Ernie rather than to brave the wilderness. While Grandfather was less impressed, he still admired Mary's (3) _____ for coming right out and telling him what she did. Grandfather laughed and admitted to (4) _____ himself on deer, not berries, during his Ta-Na-E-Ka.

LITERARY SKILLS FOCUS: THEME AND CHARACTER

DIRECTIONS: The **theme** of "Ta-Na-E-Ka" revolves around tradition, coming of age, and survival. Write a short paragraph in which you discuss the message you think the author was trying to send through her short story.

READING SKILLS FOCUS: IDENTIFYING THE THEME

DIRECTIONS: Write "Yes" after each detail listed below if it helped you **identify the theme** of the story. Write "No" if it did not.

1. Ta-Na-E-Ka is considered the "flowering of adulthood." _____

2. Grandfather's Ta-Na-E-Ka lasted for 18 days. _____

3. Mrs. Richardson admires Mary's heritage and the Kaw tradition. _____

4. Grandfather is pleased that Mary knows how to exist in a world not made for Indians. _____

5. In 1947, hamburgers cost twenty-five cents and milkshakes cost twenty. _____

Reading Standard 3.6 Identify and analyze features of themes conveyed through characters, actions, and images.

Pet Adoption Application

INFORMATIONAL TEXT FOCUS: PREPARING AN APPLICATION

Throughout your life, you will need to fill out applications for many things, from adopting a pet to applying for a new job. When filling out any application, remember the following steps:

1. **Read the application all the way through** before picking up a pen. If you are asked for references, get permission from them first. A **reference** is someone that the person reviewing the application can call to get information about you.

2. **Write and edit any long responses** on a separate sheet of paper before writing your final response on the form.

3. Always **answer questions truthfully**.

4. **Print or type carefully.** Always check your **spelling**.

5. **Fill in all the blanks on** the form. Write *n/a* ("not applicable") for questions you don't need to answer.

6. Read through what you have written to **make sure you didn't miss anything**.

7. **Sign and date** the application form.

SELECTION VOCABULARY

contribution (KAHN TRUH BYOO SHUHN) *n.:* payment given for a specific purpose.
I gave the animal shelter a contribution so that it could provide food for the animals.

occupation (AHK YOO PAY SHUHN) *n.:* work a person does regularly.
I asked what her occupation was, and she said she was an engineer.

supervisor (SOO PUHR VY ZUHR) *n.:* person in charge.
My supervisor asked me to work extra hours on Monday.

WORD STUDY

DIRECTIONS: Fill in each blank with the correct vocabulary word.

When I filled out an application to adopt a pet, I was asked what my

(1) _____ is, and how many years I have worked at that

job. The animal shelter then called my (2) _____ to ask him

if I was a good employee. Finally, the shelter asked if I would make a

(3) _____ to help fund its efforts.

Reading Standard 2.5
Follow multiple-step instructions for preparing applications (e.g., for a public library card, bank savings account, sports club, league membership).

INSTRUCTIONS: Adopter, print carefully in **WHITE AREAS ONLY**—do not write in shaded areas. **A**

Pet Adoption Application

❑ Puppy ❑ Kitten ❑ Dog ❑ Cat

		1	Program	H	T	Adoption Number	
				D	O	1	
			MTA MTD	L	R		
			❑ ❑	G	circle one	2	

Date / /	Single Adoption	Double Adoption	Age	

MTA MTD ❑ ❑ L G R circle one

❑Mr. ❑Mrs. ❑Ms. ❑Miss ❑Mr. & Mrs.

Day	Time ❑AM ❑PM	Breed	Color

			Sex	❑Adopter's Last Name First Name

Voluntary Contribution	Size: S___ M___ L___	Spay/Neuter

Cash	$	❑ Pure ❑ Mix	Vaccine Type	Street Address Apt. #

Check	$	Pet's Name	Vaccine Date	

D V M A circle one	$		Rabies Tag	City State/Zip Code

Credit A/R	($)	ASC Int. No.	Rabies Date	

Total Voluntary Contribution $ _____	Wormed	Home Phone Business Phone

X _____

	Med. Given	NMR ❑	Tech. App.	( ) - ( )

Name of Reference	Address	City	State	Telephone	
				( ) -	❑ Yes ❑ No
				( )	D V ❑ Yes M A ❑ No

1. WHOM IS THE PET FOR? Self____ Gift____ For whom? _____ Adopter's age:_____

2. IF YOU'RE SINGLE: Do you live alone? Yes____ No____ Do you live with family? Yes____ No____
   Do you work? Yes____ No____ What are your hours? _____

   IF YOU'RE MARRIED: Do you both work? Yes____ No____ Husband's hours: _____
   Wife's hours: _____ How many children at home? _____ Ages: ____, ____, ____
   Who will be responsible for the pet? Husband_____ Wife_____ Children_____ Other_____

3. DO YOU: OWN ❑ RENT ❑ HOUSE ❑ APT. ❑ Floor #____ Elevator in the building? Yes____ No____
      (CHECK ONE)   (CHECK ONE)
   If renting, does your lease allow pets? Yes___ No___ Are you moving? Yes___ No___ When?_____
   Do you have use of a private yard? Yes___ No___ Is it fenced? Yes___ No___ Fence height:____
   Where will your pet be kept? _____ / _____ Any allergy to pets? Yes___ No___
                         DAYTIME   NIGHTTIME

4. DO YOU HAVE OTHER PETS NOW? Yes____ No____ Breed: _____
   Where did you get the pet? _____ How long have you had it? _____

   HAVE YOU EVER HAD A PET BEFORE? Yes____ No____ Breed: _____
   How long did you have the pet? _____ What happened to the pet? _____
   Have you ever adopted from this shelter? Yes____ No____ Where is the pet now? _____

5. YOUR OCCUPATION: _____ Business Phone: ( ) _____
   Company: _____ Supervisor's Name: _____ **B**

VET'S NAME	CITY, STATE	ZIP CODE **C**
Adopter's Signature:		

A READING FOCUS

Read the application all the way through. What information would you need to have with you before you could complete the application?

_____

_____

_____

B VOCABULARY

Selection Vocabulary

Read the definition of *supervisor*. Why would an application require you to provide the name of your supervisor?

_____

_____

C READ AND DISCUSS

Comprehension

What do the variety and number of questions on the form tell you about adopting a pet?

North Shore Animal League Pet Adoption Application. Copyright © 2000 by North Shore Animal League. Reproduced by permission of **North Shore Animal League, Port Washington, New York.**

Pet Adoption Application

USE A PERSONAL INFORMATION CHART

Suppose that you are about to fill out an application to volunteer at a local retirement home. You know the application will ask for lots of personal information. You decide to write down some of your information beforehand so you can fill out the application quickly. In the chart below, fill out any information that you can. Remember, you can write *n/a* if a question does not apply to you.

Name	
Date of birth	
Address	
School I go to	
Previous work experience	
2 personal references	
Hobbies	
Why do I want to work here?	

Pet Adoption Application

VOCABULARY DEVELOPMENT

DIRECTIONS: Read the incomplete paragraph below. On each blank line, write a sentence that fits with the story and includes a vocabulary word from the Word Box. All three vocabulary words should be used.

Word Box

supervisor

occupation

contribution

Last Saturday, I walked to Pepper's Restaurant to apply for a job. I carefully filled out a job application and then waited five minutes for my interview.

_____

_____. She asked

me several questions about my education and past work experience. _____

_____

On my way out of the store, I noticed a box for donations to the Pepper's Restaurant Charity, which provides food to homeless shelters. _____

_____

_____

INFORMATIONAL TEXT FOCUS: PREPARING AN APPLICATION

DIRECTIONS: In the diagram below, list the steps you would take to complete an application. Circle the steps that require you to find out information before filling out the application.

Reading Standard 2.5
Follow multiple-step instructions for preparing applications (e.g., for a public library card, bank savings account, sports club, league membership).

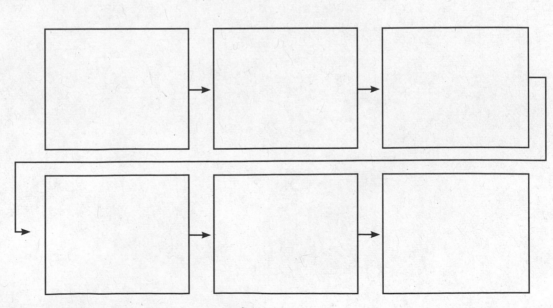

Chapter 3

VOCABULARY REVIEW

DIRECTIONS: Choose the correct vocabulary word from the Word Box to complete each sentence. Not all words will be used.

Word Box

attitude

audacity

communicate

conveyed

contribution

gorging

grimaced

illustrate

loftiest

occupation

shrewdest

supervisor

1. After three days lost at sea, the rescued sailor was _____ himself on bread, meat, and vegetables.

2. Since Maria was the _____ person on our team, we let her plan our strategy for the debate.

3. When a stranger approached me and asked for $20, I was astounded by her _____.

4. After his brother returned home safely from war, Luis made a large _____ to a local war veterans' charity.

5. My _____ is always asking me to work extra hours on the weekend.

6. At the meeting, the class president _____ her opinion about the theme of the school dance.

7. Since she is studying in Europe this year, my sister and I now _____ by email more than by telephone.

Chapter 3

LANGUAGE COACH

DIRECTIONS: Comparative adjectives, such as *wealthier,* compare two things. **Superlative** adjectives, such as *softest*, compare three or more things. Label each word below as either a comparative or superlative adjective. Then, for the last two exercises, write the comparative and superlative forms of the adjective provided. If you are unsure of how to form a comparative or superlative adjective, check a dictionary.

1. shrewdest   _____

2. cooler   _____

3. chattier   _____

4. longest   _____

5. cutest   _____

6. smaller   _____

7. cleanest   _____

8. quicker   _____

9. loud   Comparative: _____

           Superlative: _____

10. smart   Comparative: _____

           Superlative: _____

WRITING ACTIVITY

DIRECTIONS: Usually, a reader needs to carefully examine characters, conflicts, and other events to fully understand a story's theme. On a separate sheet of paper, write two paragraphs that explain the theme or themes in "Ta-Na-E-Ka." For each theme that you describe, provide at least two pieces of evidence that support your explanation.

Chapter

4

Forms of Fiction

Erosion, 2000 by Jacek Yerka/Courtesy of Agra–Art S.A.

Literary and Academic Vocabulary for Chapter 4

characteristics (KAR IHK TUH RIHS TIHKS) *n.:* important, typical parts or features.
The different forms of fiction each have defining characteristics.

concept (KAHN SEHPT) *n.:* idea of how something is or could be.
The concept of storytelling exists in all cultures.

indicate (IHN DUH KAYT) *v.:* show, express, or suggest.
The author used the detailed passage to indicate what the character was feeling.

interpret (IHN TUR PRIHT) *v.:* decide on the meaning of something.
When we interpret stories, we can learn lessons about life.

fiction *n.:* made-up stories that are purely products of the imagination.
Fiction authors often have very vivid imaginations.

genres (ZHAHN RUHZ) *n:* specific categories.
Fiction genres include mystery, romance, science fiction, historical fiction, and adventure.

novel (NAH VUHL) *n.:* long fictional story with more than one hundred pages.
To Kill a Mockingbird, a novel by Harper Lee, is often considered to be a coming-of-age story.

novella (NOH VEHL UH) *n.:* a story that is shorter than a novel but longer than a short story.
I read the "The Gold Cadillac," a novella, in only two nights.

La Bamba

by Gary Soto

LITERARY SKILLS FOCUS: FORMS OF FICTION: IDENTIFYING THE CHARACTERISTICS OF THE SHORT STORY

You can tell by its name that a **short story** is not long. It is usually between five and twenty pages long. A short story is a fictional prose narrative, which is another way of saying it is made up; it is not a poem, and it has a series of events.

READING SKILLS FOCUS: STORY AND STRUCTURE

How does a writer put together a short story? Short stories are built in the same way as other kinds of fiction. They have a character or characters dealing with a problem, or **conflict**. The main events in the story lead to a **climax**, the most exciting point in the story. Finally, the conflict is settled in the story's **resolution**. The diagram below shows the building blocks of short stories. You can use this chart to analyze the structure of most stories, but keep in mind that a short story usually has just one or two main characters and a simple plot. In fact, most short stories can be read in just one sitting.

Reading Standard 3.1
Identify the forms of fiction and describe the major characteristics of each form.

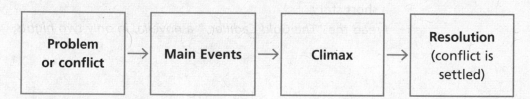

Problem or conflict → Main Events → Climax → Resolution (conflict is settled)

Vocabulary Development

La Bamba

SELECTION VOCABULARY

jammed (JAMD) *v.:* got stuck in a non-working position.

> *When the needle jammed, Mr. Roybal got angry.*

maneuvered (MUH NOO VUHRD) *v.:* moved, as a group, into position.

> *The cast members maneuvered themselves back onto the stage.*

groove (GROOV) *n.:* state of being comfortable.

> *Manuel got into the groove once he felt more comfortable on stage.*

cast (KAST) *n.:* group of performers in a play or event.

> *The audience appreciated the cast's efforts.*

WORD STUDY

DIRECTIONS: Write the vocabulary words above in the correct blanks to complete the sentences.

1. The dancers _____ around the stage.

2. The entire _____ received a standing ovation for their magnificent performance.

3. The basketball got _____ between the rim and the backboard.

4. Once she settled into a _____, the game show contestant won numerous prizes.

LA BAMBA

by Gary Soto

BACKGROUND

In this story, an elementary school student named Manuel enters a school talent show. He uses a record to play music during his show. Records are vinyl disks that contain cut grooves. Putting a needle into the grooves and rotating the record on a turntable, or record player, made the needle vibrate, which reproduced the recorded sounds. Records got scratched easily. A scratch could ruin a record, making the same bit of music play over and over.

A **LITERARY FOCUS**

Underline the words in the opening paragraph that describe the character Manuel. Circle words that provide hints about the plot of this **short story**.

B **READ AND DISCUSS**

Comprehension

What is the author letting us know about Manuel?

Manuel was the fourth of seven children and looked like a lot of kids in his neighborhood: black hair, brown face, and skinny legs scuffed from summer play. But summer was giving way to fall: The trees were turning red, the lawns brown, and the pomegranate trees were heavy with fruit. Manuel walked to school in the frosty morning, kicking leaves and thinking of tomorrow's talent show. He was still amazed that he had volunteered. He was going to pretend to sing Ritchie Valens's[1] "La Bamba" before the entire school. **A**

10   Why did I raise my hand? he asked himself, but in his heart he knew the answer. He yearned for the limelight. He wanted applause as loud as a thunderstorm and to hear his friends say, "Man, that was bad!" And he wanted to impress the girls, especially Petra Lopez, the second-prettiest girl in his class. The prettiest was already taken by his friend Ernie. Manuel knew he should be reasonable since he himself was not great-looking, just average. **B**

---

1. **Ritchie Valens** (1941–1959), the professional singer mentioned in the story, was the first Mexican American rock star. In 1959, when he was only seventeen, Valens was killed in a plane crash.

"La Bamba" from *Baseball in April and Other Stories* by Gary Soto. Copyright © 1990 by Gary Soto. Reproduced by permission of **Harcourt, Inc.**

Manuel kicked through the fresh-fallen leaves. When he got to school, he realized he had forgotten his math workbook. If the teacher found out, he would have to stay after school and miss practice for the talent show. But fortunately for him, they did drills that morning.

During lunch Manuel hung around with Benny, who was also in the talent show. Benny was going to play the trumpet in spite of the fat lip he had gotten playing football.

"How do I look?" Manuel asked. He cleared his throat and started moving his lips in pantomime. **C** No words came out, just a hiss that sounded like a snake. Manuel tried to look emotional, flailing his arms on the high notes and opening his eyes and mouth as wide as he could when he came to "Para bailar la baaaaammmba."[2]

After Manuel finished, Benny said it looked all right but suggested Manuel dance while he sang. Manuel thought for a moment and decided it was a good idea.

"Yeah, just think you're like Michael Jackson or someone like that," Benny suggested. "But don't get carried away."

During rehearsal, Mr. Roybal, nervous about his debut as the school's talent co-ordinator, cursed under his breath when the lever that controlled the speed on the record player jammed. **D**

"Darn," he growled, trying to force the lever. "What's wrong with you?"

"Is it broken?" Manuel asked, bending over for a closer look. It looked all right to him.

Mr. Roybal assured Manuel that he would have a good record player at the talent show, even if it meant bringing his own stereo from home.

Manuel sat in a folding chair, twirling his record on his thumb. He watched a skit about personal hygiene, a mother-and-daughter violin duo, five first-grade girls jumping rope, a karate kid breaking boards, three girls singing "Like a Virgin," and a skit

---

2. **para bailar la bamba** (PAH RAH BY LAHR LAH BAHM BAH): Spanish for "to dance the bamba."

C VOCABULARY

Word Study

The word *pantomime* comes from a Greek word meaning "all-imitating." In ancient Rome, a *pantomime* was an actor who used only actions and gestures, no words. Based on this information, what do you think *pantomime* means here?

_____

_____

_____

D VOCABULARY

Selection Vocabulary

Recall what the word *jammed* means. Underline Mr. Roybal's reaction to the record player getting jammed.

Academic Vocabulary

A *concept* is a general idea. What do you think is the concept behind a talent show that has many different types of acts? Why might the students and the audience like this type of show?

_____

_____

_____

_____

_____

_____

_____

B **READ AND DISCUSS**

Comprehension

How do Manuel's thoughts about his family add to what we know about him?

about the pilgrims. Ⓐ If the record player hadn't been broken, he would have gone after the karate kid, an easy act to follow, he told himself.

As he twirled his forty-five record, Manuel thought they had a great talent show. The entire school would be amazed. His mother and father would be proud, and his brothers and sisters would be jealous and pout. It would be a night to remember. Ⓑ

Benny walked onto the stage, raised his trumpet to his mouth, and waited for his cue. Mr. Roybal raised his hand like a
60 symphony conductor and let it fall dramatically. Benny inhaled and blew so loud that Manuel dropped his record, which rolled across the cafeteria floor until it hit a wall. Manuel raced after it, picked it up, and wiped it clean.

"Boy, I'm glad it didn't break," he said with a sigh.

That night Manuel had to do the dishes and a lot of homework, so he could only practice in the shower. In bed he prayed that he wouldn't mess up. He prayed that it wouldn't be like when he was a first-grader. For Science Week he had wired together a C battery and a bulb and told everyone he had discovered how a
70 flashlight worked. He was so pleased with himself that he practiced for hours pressing the wire to the battery, making the bulb wink

a dim, orangish light. He showed it to so many kids in his neighborhood that when it was time to show his class how a flashlight worked, the battery was dead. He pressed the wire to the battery, but the bulb didn't respond. He pressed until his thumb hurt and some kids in the back started snickering.

But Manuel fell asleep confident that nothing would go wrong this time. **C**

The next morning his father and mother beamed at him.
80 They were proud that he was going to be in the talent show. **D**

"I wish you would tell us what you're doing," his mother said. His father, a pharmacist who wore a blue smock with his name on a plastic rectangle, looked up from the newspaper and sided with his wife. "Yes, what are you doing in the talent show?"

"You'll see," Manuel said, with his mouth full of Cheerios.

The day whizzed by, and so did his afternoon chores and dinner. Suddenly he was dressed in his best clothes and standing next to Benny backstage, listening to the commotion as the cafeteria filled with school kids and parents. The lights dimmed,
90 and Mr. Roybal, sweaty in a tight suit and a necktie with a large knot, wet his lips and parted the stage curtains.

"Good evening, everyone," the kids behind the curtain heard him say. "Good evening to you," some of the smart-alecky kids said back to him.

"Tonight we bring you the best John Burroughs Elementary has to offer, and I'm sure that you'll be both pleased and amazed that our little school houses so much talent. And now, without further ado, let's get on with the show." **E** He turned and, with a swish of his hand, commanded, "Part the curtain." The curtains
100 parted in jerks. A girl dressed as a toothbrush and a boy dressed as a dirty gray tooth walked onto the stage and sang:

Brush, brush, brush
Floss, floss, floss
Gargle the germs away—hey! hey! hey!

After they finished singing, they turned to Mr. Roybal, who dropped his hand. The toothbrush dashed around the stage after

C (READ AND DISCUSS)

Comprehension

What does Manuel think about his upcoming performance now?

D (READING FOCUS)

Review the four stages of **a story** on the Preparing to Read page. Which stage does this paragraph fall into? Explain your answer.

_____

_____

_____

_____

_____

E (VOCABULARY)

Word Study

Ado (UH DOO), is not commonly used anymore. Look up its definition in the dictionary, then write that definition on the following lines.

_____

_____

_____

_____

Write a pronunciation guide
for the word *maneuvered*
on the following line. Then
compare it to the guide on
the Preparing to Read page.
Pronouncing words correctly
is important for building **oral
fluency.**

B **READING FOCUS**

What internal **conflict**, or
problem, is Manuel having
in this paragraph?

C **READING FOCUS**

The **climax** of the story
begins when Manuel walks
on stage. How do you think
he will do?

the dirty tooth, which was laughing and having a great time until
it slipped and nearly rolled off the stage.

Mr. Roybal jumped out and caught it just in time. "Are you
110 OK?"

The dirty tooth answered, "Ask my dentist," which drew
laughter and applause from the audience.

The violin duo played next, and except for one time when
the girl got lost, they sounded fine. People applauded, and some
even stood up. Then the first-grade girls maneuvered onto the
stage while jumping rope. A They were all smiles and bouncing
ponytails as a hundred cameras flashed at once. Mothers "awhed"
and fathers sat up proudly.

The karate kid was next. He did a few kicks, yells, and
120 chops, and finally, when his father held up a board, punched it in
two. The audience clapped and looked at each other, wide-eyed
with respect. The boy bowed to the audience, and father and son
ran off the stage.

Manuel remained behind the stage, shivering with fear. He
mouthed the words to "La Bamba" and swayed left to right. Why
did he raise his hand and volunteer? Why couldn't he have just
sat there like the rest of the kids and not said anything? While
the karate kid was onstage, Mr. Roybal, more sweaty than before,
took Manuel's forty-five record and placed it on a new record
130 player. B

"You ready?" Mr. Roybal asked.

"Yeah. . ."

Mr. Roybal walked back on stage and announced that
Manuel Gomez, a fifth-grader in Mrs. Knight's class, was going to
pantomime Ritchie Valens's classic hit "La Bamba."

The cafeteria roared with applause. Manuel was nervous
but loved the noisy crowd. He pictured his mother and father
applauding loudly and his brothers and sister also clapping,
though not as energetically.

140 Manuel walked on stage and the song started immediately. C
Glassy-eyed from the shock of being in front of so many people,

Manuel moved his lips and swayed in a made-up dance step. He couldn't see his parents, but he could see his brother Mario, who was a year younger, thumb-wrestling with a friend. Mario was wearing Manuel's favorite shirt; he would deal with Mario later. He saw some other kids get up and head for the drinking fountain, and a baby sitting in the middle of an aisle sucking her thumb and watching him intently.

What am I doing here? thought Manuel. This is no fun at

150   all. Everyone was just sitting there. Some people were moving to the beat, but most were just watching him, like they would a monkey at the zoo. **D**

But when Manuel did a fancy dance step, there was a burst of applause and some girls screamed. Manuel tried another dance step. He heard more applause and screams and started getting into the groove as he shivered and snaked like Michael Jackson around the stage. But the record got stuck, and he had to sing

Para bailar la bamba
Para bailar la bamba
160   *Para bailar la bamba*
Para bailar la bamba
again and again. **E**

Manuel couldn't believe his bad luck. The audience began to laugh and stand up in their chairs. Manuel remembered how the forty-five record had dropped from his hand and rolled across the cafeteria floor. It probably got scratched, he thought, and now it was stuck, and he was stuck dancing and moving his lips to the same words over and over. He had never been so embarrassed. He would have to ask his parents to move the family out of town.

170   After Mr. Roybal ripped the needle across the record, Manuel slowed his dance steps to a halt. He didn't know what to do except bow to the audience, which applauded wildly, and scoot off the stage, on the verge of tears. This was worse than the homemade flashlight. At least no one laughed then; they just snickered.

Manuel stood alone, trying hard to hold back the tears as Benny, center stage, played his trumpet. Manuel was jealous

D READ AND DISCUSS

Comprehension

What does Manuel mean that people "were watching him like they would watch a monkey at the zoo"?

E LITERARY FOCUS

One characteristic of the **short story** is that it has a series of events. What events have brought Manuel to this point in the story?

_____
_____
_____
_____
_____
_____

A VOCABULARY

Selection Vocabulary

The word *cast* means "a group of performers in a play or event." For what event did this cast perform?

_____

_____

B READ AND DISCUSS

Comprehension

What's the reaction to Manuel's performance? **Follow-up:** Explain whether this matches his view of what happened.

C VOCABULARY

Academic Vocabulary

What do the compliments that Manuel receives in line 186 *indicate*—show or point out—about his performance?

_____

_____

_____

_____

Ritchie Valens   © Bettmann/Corbis

because he sounded great, then mad as he recalled that it was Benny's loud trumpet playing that made the forty-five record fly
180   out of his hands. But when the entire cast lined up for a curtain call, Manuel received a burst of applause that was so loud it shook the walls of the cafeteria. **A** Later, as he mingled with the kids and parents, everyone patted him on the shoulder and told him, "Way to go. You were really funny." **B**

Funny? Manuel thought. Did he do something funny? Funny. Crazy. Hilarious. **C** These were the words people said to him. He was confused but beyond caring. All he knew was that people were paying attention to him, and his brother and sisters looked at him with a mixture of jealousy and awe.
190   He was going to pull Mario aside and punch him in the arm for wearing his shirt, but he cooled it. He was enjoying the limelight. A teacher brought him cookies and punch, and the popular kids who had never before given him the time of day now clustered

around him. Ricardo, the editor of the school bulletin, asked him how he made the needle stick.

"It just happened," Manuel said, crunching on a star-shaped cookie.

At home that night his father, eager to undo the buttons on his shirt and ease into his La-Z-Boy recliner, asked Manuel
200 the same thing, how he managed to make the song stick on the words "Para bailar la bamba."

Manuel thought quickly and reached for scientific jargon he had read in magazines. "Easy, Dad. I used laser tracking with high optics and low functional decibels per channel." **D** His proud but confused father told him to be quiet and go to bed.

"Ah, que niños tan truchas,"[3] he said as he walked to the kitchen for a glass of milk. "I don't know how you kids nowadays get so smart."

Manuel, feeling happy, went to his bedroom, undressed, and
210 slipped into his pajamas. He looked in the mirror and began to pantomime "La Bamba," but stopped because he was tired of the song. He crawled into bed. The sheets were as cold as the moon that stood over the peach tree in their backyard.

He was relieved that the day was over. Next year, when they asked for volunteers for the talent show, he wouldn't raise his hand. Probably. **E**

© Royalty-Free/CORBIS.

---

3. **que niños tan truchas** (KAY NEEN YOHS TAHN TROO CHAHS): Spanish for "what smart kids."

D VOCABULARY

Word Study

Jargon is the special language of people who work in the same profession. Underline the words here that are examples of jargon. Why does Manuel use jargon here?

_____

_____

_____

_____

_____

_____

_____

E READ AND DISCUSS

Comprehension

What does it tell us about Manuel that he *probably* won't volunteer for the talent show next year?

_____

_____

_____

_____

_____

_____

_____

_____

Skills Practice

La Bamba

USE A STORY STRUCTURE CHART

Recall the parts of the **short story** that you learned in the Preparing to Read section. Fill in the details about "La Bamba" for each box.

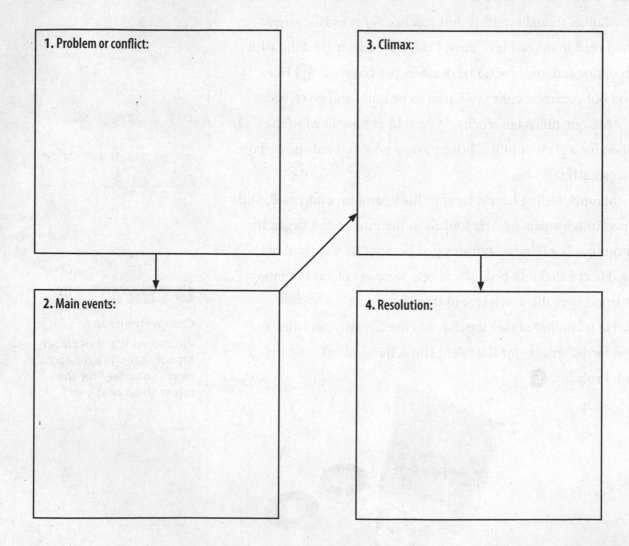

1. Problem or conflict:

2. Main events:

3. Climax:

4. Resolution:

Applying Your Skills

La Bamba

VOCABULARY DEVELOPMENT

DIRECTIONS: Match each vocabulary word with its correct synonym. A synonym is a word that has the same or nearly the same meaning as another word. For example, *happy* is a synonym of *glad*.

1. _____ jammed   a. moved
2. _____ maneuvered   b. group
3. _____ groove   c. stuck
4. _____ cast   d. comfort

LITERARY SKILLS FOCUS: FORMS OF FICTION: IDENTIFYING THE CHARACTERISTICS OF THE SHORT STORY

DIRECTIONS: Which of the following are characteristics of **short stories**? Put a check mark next to the correct answers.

1. ____ they are usually longer than twenty-five pages
2. ____ they can be poems
3. ____ they are made-up
4. ____ they are strictly factual
5. ____ they have a series of events

READING SKILLS FOCUS: STORY AND STRUCTURE

DIRECTIONS: Answer the following questions in complete sentences.

1. What is the **climax** of the short story "La Bamba"?

_____

_____

2. What clues in the story help you figure this out? (Hint: Remember that a story's climax is its most exciting point, when something important happens.)

_____

_____

Reading Standard 3.1 Identify the forms of fiction and describe the major characteristics of each form.

The Gold Cadillac

by Mildred D. Taylor

LITERARY SKILLS FOCUS: FORMS OF FICTION: IDENTIFYING THE CHARACTERISTICS OF THE NOVELLA

Like the novel and short story, a **novella** has plot, characters, and setting. A novella is usually longer than a short story but shorter than a novel. It is short enough to be published with other stories, but long enough to be published by itself. The length of the story, though, is not as important as the story it tells. Many novellas relate one important lesson or journey that takes place over a fairly short period of time.

READING SKILLS FOCUS: MAKING AND ADJUSTING PREDICTIONS

When you read, you use clues from the text and your own experiences to **make predictions**, or educated guesses, about what will happen next in a story. As you continue to read, new information may cause you to change, or **adjust**, your predictions.

As you read *The Gold Cadillac,* write down clues and predictions in a chart like the one below. Give reasons for your predictions as well. Remember to adjust your predictions if necessary.

In the story...	I predict...	Because...
The narrator and her sister see the Cadillac.	That the father bought it.	The father drives up in it and then is grinning and happy.
Mother sees the Cadillac.		

Reading Standard 3.1
Identify the forms of fiction and describe the major characteristics of each form.

Vocabulary Development

The Gold Cadillac

SELECTION VOCABULARY

evident (EHV UH DUHNT) *adj.*: easily seen or understood; obvious.
It's evident from the scowl on her face that Dee is angry.

rural (RUR UHL) *adj.*: having to do with country life.
The narrator's grandparents live in a rural area on a big farm.

dusk (DUHSK) *n.*: the period of time when the sky darkens as the sun goes down.
As dusk approached, 'lois became frightened of the growing darkness.

ignorance (IHG NUHR UHNS) *n.*: lack of knowledge.
Her father says that people sometimes pass unfair laws out of ignorance.

WORD STUDY

DIRECTIONS: Write words from the vocabulary list above in the correct blanks below.

The Gold Cadillac is a novella that takes place around 1950. In the story, 'lois, the main character, leaves her home in Toledo, Ohio. She travels with her family to visit her grandparents in the (1) _____ South, on a farm in Mississippi. During this road trip, 'lois learns about unfair laws against black people. Her father explains that they are due to some people's (2) _____. One day during the trip, 'lois's father is harassed by policemen, and it becomes (3) _____ that the police are prejudiced. As the daylight fades and (4) _____ sets in, 'lois and her family leave Mississippi.

THE GOLD CADILLAC

by Mildred D. Taylor

BACKGROUND

The novella *The Gold Cadillac* takes place around 1950.
African Americans, especially those living in the South during
this time, were treated unfairly. Experiences like the one the
family in the story has when entering Mississippi outraged
blacks and many whites. During the Civil Rights Era of the
mid-1950s and 1960s, many people demanded changes in the
laws across the nation.

A **READING FOCUS**

How do you **predict** 'lois,
Wilma, and their mother will
feel about the new Cadillac?

_____

_____

_____

_____

_____

_____

My sister and I were playing out on the front lawn when the gold
Cadillac rolled up and my father stepped from behind the wheel.

We ran to him, our eyes filled with wonder. "Daddy, whose
Cadillac?" I asked.

And Wilma demanded, "Where's our Mercury?"

My father grinned. "Go get your mother and I'll tell you all
about it."

"Is it ours?" I cried. "Daddy, is it ours?"

"Get your mother!" he laughed. "And tell her to hurry!"

10   Wilma and I ran off to obey, as Mr. Pondexter next door
came from his house to see what this new Cadillac was all about.
We threw open the front door, ran through the downstairs front
parlor and straight through the house to the kitchen, where my
mother was cooking and one of my aunts was helping her. "Come
on, Mother-Dear!" we cried together. "Daddy say come on out
and see this new car!" **A**

"What?" said my mother, her face showing her surprise.
"What're you talking about?"

"A Cadillac!" I cried.

20   "He said hurry up!" relayed Wilma.

© National Motor Museum, Beaulieu

B VOCABULARY

Word Study

The word *unison* has to do with togetherness. Look up other words beginning with *uni-* in the dictionary. What do they have in common?

_____

_____

_____

C READ AND DISCUSS

Comprehension

What has the author set up for us?

And then we took off again, up the back stairs to the second floor of the duplex. Running down the hall, we banged on all the apartment doors. My uncles and their wives stepped to the doors. It was good it was a Saturday morning. Everybody was home.

"We got us a Cadillac! We got us a Cadillac!" Wilma and I proclaimed in unison.[1] B C

We had decided that the Cadillac had to be ours if our father was driving it and holding on to the keys. "Come on see!" Then we raced on, through the upstairs sunroom, down
30　the front steps, through the downstairs sunroom, and out to the Cadillac. Mr. Pondexter was still there. Mr. LeRoy and Mr. Courtland from down the street were there too, and all were admiring the Cadillac as my father stood proudly by, pointing out the various features.

"Brand-new 1950 Coupe deVille!" I heard one of the men saying.

"Just off the showroom floor!" my father said. "I just couldn't resist it."

My sister and I eased up to the car and peeked in. It was all
40　gold inside. Gold leather seats. Gold carpeting. Gold dashboard. It was like no car we had owned before. It looked like a car for rich folks.

"Daddy, are we rich?" I asked. My father laughed.

1.　**in unison** (IHN YOO NUH SUHN): in chorus; in the same words, spoken at the same time.

A LITERARY FOCUS

By now you know that 'lois is the main character of this **novella**. What information have you already learned about her?

_____

_____

_____

_____

_____

B READ AND DISCUSS

Comprehension

What does the author show us about the relationship between the sisters and their father?

C VOCABULARY

Academic Vocabulary

Interpret means "understand or find out the meaning of." Circle any clues in lines 61–76 that help you to interpret Dee's reaction to the Cadillac.

"Daddy, it's ours, isn't it?" asked Wilma, who was older and more practical than I. She didn't intend to give her heart too quickly to something that wasn't hers. **A**

"You like it?"

"Oh, Daddy, yes!"

He looked at me. "What 'bout you, 'lois?"

50   "Yes, sir!"

My father laughed again. "Then I expect I can't much disappoint my girls, can I? It's ours, all right!" **B**

Wilma and I hugged our father with our joy. My uncles came from the house, and my aunts, carrying their babies, came out too. Everybody surrounded the car and owwed and ahhed. Nobody could believe it.

Then my mother came out.

Everybody stood back grinning as she approached the car. There was no smile on her face. We all waited for her to speak.

60   She stared at the car, then looked at my father, standing there as proud as he could be. Finally she said, "You didn't buy this car, did you, Wilbert?"

"Gotta admit I did. Couldn't resist it."

"But . . . but what about our Mercury? It was perfectly good!"

"Don't you like the Cadillac, Dee?"

"That Mercury wasn't even a year old!"

My father nodded. "And I'm sure whoever buys it is going to get themselves a good car. But we've got ourselves a better one. Now stop frowning, honey, and let's take ourselves a ride in our

70   brand-new Cadillac!"

My mother shook her head. "I've got food on the stove," she said and, turning away, walked back to the house. **C**

There was an awkward silence, and then my father said, "You know Dee never did much like surprises. Guess this here Cadillac was a bit too much for her. I best go smooth things out with her."

Everybody watched as he went after my mother. But when he came back, he was alone.

"Well, what she say?" asked one of my uncles.

80　　　My father shrugged and smiled. "Told me I bought this
Cadillac alone, I could just ride in it alone."

　　　Another uncle laughed. "Uh-oh! Guess she told you!"

　　　"Oh, she'll come around," said one of my aunts. "Any woman
would be proud to ride in this car."

　　　"That's what I'm banking on," said my father as he
went around to the street side of the car and opened the door.
"All right! Who's for a ride?" **D**

　　　"We are!" Wilma and I cried.

　　　All three of my uncles and one of my aunts, still holding
90　her baby, and Mr. Pondexter climbed in with us, and we took off
for the first ride in the gold Cadillac. It was a glorious ride, and
we drove all through the city of Toledo. We rode past the church
and past the school. We rode through Ottawa Hills, where the
rich folks lived, and on into Walbridge Park and past the zoo,
then along the Maumee River. But none of us had had enough
of the car, so my father put the car on the road and we drove all
the way to Detroit. We had plenty of family there, and everybody
was just as pleased as could be about the Cadillac. My father told
our Detroit relatives that he was in the doghouse with my mother
100　about buying the Cadillac. My uncles told them she wouldn't
ride in the car. All the Detroit family thought that was funny, and
everybody, including my father, laughed about it and said my
mother would come around.

　　　It was early evening by the time we got back home, and
I could see from my mother's face she had not come around. **E**
She was angry now not only about the car, but that we had been
gone so long. I didn't understand that, since my father had called
her as soon as we reached Detroit to let her know where we were.
I had heard him myself. I didn't understand either why she did
110　not like that fine Cadillac and thought she was being terribly
disagreeable with my father. That night, as she tucked Wilma and
me in bed, I told her that too.

　　　"Is this your business?" she asked.

　　　"Well, I just think you ought to be nice to Daddy. I think
you ought to ride in that car with him! It'd sure make him happy."

D READ AND DISCUSS

Comprehension
What's going on with Dee in this scene?

E READ AND DISCUSS

Comprehension
What does 'lois mean by, "I could see from my mother's face she had not come around"?

The Gold Cadillac　　**113**

A   **READING FOCUS**

Predict whether or not the father will keep the new Cadillac. Explain your answer.

_____

_____

_____

_____

_____

B   **READ AND DISCUSS**

Comprehension

What does this segment show us about Dee's anger toward the Cadillac purchase?

"I think you ought to go to sleep," she said and turned out the light.

Later I heard her arguing with my father. "We're supposed to be saving for a house!" she said.

120   "We've already got a house!" said my father.

"But you said you wanted a house in a better neighborhood. I thought that's what we both said!"

"I haven't changed my mind."

"Well, you have a mighty funny way of saving for it, then. Your brothers are saving for houses of their own, and you don't see them out buying new cars every year!"

"We'll still get the house, Dee. That's a promise!"

"Not with new Cadillacs we won't!" said my mother, and then she said a very loud good night, and all was quiet. **A**

130   The next day was Sunday, and everybody figured that my mother would be sure to give in and ride in the Cadillac. After all, the family always went to church together on Sunday. But she didn't give in. What was worse, she wouldn't let Wilma and me ride in the Cadillac either. She took us each by the hand, walked past the Cadillac where my father stood waiting, and headed on toward the church three blocks away. I was really mad at her now. I had been looking forward to driving up to the church in that gold Cadillac and having everybody see. **B**

140   On most Sunday afternoons during the summertime, my mother, my father, Wilma, and I would go for a ride. Sometimes we just rode around the city and visited friends and family. Sometimes we made short trips over to Chicago or Peoria or Detroit to see relatives there or to Cleveland, where we had relatives too, but we could also see the Cleveland Indians play. Sometimes we joined our aunts and uncles and drove in a caravan[2] out to the park or to the beach. At the park or the beach, Wilma and I would run and play. My mother and my aunts would spread a picnic, and my father and my uncles would shine their cars.

---

2.   **caravan** (KAR UH VAN): group of vehicles traveling together.

150   But on this Sunday afternoon, my mother refused to ride
anywhere. She told Wilma and me that we could go. So we left
her alone in the big, empty house, and the family cars, led by the
gold Cadillac, headed for the park. **C** For a while I played and
had a good time, but then I stopped playing and went to sit with
my father. Despite his laughter he seemed sad to me. I think he
was missing my mother as much as I was.

That evening, my father took my mother to dinner down at
the corner cafe. They walked. Wilma and I stayed at the house,
chasing fireflies in the backyard. My aunts and uncles sat in
160   the yard and on the porch, talking and laughing about the day
and watching us. It was a soft summer's evening, the kind that
came every day and was expected. The smell of charcoal and of
barbecue drifting from up the block, the sound of laughter and
music and talk drifting from yard to yard were all a part of it.
Soon one of my uncles joined Wilma and me in our chase of
fireflies, and when my mother and father came home, we were
at it still. My mother and father watched us for a while, while
everybody else watched them to see if my father would take out
the Cadillac and if my mother would slide in beside him to take a
170   ride. But it soon became evident that the dinner had not changed
my mother's mind. She still refused to ride in the Cadillac. I just
couldn't understand her objection to it. **D**

Though my mother didn't like the Cadillac, everybody else
in the neighborhood certainly did. That meant quite a few folks
too, since we lived on a very busy block. On one corner was a
grocery store, a cleaner's, and a gas station. Across the street was
a beauty shop and a fish market, and down the street was a bar,
another grocery store, the Dixie Theater, the cafe, and a drug-
store. There were always people strolling to or from one of these
180   places, and because our house was right in the middle of the
block, just about everybody had to pass our house and the gold
Cadillac. Sometimes people took in the Cadillac as they walked,
their heads turning for a longer look as they passed. Then there
were people who just outright stopped and took a good look
before continuing on their way. I was proud to say that car

C **VOCABULARY**

Word Study

What does the fact that
the gold Cadillac leads the
caravan on this day tell you
about the meaning of the
car to 'lois's family members?

_____

_____

_____

_____

_____

_____

D **READ AND DISCUSS**

Comprehension

How have these scenes
added to what we know
about 'lois's father and
mother?

A (READ AND DISCUSS)

Comprehension
What does this segment show us about 'lois?

B (READ AND DISCUSS)

Comprehension
What does the conversation between 'lois's father and his relatives show us about their lives?

belonged to my family. I felt mighty important as people called to me as I ran down the street. "'Ey, 'lois! How's that Cadillac, girl? Riding fine?" I told my mother how much everybody liked that car. She was not impressed and made no comment. **A**

190   Since just about everybody on the block knew everybody else, most folks knew that my mother wouldn't ride in the Cadillac. Because of that, my father took a lot of good-natured kidding from the men. My mother got kidded too, as the women said if she didn't ride in that car, maybe some other woman would. And everybody laughed about it and began to bet on who would give in first, my mother or my father. But then my father said he was going to drive the car south into Mississippi to visit my grandparents, and everybody stopped laughing.

My uncles stopped.

200   So did my aunts.

Everybody.

"Look here, Wilbert," said one of my uncles, "it's too dangerous. It's like putting a loaded gun to your head."

"I paid good money for that car," said my father. "That gives me a right to drive it where I please. Even down to Mississippi."

My uncles argued with him and tried to talk him out of driving the car south. So did my aunts, and so did the neighbors, Mr. LeRoy, Mr. Courtland, and Mr. Pondexter. They said it was a dangerous thing, a mighty dangerous thing, for a black man to

210   drive an expensive car into the rural South.

"Not much those folks hate more'n to see a northern Negro coming down there in a fine car," said Mr. Pondexter. "They see those Ohio license plates, they'll figure you coming down uppity, trying to lord your fine car over them!" **B**

I listened, but I didn't understand. I didn't understand why they didn't want my father to drive that car south. It was his.

"Listen to Pondexter, Wilbert!" cried another uncle. "We might've fought a war to free people overseas, but we're not free

here! Man, those white folks down south'll lynch[3] you soon's look
at you. You know that!"

Wilma and I looked at each other. Neither one of us knew
what lynch meant, but the word sent a shiver through us. We
held each other's hand.

My father was silent, then he said: "All my life I've had to
be heedful of what white folks thought. Well, I'm tired of that.
I worked hard for everything I got. Got it honest, too. Now I got
that Cadillac because I liked it and because it meant something to
me that somebody like me from Mississippi could go and buy it.
It's my car, I paid for it, and I'm driving it south." **C**

My mother, who had said nothing through all this, now
stood. "Then the girls and I'll be going too," she said.

"No!" said my father.

My mother only looked at him and went off to the kitchen.

My father shook his head. It seemed he didn't want us to go.
My uncles looked at each other, then at my father. "You set on
doing this, we'll all go," they said. "That way we can watch out
for each other." My father took a moment and nodded. Then my
aunts got up and went off to their kitchens too.

All the next day, my aunts and my mother cooked and the
house was filled with delicious smells. They fried chicken and
baked hams and cakes and sweet potato pies and mixed potato
salad. They filled jugs with water and punch and coffee. Then
they packed everything in huge picnic baskets, along with bread
and boiled eggs, oranges and apples, plates and napkins, spoons
and forks and cups. They placed all that food on the back seats of
the cars. It was like a grand, grand picnic we were going on, and
Wilma and I were mighty excited. We could hardly wait to start.

My father, my mother, Wilma, and I got into the Cadillac. My
uncles, my aunts, my cousins got into the Ford, the Buick, and the
Chevrolet, and we rolled off in our caravan headed south. Though
my mother was finally riding in the Cadillac, she had no praise for
it. In fact, she said nothing about it at all. She still seemed upset,

---

3. **lynch** (LIHNCH): kill a person without legal authority, usually by
    hanging. Lynchings are usually committed by violent mobs that have
    taken the law into their own hands.

C READING FOCUS

Do you **predict** that 'lois's father's attitude will change or remain the same once he arrives in the South? Why?

_____

_____

_____

_____

_____

_____

_____

A **READ AND DISCUSS**

Comprehension

What is 'lois thinking about during the trip?

B **READ AND DISCUSS**

Comprehension

What is 'lois thinking about the grand picnic now?

C **VOCABULARY**

Word Study

Usually, the word *eyeball* is used as a noun that means "a part of the eye." In this sentence, *eyeballed* is used as a verb that means "look over carefully." How are the two definitions similar?

_____

_____

_____

_____

_____

_____

and since she still seemed to feel the same about the car, I wondered why she had insisted upon making this trip with my father. **A**

We left the city of Toledo behind, drove through Bowling Green and down through the Ohio countryside of farms and small towns, through Dayton and Cincinnati, and across the Ohio River into Kentucky. On the other side of the river, my father stopped the car and looked back at Wilma and me and said, "Now from here on, whenever we stop and there're white people around, I don't want either one of you to say a word. *Not one word!* Your mother and I'll do the talking. That understood?"

"Yes, sir," Wilma and I both said, though we didn't truly understand why.

My father nodded, looked at my mother, and started the car again. We rolled on, down Highway 25 and through the bluegrass hills of Kentucky. Soon we began to see signs. Signs that read: "White Only, Colored Not Allowed." Hours later, we left the Bluegrass State and crossed into Tennessee. Now we saw even more of the signs saying: "White Only, Colored Not Allowed." We saw the signs above water fountains and in restaurant windows. We saw them in ice cream parlors and at hamburger stands. We saw them in front of hotels and motels, and on the restroom doors of filling stations. I didn't like the signs. I felt as if I were in a foreign land.

I couldn't understand why the signs were there, and I asked my father what the signs meant. He said they meant we couldn't drink from the water fountains. He said they meant we couldn't stop to sleep in the motels. He said they meant we couldn't stop to eat in the restaurants. I looked at the grand picnic basket I had been enjoying so much. Now I understood why my mother had packed it. Suddenly the picnic did not seem so grand. **B**

Finally we reached Memphis. We got there at a bad time. Traffic was heavy and we got separated from the rest of the family. We tried to find them but it was no use. We had to go on alone. We reached the Mississippi state line, and soon after, we heard a police siren. A police car came up behind us. My father slowed the Cadillac, then stopped. Two white policemen got out of their car. They eyeballed the Cadillac and told my father to get out. **C**

"Whose car is this, boy?" they asked.

290   I saw anger in my father's eyes. "It's mine," he said.

"You're a liar," said one of the policemen. "You stole this car."

"Turn around, put your hands on top of that car, and spread-eagle," said the other policeman.

My father did as he was told. They searched him and I didn't understand why.

I didn't understand either why they had called my father a liar and didn't believe that the Cadillac was his. I wanted to ask, but I remembered my father's warning not to say a word, and I obeyed that warning.

300   The policemen told my father to get in the back of the police car. My father did. One policeman got back into the police car. The other policeman slid behind the wheel of our Cadillac. The police car started off. The Cadillac followed. Wilma and I looked at each other and at our mother. We didn't know what to think. We were scared.

The Cadillac followed the police car into a small town and stopped in front of the police station. The policeman stepped out of our Cadillac and took the keys. The other policeman took my father into the police station.

310   "Mother-Dear!" Wilma and I cried. "What're they going to do to our daddy? They going to hurt him?"

"He'll be all right," said my mother. "He'll be all right." But she didn't sound so sure of that. She seemed worried. **D**

We waited. More than three hours we waited. Finally my father came out of the police station. We had lots of questions to ask him. He said the police had given him a ticket for speeding and locked him up. But then the judge had come. My father had paid the ticket and they had let him go.

He started the Cadillac and drove slowly out of the town,
320   below the speed limit. The police car followed us. People standing on steps and sitting on porches and in front of stores stared at us as we passed. Finally we were out of the town. The police car still followed. Dusk was falling. **E** The night grew black, and finally the police car turned around and left us.

D READ AND DISCUSS

Comprehension

How does 'lois handle the unfolding events with the police?

E LANGUAGE COACH

The noun *dusk* means "the period of time when the sky darkens as the sun goes down." If we add a *y* to the end of the word, it changes **form** and becomes an adjective with a similar meaning. What do you think *dusky* means? Look up the word to confirm your guess.

_____

_____

_____

A READ AND DISCUSS

Comprehension

What is going on now?

B READ AND DISCUSS

Comprehension

What kind of mood does the conversation between 'lois and her father create?

We drove and drove. But my father was tired now and my grandparents' farm was still far away. My father said he had to get some sleep, and since my mother didn't drive, he pulled into a grove of trees at the side of the road and stopped.

"I'll keep watch," said my mother.

330 "Wake me if you see anybody," said my father.

"Just rest," said my mother.

So my father slept. But that bothered me. I needed him awake. I was afraid of the dark and of the woods and of whatever lurked there. My father was the one who kept us safe, he and my uncles. But already the police had taken my father away from us once today, and my uncles were lost.

"Go to sleep, baby," said my mother. "Go to sleep." **A**

But I was afraid to sleep until my father woke. I had to help my mother keep watch. I figured I had to help protect us too,

340 in case the police came back and tried to take my father away again. There was a long, sharp knife in the picnic basket, and I took hold of it, clutching it tightly in my hand. Ready to strike, I sat there in the back of the car, eyes wide, searching the blackness outside the Cadillac. Wilma, for a while, searched the night too, then she fell asleep. I didn't want to sleep, but soon I found I couldn't help myself as an unwelcome drowsiness came over me. I had an uneasy sleep, and when I woke, it was dawn and my father was gently shaking me. I woke with a start and my hand went up, but the knife wasn't there. My mother had it. My father

350 took my hand. "Why were you holding the knife, 'lois?" he asked.

I looked at him and at my mother. "I—I was scared," I said. **B**

My father was thoughtful. "No need to be scared now, sugar," he said. "Daddy's here and so is Mother-Dear."

Then after a glance at my mother, he got out of the car, walked to the road, looked down it one way, then the other.

When he came back and started the motor, he turned the Cadillac north, not south.

"What're you doing?" asked my mother.

Courtesy of the James Cox Gallery at Woodstock

"Heading back to Memphis," said my father. "Cousin
360   Halton's there. We'll leave the Cadillac and get his car. Driving
this car any farther south with you and the girls in the car, it's just
not worth the risk."

And so that's what we did. Instead of driving through
Mississippi in golden splendor, we traveled its streets and roads
and highways in Cousin Halton's solid, yet not so splendid,
four-year-old Chevy. When we reached my grandparents' farm,
my uncles and aunts were already there. Everybody was glad to
see us. They had been worried. They asked about the Cadillac.
My father told them what had happened, and they nodded and
370   said he had done the best thing.

We stayed one week in Mississippi. During that week I often
saw my father, looking deep in thought, walk off alone across the
family land. I saw my mother watching him. One day I ran after
my father, took his hand, and walked the land with him. I asked
him all the questions that were on my mind. I asked him why
the policemen had treated him the way they had and why people
didn't want us to eat in the restaurants or drink from the water
fountains or sleep in the hotels. I told him I just didn't understand all that.

380   My father looked at me and said that it all was a difficult
thing to understand and he didn't really understand it himself.
He said it all had to do with the fact that black people had once
been forced to be slaves. He said it had to do with our skins being
colored. He said it had to do with stupidity and ignorance. He

Selection Vocabulary
'lois's father says that black
people are treated unfairly
because of *ignorance*, which
means "lack of knowledge."
What knowledge do you
think some white people in
the South lack at this time?

_____

_____

_____

_____

_____

_____

_____

Have you had to **adjust** your **prediction** about whether the father will keep the car? Why or why not?

_____

_____

_____

_____

_____

_____

_____

said it had to do with the law, the law that said we could be treated like this here in the South. And for that matter, he added, any other place in these United States where folks thought the same as so many folks did here in the South. But he also said, "I'm hoping one day though we can drive that long road down here

390 and there won't be any signs. I'm hoping one day the police won't stop us just because of the color of our skins and we're riding in a gold Cadillac with northern plates."

When the week ended, we said a sad goodbye to my grand-parents and all the Mississippi family and headed in a caravan back toward Memphis. In Memphis, we returned Cousin Halton's car and got our Cadillac. Once we were home, my father put the Cadillac in the garage and didn't drive it. I didn't hear my mother say any more about the Cadillac. I didn't hear my father speak of it either.

400 Some days passed, and then on a bright Saturday afternoon while Wilma and I were playing in the backyard, I saw my father go into the garage. He opened the garage doors wide so the sunshine streamed in and began to shine the Cadillac. I saw my mother at the kitchen window staring out across the yard at my father. For a long time, she stood there watching my father shine his car. Then she came out and crossed the yard to the garage, and I heard her say, "Wilbert, you keep the car." He looked at her as if he had not heard. **A**

"You keep it," she repeated and turned and walked back to

410 the house.

My father watched her until the back door had shut behind her. Then he went on shining the car and soon began to sing. About an hour later he got into the car and drove away. That evening when he came back, he was walking. The Cadillac was nowhere in sight.

"Daddy, where's our new Cadillac?" I demanded to know. So did Wilma.

He smiled and put his hand on my head. "Sold it," he said as my mother came into the room.

420 "But how come?" I asked. "We poor now?"

© Michael Nelson/Getty Images

B (READ AND DISCUSS)

Comprehension

What's going on with the family and the Cadillac?

"No, sugar. We've got more money towards our new house now, and we're all together. I figure that makes us about the richest folks in the world." He smiled at my mother, and she smiled too and came into his arms.

After that, we drove around in an old 1930s Model A Ford my father had. He said he'd factory-ordered us another Mercury, this time with my mother's approval. Despite that, most folks on the block figured we had fallen on hard times after such a splashy showing of good times, and some folks even laughed at us as the

430 Ford rattled around the city. I must admit that at first I was pretty much embarrassed to be riding around in that old Ford after the splendor of the Cadillac. But my father said to hold my head high. We and the family knew the truth. As fine as the Cadillac had been, he said, it had pulled us apart for a while. Now, as ragged and noisy as that old Ford was, we all rode in it together, and we were a family again. So I held my head high. **B**

Still, though, I thought often of that Cadillac. We had had the Cadillac only a little more than a month, but I wouldn't soon forget its splendor or how I'd felt riding around inside it.

440 I wouldn't soon forget either the ride we had taken south in it. I wouldn't soon forget the signs, the policemen, or my fear. I would remember that ride and the gold Cadillac all my life.

Skills Practice

The Gold Cadillac

USE A TABLE

Like a novel or a short story, a **novella** has characters, a plot, and settings. In the table below, list all the characters from *The Gold Cadillac*. Then explain the plot, and describe one of the settings. Be as specific as possible.

The Gold Cadillac	
Characters	1.
Plot	2.
Setting	3.

Applying Your Skills

The Gold Cadillac

VOCABULARY DEVELOPMENT

DIRECTIONS: Review the meaning of each of the words from the Word Box.
Then, write your own sentences using each word.

Word Box

dusk

rural

ignorance

evident

1. _____
2. _____
3. _____
4. _____

LITERARY SKILLS FOCUS: FORMS OF FICTION: IDENTIFYING THE CHARACTERISTICS OF THE NOVELLA

DIRECTIONS: The **novella** *The Gold Cadillac* has several different settings.
Copy the concept web below on to a separate sheet of paper. List four of
those settings in the concept web. Then, give details about what takes place
in each setting.

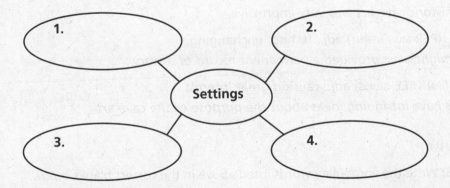

1.

2.

Settings

3.

4.

READING SKILLS FOCUS: MAKING AND ADJUSTING PREDICTIONS

DIRECTIONS: In the table below, list a **prediction** you made while reading
the story. Did it need to be **adjusted**? If so, explain why.

My prediction:	Why I needed to adjust:

Reading Standard 3.1 Identify the forms of fiction and describe the major characteristics of each form.

Making It Up as We Go

by Jennifer Kroll

INFORMATIONAL TEXT FOCUS: STRUCTURAL FEATURES OF POPULAR MEDIA: MAGAZINES

Look for the following **features** when you read a **magazine:**

Cover Announces the main articles inside.

Contents page Tells what page numbers all articles are on.

Title Has large lettering to catch your attention.

Subtitle Better explains what the article is about.

Headings Have lettering that is set off from the rest of the text. They break up the text into sections based on different topics, which are often the main points of the article.

Illustrations Graphs, drawings, maps, and photographs give you more information in a visual way. **Captions,** found near illustrations, help explain what you are looking at.

SELECTION VOCABULARY

prehistoric (PREE HIH STAWR RIHK) *adj.:* relating to the time before written history.
The prehistoric cave art was very impressive.

permanent (PER MUH NEHNT) *adj.:* lasting; unchanging.
The art might have provided a permanent record of a story.

intriguing (IHN TREE GIHNG) *adj.:* causing great interest.
Scientists have intriguing ideas about the purpose of the cave art.

WORD STUDY

DIRECTIONS: Write the vocabulary words listed above in the correct blanks below.

In the magazine article "Making It Up as We Go," the author discusses how (1) _____ peoples passed on their stories. Since there was not yet a system of writing, stories were not recorded in a (2) _____ way, but instead passed down by word of mouth. The idea of passing information on in this way is especially (3) _____ today, when we are so used to different versions of written information, from e-mail to text messaging.

Reading Standard 2.1 Identify the structural features of popular media (e.g., newspapers, magazines, online information) and use the features to obtain information.

MAKING IT UP AS WE GO: THE HISTORY OF STORYTELLING

by Jennifer Kroll

On an autumn day in 1879, eight-year-old Maria Sanz de Sautuola explored a cave on her family's land in Altamira, Spain. As her candle lit up a large chamber, Maria was startled and called to her father. "Look, Papa! Oxen!" she cried. The chamber was filled with animal paintings. From where she stood, oxen seemed to be running across the ceiling.

Similar paintings have since been found in more than 200 caves in Spain and France. The artwork shows such animals as mammoths, reindeer, and horses. Sometimes, symbols have been drawn on or near the creatures. At a cave called Font-du-Gaume, these symbols include upside-down *T*s and side-by-side circles with arches above them.

What did these pictures and symbols mean to the people who made them? We cannot know. But it is reasonable to wonder whether the images were used as a way of preserving stories—or as an aid in telling them. **(A)**

Headings break up the text into sections.

STONE-AGE STORYTELLERS

Maria and her father, Marcelino, found stone tools, pieces of pottery, oyster shells, and animal bones nearby before uncovering the art. Marcelino figured the items, and therefore the artwork, were created by prehistoric people called Cro-Magnons. Cro-Magnons were **(B)**

Marcelino Sanz de Sautuola and his daughter Maria discover the cave paintings at Altamira.

hunters and gatherers who lived from about 40,000 to 10,000 years ago. They did not have written language as we do. But surely they had stories.

Imagine a Cro-Magnon storyteller standing in the Altamira cave, lighting up pictures to show parts of a story. Perhaps he stood where Maria stood. Maybe the flicker of fire from his torch made the oxen seem to run. **(C)**

PASS IT ON, PASS IT DOWN

Writing is a recent invention, only about 5,000 to 6,000 years old. Among the first people to develop a writing system were the Sumerians. They lived in the region that is now Iraq. Their writing system, called

A READ AND DISCUSS

Comprehension

What has the author told us in this first section?

B VOCABULARY

Selection Vocabulary

Examine the word *prehistoric*. It uses the prefix *pre-*. Think of other words that use the same prefix. What do the definitions of all these words have in common?

_____

_____

_____

_____

C READ AND DISCUSS

Comprehension

How does this new information add to what we already learned?

READING FOCUS

What does this **caption** tell you about the illustration?

_____

_____

_____

_____

_____

B **READ AND DISCUSS**

Comprehension

The author has given us a number of facts here. What's the point of this information?

FROM DRAWING TO WRITING

The Sumerians first wrote by using pictures to represent things and ideas. Gradually, the pictures became more like abstract symbols and less like illustrations of what they represented. These examples show how Sumerian writing changed over time. **A**

Illustrations help you picture things described in the article.

	3300 BC	2800 BC	2400 BC	1800 BC
Heaven				
Grain				
Fish				
Bird				
Water				

THE RARE AND WONDERFUL WRITTEN WORD

JUST HOW NEW AND NOVEL IS WRITING? CONSIDER THESE FACTS:

- Modern humans (*Homo sapiens*) have existed for between 100,000 and 150,000 years. The earliest written language, though, dates from only 5,000 to 6,000 years ago.
- Perhaps tens of thousands of different languages have existed in human history. Stories have been told orally in most of these languages. But *written* stories exist in only a small percentage of all languages—about 106!
- About 6,000 languages are spoken in the world today. Only about 78 of them have a written form that is used for recording and saving stories.
- Even today, hundreds of languages with no written form are being used all over the world. **B**

cuneiform, dates back to before 3000 B.C.  The Sumerians wrote by pressing marks into moist clay tablets with a sharp reed. The tablets would be baked, hardening the clay so that it would last. They kept detailed business and government records. The Sumerians also wrote down stories. The *Epic of Gilgamesh* is a Sumerian story that's still told today. It was written on clay tablets that have lasted thousands of years.

Before developing writing, the Sumerians kept stories alive in the way most groups have throughout time. They passed on tales by word of mouth. Many of these ancient stories were written into the *Epic of Gilgamesh*. But the tales were passed from person to person for years before being pressed into clay.

A culture that passes on stories by word of mouth is said to have an *oral tradition*. The stories of such a culture differ from those of a *chirographic* (ky ruh GRAF ihk), or writing, culture in some ways. For one thing, written stories remain the same with each reading. But unwritten stories change with every telling. Each storyteller cannot help but give each story his or her own twist.

PREHISTORIC BLOGGERS?

The idea that a story may never be told the same twice might seem to go against the belief that a story is a permanent creation. Then again, maybe not. After all, we're used to seeing stories change as they shift forms—when a novel is made into a film, for example, or a film into a comic book.

The **caption** explains what is shown in an illustration.

American tall tales, like those about Paul Bunyan and Babe the Blue Ox (the subjects of this California sculpture) are examples of stories spread by word of mouth.

We still pass on stories by word of mouth, just as our ancestors did. Think of campers telling scary stories around a fire or fishers swapping "biggest catch" stories. Most people like to give a story their own "spin." Think of news passed around the school cafeteria or by Internet bloggers. Most Web writers don't just tell you what happened; they tell you what they *think* about what happened. The journalists Gregory Curtis and Daniel Burnstein have (separately) suggested that the Cro-Magnons might have done something similar when they drew symbols around cave paintings. Could the symbols be comments added to a story by later viewers or tellers? It is an intriguing idea. What do you think?

Read with a Purpose
What's something that has stayed the same throughout the history of storytelling?

C LANGUAGE COACH

The word *cuneiform* comes from the Latin words *cuneus*, which means "wedge," and *forma* which means "shape or figure." The word was created to describe ancient writing, which was often done with a wedge-shaped tool. Why are these Latin words used to describe this kind of writing?

_____

_____

_____

_____

D READING FOCUS

Re-read each of the **headings** in this article. How do they help you follow the flow of information in the article?

_____

_____

_____

_____

E READING FOCUS

Now that you are finished reading, do you feel that the **title** does a good job of describing the article? What other titles would you suggest for this article?

_____

_____

_____

_____

Iraqi Treasures Hunted

by Barbara Bakowski

INFORMATIONAL TEXT FOCUS: STRUCTURAL FEATURES OF POPULAR MEDIA: NEWSPAPERS

Look for the following **features** when you read a **newspaper:**

Sections Organize a newspaper by specific topics.

Headlines Tell what an article is about in large, bold-faced print.

Byline/Dateline Give the name of the reporter (byline) and describe where and when the event described in the article happened (dateline).

Lead Begins an article and answers at least one of the questions *who? what? where? when? why?* and *how?*

Captions Explain photographs and other graphics.

Sidebars Explain additional information in the margins of an article.

SELECTION VOCABULARY

recovered (RIH KUH VUHRD) *v.:* got back something lost.
Amy recovered her toy the day after she lost it.

civilizations (SIH VIH LUH ZAY SHUHNZ) *n.:* advanced cultures that are characteristic of particular times and places.
Some of the earliest civilizations were located in Mesopotamia.

authorities (UH THAWR UH TEEZ) *n.:* people with official responsibility for something.
Shawn reported the crime to the authorities.

WORD STUDY

DIRECTIONS: Write words from the vocabulary list above in the correct blanks below.

The newspaper article "Iraqi Treasures Hunted" explains how many artifacts stolen from Iraq's National Museum have been found, or

(1) _____, since the museum was looted. The article

describes how, despite the best efforts of (2) _____,

many artifacts remain in the wrong hands. Many of the lost artifacts date

back to the time of ancient (3) _____.

Reading Standard 2.1
Identify the structural features of popular media (e.g., newspapers, magazines, online information) and use the features to obtain information.

by Barbara Bakowski

NEWSPAPER ARTICLE

The **headline** tells you what the news story is about.

Iraqi workers repair a damaged statue.

IRAQI TREASURES HUNTED

Long after the looting of the National Museum, Iraq's treasures remain at risk. A

The **byline** tells you who wrote the article.

by Barbara Bakowski

THE WORLD ALMANAC

A **READING FOCUS**

Re-read the **headline**. Then, in your own words, write what you think this article will be about.

_____

_____

_____

_____

_____

_____

_____

_____

STONY BROOK, N.Y., January 14 — Nearly four years have passed since looters removed thousands of items from Iraq's National Museum. Many of the missing pieces have been recovered. Historians and art experts, however, say Iraq's historical artifacts are still in danger.

After the robberies, museum director Donny George walled off much of the collection to protect the remains. George left Iraq in 2006 and is serving as a visiting professor at New York's Stony Brook University. Now looters are stealing items from throughout Iraq, says his Stony Brook colleague Dr. Elizabeth Stone, an expert in the archaeology of the Middle East. Dig sites are the new targets. Some of the objects being taken date back to the world's earliest civilizations.

"Mesopotamia had the world's first cities, first writing," Stone says. "All our ideas of how we live in cities came from there." **B**

The **lead** presents the most important information.

Birthplace of Civilization **C**

Present-day Iraq occupies the land once called Mesopotamia. The name comes from a Greek word meaning "the land between rivers." In the plains between the Tigris and Euphrates rivers, some of the world's earliest settlements were founded: Sumer, Babylonia, and Assyria. "It was the cradle of civilization" more than 5,000 years ago, Stone says.

Early Mesopotamians were ahead of their time in many ways. They improved farming methods, created irrigation systems, learned how to measure time, wrote a set of laws, and invented the wheeled chariot. The Sumerians also invented cuneiform, one of the first writing systems in the world, before 3000 B.C. *The Epic of Gilgamesh*, a famous work of Sumerian literature, was recorded on clay tablets that still survive. It was written down in about 2000 B.C. **D**

Ancient Objects Stolen

Iraq's National Museum, founded in 1923, held the physical record of Mesopotamia's long history. The museum housed at least 500,000 valuable items. Then, in April 2003, U.S.-led troops moved into Baghdad. Looters used the resulting confusion as an opportunity to steal statues, coins, and more. In the final count, about 14,000 items from the museum were stolen, including the 5,000-year-old Warka mask and a copper sculpture known as the Bassetki statue.

Iraqi authorities, the United Nations, the U.S. government, and international law-enforcement officials began a search. Researchers at the Oriental Institute at the University of Chicago listed photographs and descriptions of the stolen objects on a Web site to aid in their recovery.

Relics Returned

Officials adopted a "no-questions-asked" policy to encourage the safe return of the missing

---

A **READING FOCUS**

Which of the following questions does the **lead** of this **article** (lines 1–5) answer: *who? what? where? when? why? how?*

B **READ AND DISCUSS**

Comprehension

What has the author set up for us in these first three paragraphs?

C **LANGUAGE COACH**

A **base word** can stand alone. It is a complete word by itself, but other word parts may be added to it to make new words. You know the word *civilization*. What is the base word of *civilization*?

D **READ AND DISCUSS**

Comprehension

What do all of these inventions indicate, or show, about the early Mesopotamians?

Riches from the Ruins

The full-page sidebar goes into greater detail about a point in the article.

E

Status: Found

Warka Mask—5,000-year-old marble mask from the Sumerian city of Uruk; one of the world's oldest realistic carvings and one of the world's oldest masks

Warka Vase—Stone (alabaster) vase from about 3000 B.C.; badly damaged during theft

Bassetki Statue—Copper sculpture from about 2300 B.C.

Nimrud Gold—Gold jewelry and precious stones dating from the eight and ninth centuries B.C.

Golden Harp of Ur—Gold and ivory harp from about 2600 B.C.; also badly damaged during looting

Clay Pot from Tall Hassuna—clay pot dating to the sixth millennium B.C., at least 1,500 years before the invention of the wheel

Status: Still Missing

Nimrud Lioness—Carved ivory and gold plaque dating to 800 B.C.

Hatra Goddess of Victory—Life-size head, made of copper, from the third century B.C.

Ninhursag Bull—One of two copper bulls from a temple built by the King of Ur around 2475 B.C.; the other has been recovered.

©Samir Mezban/Associated Press.

The 5,000-year-old "Warka mask," one of the most important artifacts stolen from Iraq's National Museum, is held up by Iraqi Minister of Culture Mufeed Muhammad Jawad Al Jazairee after it was found and returned to the police.

Lagash Statue—Headless inscribed limestone statue from about 2450 B.C.

Hatra Heads—Five statue heads from a city that thrived in the first century A.D.

Cuneiform Bricks—Nine bricks bearing royal inscriptions from the ancient Akkadian, Babylonian, and Sumerian empires.

E READING FOCUS

Why do you think the author chose to put this information in a full-page **sidebar**?

_____

_____

_____

_____

_____

_____

A VOCABULARY

Academic Vocabulary

A *concept* is a general notion or idea. Explain the concept behind the "no questions-asked" policy.

_____

_____

_____

_____

_____

_____

_____

_____

B READ AND DISCUSS

Comprehension

How do archeological digs figure into the puzzle of stolen objects?

A treasures. A few months after the looting, the Warka mask was returned to the museum. A police raid later in the year turned up the Bassetki statue. It had been hidden in a sewer in Iraq. A headless stone statue of a Sumerian king was recovered by American agents after it had been smuggled through Syria into the United States. Other treasures were found in the Netherlands, Britain, and Italy and were returned to Baghdad.

More than 5,000 of the stolen artifacts have been recovered. Experts say it may take decades to locate the rest. Some may never be found. Meanwhile, the National Museum remains closed to the public.

Looting Goes On

Experts in the United States and other countries say dig sites in Iraq are still being raided. "One of the many unfortunate consequences [of instability in Iraq is] widespread looting of archaeological sites," says Susan B. Downey. She is an art historian at the University of California, Los Angeles.

Iraqi law makes it illegal to remove artifacts from dig sites without government permission.

> The photographer's **credit** is usually printed along the side of the photo.

> The **caption** explains what is shown in a picture.

The head of a broken sculpture lies in a pile of rubble after looters plundered Iraq's National Museum for its treasures.

But thieves digging at any of thousands of sites may be able to smuggle priceless goods out of the country. Those objects have not yet been recorded or photographed, and therefore will be easier for smugglers to sell. **B**

Read with a Purpose

What specific efforts have been made to save ancient Iraqi art?

Skills Practice

Iraqi Treasures Hunted

DIRECTIONS: Fill in the second column with the **features** from the selection you just read.

Newspaper Feature	Iraqi Treasures Hunted
Headline	Iraqi Treasures Hunted: Long after the looting at the National Museum, Iraq's treasures remain at risk.
Byline	1.
Dateline	2.
Lead	3.
Sections	4.
Caption	5.

Preparing to Read

CAVE Online

INFORMATIONAL TEXT FOCUS: STRUCTURAL FEATURES OF POPULAR MEDIA: WEB SITE

Web sites are part of the Internet. They can help you research a topic. Each Web site has a URL, or address. You can use a **search engine** to find Web sites. Search engines give you a list of Web sites related to your topic. Look for the following **features** when you read a Web site:

Home page Gives basic information about the site.

Table of contents Lists the site's other pages. This often appears on the side of the home page. You can usually click on the names of the other pages to reach them.

Links Clickable names of Web sites related to the one you are exploring. You can get to these Web sites by clicking on their names which may be boldfaced, underlined, or in a different color from the rest of the text.

SELECTION VOCABULARY

techniques (TEHK NEEKS) *n.:* ways of doing complex activities.
> *The new techniques will create better images of the cave art.*

projection (PRUH JEHKT SHUHN) *n.:* display of an image made by shining light through a small version of the image.
> *The projection of the cave paintings made it seem as if I was in the actual cave.*

vivid (VIH VIHD) *adj.:* producing strong, clear images.
> *The vivid images of the cave drawings look like the real thing.*

WORD STUDY

DIRECTIONS: Write the vocabulary words from above on the correct blanks to complete the paragraph.

The CAVE Web site article discusses artists who are copying prehistoric cave art using advanced (1) _____ to help audiences experience the art without actually being in the cave. One way they do this is with photographic (2) _____. This method uses light to give audiences a very real idea of what the original art looks like. In some cases, the art will be very (3) _____, or clear.

Reading Standard 2.1
Identify the structural features of popular media (e.g., newspapers, magazines, online information) and use the features to obtain information.

CAVE ONLINE

WEB SITE

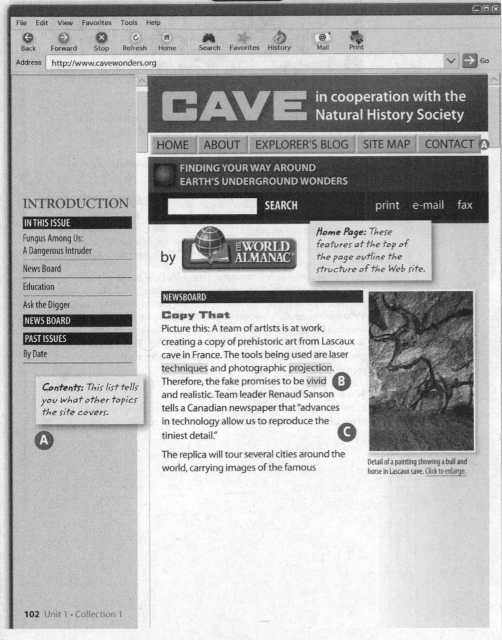

File   Edit   View   Favorites   Tools   Help

Back   Forward   Stop   Refresh   Home   Search   Favorites   History   Mail   Print

Address   http://www.cavewonders.org   Go

CAVE in cooperation with the Natural History Society

HOME   ABOUT   EXPLORER'S BLOG   SITE MAP   CONTACT Ⓐ

FINDING YOUR WAY AROUND EARTH'S UNDERGROUND WONDERS

SEARCH   print   e-mail   fax

by THE WORLD ALMANAC

Home Page: These features at the top of the page outline the structure of the Web site.

INTRODUCTION

IN THIS ISSUE

Fungus Among Us:
A Dangerous Intruder

News Board

Education

Ask the Digger

NEWS BOARD

PAST ISSUES

By Date

Contents: This list tells you what other topics the site covers.

Ⓐ

NEWSBOARD

Copy That

Picture this: A team of artists is at work, creating a copy of prehistoric art from Lascaux cave in France. The tools being used are laser techniques and photographic projection. Therefore, the fake promises to be vivid Ⓑ and realistic. Team leader Renaud Sanson tells a Canadian newspaper that "advances in technology allow us to reproduce the tiniest detail." Ⓒ

The replica will tour several cities around the world, carrying images of the famous

Detail of a painting showing a bull and horse in Lascaux cave. Click to enlarge.

102 Unit 1 · Collection 1

Artists work to create a replica of the Lascaux cave art.

17,000-year-old cave art to a wide audience. If all goes as planned, the exhibit will be ready for showing in 2008. It will begin its tour near the Eiffel Tower in Paris.

Lascaux cave in southwestern France was an accidental discovery made by teens in 1940. It has astounded the art world and the public ever since. **A** Rock paintings show bison, horses, stags, and other animals. The different stages of a hunt are clearly visible, as are the talents of those who did the artwork.

> **FACTOID**
> ❝[The Lascaux cave] has been closed to the public since 1963 to protect the paintings.❞

The site has been closed to the public since 1963 to protect the paintings. It attracted so many people—over a thousand a day—that the paintings were being damaged by the carbon dioxide from visitors' breath! That's why a professor of fine arts, Benjamin Britton, decided to design software in 1990 that would allow people to go on "virtual visits" of Lascaux. Britton, who had to work from photographs, became a finalist for a 1995 Discover Award. Sanson has been able to go one better than Britton: He has been given special permission to enter the cave to complete this latest high-tech project. **B**

Not the First Replica

In 1983, long before Renaud Sanson began his painstaking reproduction of the Lascaux cave paintings, a replica of Lascaux opened not far from the

A visitor to Lascaux II. This replica of two of the finest cave rooms opened in 1983.
Click to enlarge. **C**

original site. This replica, called Lascaux II, is an accurate copy of two of the most famous sections of the cave: the Great Hall of the Bulls and the Painted Gallery. (Lascaux is really a system of caves. Other sections of the cave system have been given colorful names based on the type of art found in them: the Shaft of the Dead Man, the Chamber of Felines, and the Chamber of Engravings.) Visitors can go inside the Great Hall of the Bulls, where paintings covering a huge area of the cave walls show horses, bulls, stags, and a creature with twisted horns that is sometimes called "the unicorn." They can also see what is probably the largest single cave-art image in the world—a seventeen-foot-long bull. True to the original cave paintings, these animals are colorfully drawn in red, black, and a dark yellow-gold color called ocher (OH kuhr). Visitors to Lascaux II can also see the Painted Gallery, which features what many art historians see as the finest paintings. Wild oxen, horses, bison, ibexes, cows, and a stag cover nearly one hundred feet of wall space—including the ceiling.

And the replicas don't end there. Tourists can go to Le Thot, France, to see more reproductions of Lascaux cave paintings at the Center of Prehistoric Art. **D**

Internet

104 Unit 1 • Collection 1

C READING FOCUS

How might this **feature** add to your understanding of the article?

_____

_____

_____

_____

_____

D VOCABULARY

Academic Vocabulary

Indicate means "show or point out." What does this paragraph *indicate* about the future of the Lascaux cave paintings?

_____

_____

_____

_____

_____

_____

Skills Practice

CAVE Online

USE A CHART

DIRECTIONS: Online news articles, such as the one you just read, often contain the structural **features** of both a Web site *and* a newspaper article. Fill in the second column with the newspaper and Web site features from CAVE Online.

Structural Feature	CAVE Online
Contents	1.
Byline	2.
Sections	3.
Links	4.
Caption	5.
Home page	6.

Applying Your Skills

Making It Up As We Go, Iraqi Treasures Hunted, and CAVE Online

VOCABULARY DEVELOPMENT

DIRECTIONS: In each exercise, circle the word that isn't related to the other two words. Then, on the blank lines, explain how the circled word is different.

1. intriguing/interesting/gigantic

_____
_____

2. blurry/faint/vivid

_____
_____

3. recovered/dropped/found

_____
_____

INFORMATIONAL TEXT FOCUS: STRUCTURAL FEATURES OF POPULAR MEDIA: MAGAZINES, NEWSPAPERS, AND WEB SITES

DIRECTIONS: Write a brief paragraph discussing how information was presented in the **newspaper** article, **magazine** article, and **Web site** that you just read.

_____
_____
_____
_____
_____
_____
_____
_____
_____
_____
_____

Reading Standard 2.1 Identify the structural features of popular media (e.g., newspapers, magazines, online information) and use the features to obtain information.

Chapter 4

VOCABULARY REVIEW

DIRECTIONS: Use context clues to figure out the meaning of the boldfaced vocabulary word. Circle the letter next to the correct definition.

1. It was **evident** from her reaction that she was not happy about the new car.

   a. obvious

   b. unclear

   c. helpful

   d. unhappy

2. A passing grade on the test would **indicate** that Roger understood subject matter.

   a. learn

   b. counter

   c. suggest

   d. disregard

3. The art museum has a **permanent** exhibit about the Renaissance, so we can see it any time.

   a. changing

   b. boring

   c. interesting

   d. lasting

4. After the robbery, I reported the crime to the **authorities**.

   a. thieves

   b. officials

   c. workers

   d. children

Skills Review

Chapter 4

LANGUAGE COACH

Sometimes it is easy to see how a word is related to other words. For example, many adjectives are constructed simply by adding a letter to another word, such as changing *snow* to *snowy*. However, other words need a little more work in order to change them into related words. Think of the changes needed to transform the verb *dare* into the noun *daring*.

DIRECTIONS: Look at the **base words** listed in the table. Write as many related noun, adjective, or verb forms of each word as you can think of. Use a dictionary if you need help.

Word	Related nouns, verbs, and adjectives
recover	1.
civil	2.
indicate	3.
laugh	4.
intrigue	5.
concept	6.

ORAL LANGUAGE ACTIVITY

DIRECTIONS: Work with a partner to answer the questions below about the stories and articles in Chapter 4. For each question, one partner should read aloud the sentences in the story or article that help answer the question. The other partner should then rephrase those sentences out loud in his or her own words. Take turns reading and rephrasing.

1. Why did Benjamin Britton decide to create software that allows people to virtually visit the Lascaux cave art? (CAVE Online article)

2. Why is 'lois's mother angry about the new Cadillac 'lois's father bought? ("The Gold Cadillac")

3. What are the headings in the article "Iraqi Treasures Hunted"?

4. Why did Manuel volunteer for the talent show? ("La Bamba")

Chapter 5

Elements of Poetry

© Greg Pease/Getty Images

Literary and Academic Vocabulary for Chapter 5

appreciate (UH PREE SHEE AYT) *v.:* understand and enjoy the good qualities or value of something.

I appreciate your help unloading the boxes.

detect (DIH TEHKT) *v.:* notice or discover, especially something that is not easy to see, hear, and so on.

I detect smoke in the kitchen.

device (DIH VYS) *n.:* way of achieving a particular purpose.

The author used figurative language as a device to make readers feel sympathy for the characters.

visual (VIHZH OO UHL) *adj.:* related to seeing or to sight.

My writing is very visual because I describe things in a way that makes it seem as though you are actually looking at them.

rhyme (RYM) *n.:* repetition of stressed vowel sounds and their accompanying consonant sounds.

She came up with a rhyme to help her remember her vocabulary words.

simile (SIHM UH LEE) *n.:* comparison between two things using words of comparison, such as *like* or *as.*

The poem "Ode to Mi Gato" uses similes such as "He's white/As spilled milk."

metaphor (MEHT UH FAWR) *n.:* direct comparison of two unlike things.

"The moon is a pearl on the dark cloth of night" is an example of a metaphor.

tone (TOHN) *n.:* attitude toward someone or something.

I could tell by the tone Mom used when speaking to me that she was very angry.

The Sneetches

by Dr. Seuss (Theodor Geisel)

LITERARY SKILLS FOCUS: RHYTHM AND RHYME

You probably know a lot about rhythm and rhymes from games, commercials, and songs. Words that rhyme end with the same vowel or consonant sound. **Rhythm** is the musical quality created by repeated sound patterns. A poem's **meter**—a regular pattern of stressed and unstressed syllables—is an important part of its rhythm. **Rhymes** are two or more words that have the same ending sounds, like *heat* and *sheet*. Dr. Seuss sometimes makes up words to rhyme with real words. For example, he rhymes the real word *stars* with the made-up word *thars*. Dr. Seuss uses rhythm and rhyme to give the poem a silly sound, but don't be fooled! A serious **tone**, or attitude, lies beneath the poem's surface.

READING SKILLS FOCUS: READING A POEM

The first time you **read a poem**, just enjoy it for its language. Then read it again, paying closer attention to its individual parts, such as title, punctuation, rhythm, and rhyme scheme. **Rhyme scheme** refers to a pattern of **end rhymes**, which are the rhymes made by words at the end of the lines. Patterns of rhymes are indicated by letters of the alphabet. For example, a four-line section of a poem with an *abab* pattern has two rhymes. The first line (*a*) rhymes with the third line; the second line (*b*) rhymes with the fourth line.

While reading "The Sneetches," keep the following hints for reading a poem in mind:

- **Scan** the poem to identify its meter. Mark stressed syllables with the ´ symbol and unstressed syllables with the ˘ symbol.

- **Read to enjoy.** Even serious poems should be enjoyable. Poets play with words, sounds, rhymes, rhythms, and punctuation.

- **Read aloud.** Read the poem in a normal voice as if you were talking to a friend. Only pause at the end of a line if the punctuation tells you to do so.

- **Pay attention to each word.** Each word in a poem is important to its meaning. Use a dictionary if you need to, and make sure word meanings are clear before you continue.

Reading Standard 3.4
Define how tone or meaning is conveyed in poetry through word choice, figurative language, sentence structure, line length, punctuation, rhythm, repetition, and rhyme.

Vocabulary Development

The Sneetches

SELECTION VOCABULARY

keen (KEEN) *adj.:* eager; enthusiastic.
> *McBean tells the Sneetches in a keen voice that he can help them.*

guaranteed (GAR UHN TEED) *v.* used as *adj.:* subject to a promise that something will be paid for or replaced if it is not satisfactory or acceptable.
> *Anything you buy from me is guaranteed, so you will never have to worry about buying a replacement.*

peculiar (PIH KYOOL YUHR) *adj.:* strange.
> *McBean shows the Sneetches a peculiar machine.*

WORD STUDY

DIRECTIONS: Match each vocabulary word in the first column with that which it best describes in the second column.

_____ **1.** keen   **a.** a talking dog

_____ **2.** guaranteed   **b.** a real estate agent looking to make a sale

_____ **3.** peculiar   **c.** a new computer with a one-year replacement offer

THE SNEETCHES

by Dr. Seuss (Theodor Geisel)

A READING FOCUS

What is the **rhyme scheme** of this stanza, or section, of the poem?

_____

Now, the Star-Belly Sneetches
Had bellies with stars.
The Plain-Belly Sneetches
Had none upon thars.

5   Those stars weren't so big. They were really so small
You might think such a thing wouldn't matter at all.

But, because they had stars, all the Star-Belly Sneetches
Would brag, "We're the best kind of Sneetch on the beaches."
With their snoots in the air, they would sniff and they'd snort
10 "We'll have nothing to do with the Plain-Belly sort!"
And whenever they met some, when they were out walking,
They'd hike right on past them without even talking. **A**

When the Star-Belly children went out to play ball,
Could a Plain Belly get in the game . . . ? Not at all.
15 You only could play if your bellies had stars
And the Plain-Belly children had none upon thars.

When the Star-Belly Sneetches had frankfurter roasts

Or picnics or parties or marshmallow toasts,

They never invited the Plain-Belly Sneetches.

20 They left them out cold, in the dark of the beaches.

They kept them away. Never let them come near.

And that's how they treated them year after year. **B**

Then ONE day, it seems . . . while the Plain-Belly Sneetches

Were moping and doping alone on the beaches,

25 Just sitting there wishing their bellies had stars . . .

A stranger zipped up in the strangest of cars!

"My friends," he announced in a voice clear and keen,

"My name is Sylvester McMonkey McBean.

And I've heard of your troubles. I've heard you're unhappy.

30 But I can fix that. I'm the Fix-it-Up Chappie. **C**

I've come here to help you. I have what you need.

And my prices are low. And I work at great speed.

And my work is one hundred per cent guaranteed!"

Then, quickly, Sylvester McMonkey McBean

35 Put together a very peculiar machine. **D**

And he said, "You want stars like a Star-Belly Sneetch . . . ?

My friends, you can have them for three dollars each!" **E**

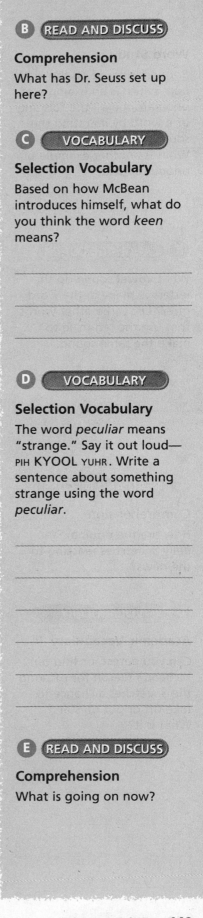

B READ AND DISCUSS

Comprehension

What has Dr. Seuss set up here?

C VOCABULARY

Selection Vocabulary

Based on how McBean introduces himself, what do you think the word *keen* means?

_____

_____

_____

D VOCABULARY

Selection Vocabulary

The word *peculiar* means "strange." Say it out loud— PIH KYOOL YUHR . Write a sentence about something strange using the word *peculiar*.

_____

_____

_____

_____

_____

E READ AND DISCUSS

Comprehension

What is going on now?

A VOCABULARY

Word Study

Bopped is based on the word *bop*, which is an example of onomatopoeia—the forming of a word by imitating the sound the word is related to. What is another example of onomatopoeia?

_____

_____

B LANGUAGE COACH

What **vowel sound** do the letters *ie* make in the word *grief*? List three other words that use the letters *ie* to make the same sound.

_____

_____

_____

C READ AND DISCUSS

Comprehension

How are the original Star-Belly Sneetches reacting to the news?

D VOCABULARY

Academic Vocabulary

Can you *detect*, or find out, McBean's reason for offering the Sneetches a chance to take off or put on stars? What is it?

_____

_____

_____

_____

"Just pay me your money and hop right aboard!"

So they clambered inside. Then the big machine roared

40 And it klonked. And it bonked. And it jerked. And it berked

And it bopped them about. **A** But the thing really worked!

When the Plain-Belly Sneetches popped out, they had stars!

They actually did. They had stars upon thars!

Then they yelled at the ones who had stars at the start.

45 "We're exactly like you! You can't tell us apart.

We're all just the same, now, you snooty old smarties!

And now we can go to your frankfurter parties."

"Good grief!" groaned the ones who had stars at the first. **B**

"We're *still* the best Sneetches and they are the worst.

50 But, now, how in the world will we know," they all frowned,

"If which kind is what, or the other way round?" **C**

Then up came McBean with a very sly wink

And he said, "Things are not quite as bad as you think.

So you don't know who's who. That is perfectly true.

55 But come with me, friends. Do you know what I'll do?

I'll make you, again, the best Sneetches on beaches

And all it will cost you is ten dollars eaches." **D**

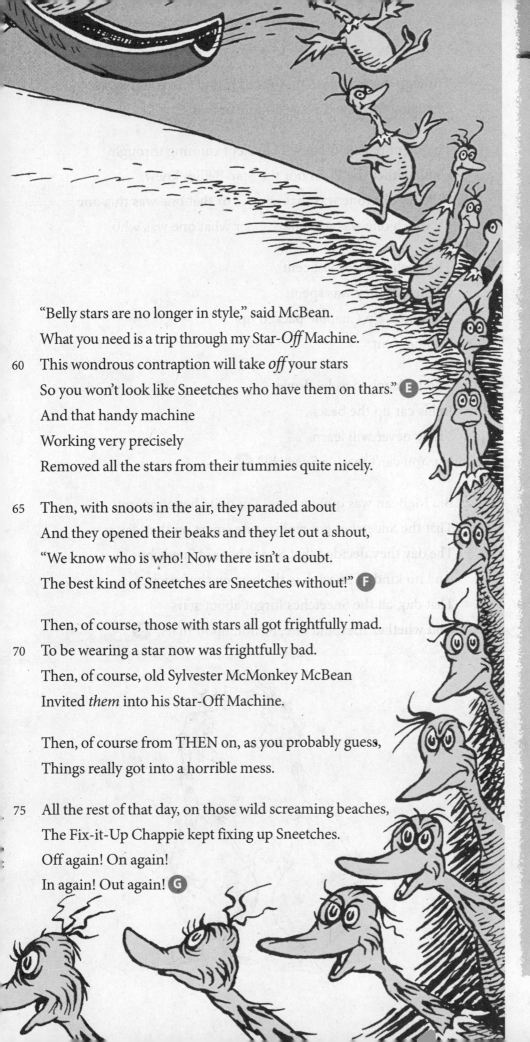

"Belly stars are no longer in style," said McBean.

What you need is a trip through my Star-*Off* Machine.

60 This wondrous contraption will take *off* your stars

So you won't look like Sneetches who have them on thars." **E**

And that handy machine

Working very precisely

Removed all the stars from their tummies quite nicely.

65 Then, with snoots in the air, they paraded about

And they opened their beaks and they let out a shout,

"We know who is who! Now there isn't a doubt.

The best kind of Sneetches are Sneetches without!" **F**

Then, of course, those with stars all got frightfully mad.

70 To be wearing a star now was frightfully bad.

Then, of course, old Sylvester McMonkey McBean

Invited *them* into his Star-Off Machine.

Then, of course from THEN on, as you probably guess,

Things really got into a horrible mess.

75 All the rest of that day, on those wild screaming beaches,

The Fix-it-Up Chappie kept fixing up Sneetches.

Off again! On again!

In again! Out again! **G**

E **VOCABULARY**

Word Study

Underline the word in this stanza that is a synonym, or word with the same meaning, for *contraption*.

F **LITERARY FOCUS**

What words in this stanza **rhyme**?

_____

_____

G **READING FOCUS**

Scan lines 77–78. Mark stressed syllables with the ´ symbol and unstressed syllables with the ˘ symbol.

_____

_____

_____

_____

_____

A READING FOCUS

A **rhyme scheme** like the one in this stanza is usually called *abxb*. What do you think the "x" is supposed to mean?

_____

_____

_____

B READ AND DISCUSS

Comprehension

How does McBean influence the behavior of the Sneetches?

Through the machines they raced round and about again,

80   Changing their stars every minute or two.

They kept paying money. They kept running through

Until neither the Plain nor the Star-Bellies knew

Whether this one was that one . . . or that one was this one

Or which one was what one . . . or what one was who.

85   Then, when every last cent

Of their money was spent,

The Fix-it-Up Chappie packed up

And he went.

And he laughed as he drove

90   In his car up the beach,

"They never will learn.

No. You can't teach a Sneetch!" **A**

But McBean was quite wrong. I'm quite happy to say

That the Sneetches got really quite smart on that day,

95   The day they decided that Sneetches are Sneetches

And no kind of Sneetch is the best on the beaches.

That day, all the Sneetches forgot about stars

And whether they had one, or not, upon thars. **B**

Applying Your Skills

The Sneetches

VOCABULARY DEVELOPMENT

DIRECTIONS: Write "Yes" after each sentence below if the boldfaced vocabulary word is being used correctly. If it is used incorrectly, write "No" and rewrite the sentence so that the word is used correctly.

1. The Plain-Belly Sneetches were **keen** to have stars on their bellies.

   _____

   _____

2. McBean said his plan was **guaranteed** to fix the Star-Belly Sneetches' problem. _____

   _____

3. The Plain-Belly Sneetches liked to **peculiar** in the street.

   _____

   _____

LITERARY SKILLS FOCUS: RHYTHM AND RHYME

DIRECTIONS: Using what you learned about **rhyme**, write four lines about the Sneetches with an *aabb* rhyme scheme.

   _____

   _____

   _____

READING SKILLS FOCUS: READING A POEM

DIRECTIONS: Circle the answer that correctly completes each statement below.

1. If you're not sure what a certain word means, you should

   a. finish reading the poem, then ask your teacher about the word.

   b. look the word up in a dictionary before continuing.

2. When reading a poem aloud, you'll probably read words differently if they're

   a. italicized (*like this*).

   b. in all capitalized letters (LIKE THIS).

   c. followed by an exclamation mark (like this!).

   d. all of the above.

Reading Standard 3.4
Define how tone or meaning is conveyed in poetry through word choice, figurative language, sentence structure, line length, punctuation, rhythm, repetition, and rhyme.

Preparing to Read

John Henry

by an Anonymous African American

LITERARY SKILLS FOCUS: REPETITION AND REFRAIN

Words, phrases, stanzas, sounds, and patterns of words are often repeated in poems and songs. This repeating, or **repetition**, is a tool that creates rhythm, a mood, and even suspense. Repetition also helps a poet or songwriter emphasize an idea, and it helps to express **tone**, or an attitude toward someone or something.

One type of repetition is the refrain. A **refrain** is a word, phrase, line, or group of lines repeated regularly in a poem or song.

Use the Skill   Below is an example of repetition in "John Henry" and an explanation of its effect.

Text Example:

John Henry was about three days old

Sittin' on his papa's knee.

He picked up a hammer and a little piece of steel

Said, "<u>Hammer's gonna be the death of me</u>, Lord, Lord!

<u>Hammer's gonna be the death of me</u>."

> **Explanation:** The repetition makes the line more dramatic—especially because it's spoken by a baby predicting his own death.

Reading Standard 3.4
Define how tone or meaning is conveyed in poetry through word choice, figurative language, sentence structure, line length, punctuation, rhythm, repetition, and rhyme.

Preparing to Read

John Henry

READING SKILLS FOCUS: QUESTIONING

As you read this song, pause to ask **questions**. Doing so will allow you to reflect on and think about the text. Writing your questions down will also be helpful for reviewing the song after you've finished reading it. Sometimes you'll ask yourself questions that you can answer immediately. Other times, you'll have to keep your questions in mind and read ahead to find the answers. Below are a few lines from the song and examples of questions you may ask while reading it.

Text Example:

John Henry was about three days old

Sittin' on his papa's knee.

He picked up a hammer and a little piece of steel

Said, "Hammer's gonna be the death of me, Lord, Lord!

Hammer's gonna be the death of me."

> **My question:** Why does John Henry think the hammer will be the cause of his death?

Text Example:

The captain said to John Henry,

"Gonna bring that steam drill 'round

Gonna bring that steam drill out on the job

Gonna whop that steel on down, Lord, Lord!

Whop that steel on down."

> **My question:** What does the captain want John Henry to do?

JOHN HENRY

by an Anonymous African American

BACKGROUND

Nobody knows whether John Henry was a real person but people began singing about him in the early 1870s. He is said to have been an African American laborer in the crew constructing the Big Bend Tunnel of the Chesapeake and Ohio Railroad. According to the legend, someone set up a contest between John Henry and a steam drill. If you ever have a chance to do so, listen to a recording of the song "John Henry."

A READ AND DISCUSS

Comprehension

What have you learned about John Henry so far?

B LITERARY FOCUS

Underline examples of **repetition** in lines 6–15. What effect does the use of repetition have?

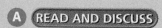

_____

_____

_____

_____

_____

John Henry was about three days old

Sittin' on his papa's knee.

He picked up a hammer and a little piece of steel

Said, "Hammer's gonna be the death of me, Lord, Lord!

5 Hammer's gonna be the death of me."

The captain said to John Henry,

"Gonna bring that steam drill 'round

Gonna bring that steam drill out on the job

Gonna whop that steel on down, Lord, Lord!

10 Whop that steel on down."

John Henry told his captain,

"A man ain't nothin' but a man

But before I let your steam drill beat me down

I'd die with a hammer in my hand, Lord, Lord!

15 I'd die with a hammer in my hand." **A** **B**

The Museum of African American Art, Los Angeles, California, Palmer C. Hayden Collection, Gift of Miriam A. Hayden

John Henry said to his shaker,[1]

"Shaker, why don't you sing?

I'm throwing thirty pounds from my hips on down

Just listen to that cold steel ring, Lord, Lord!

20   Listen to that cold steel ring." C

John Henry said to his shaker,

"Shaker, you'd better pray

'Cause if I miss that little piece of steel

Tomorrow be your buryin' day, Lord, Lord!

25   Tomorrow be your buryin' day." D

The shaker said to John Henry,

"I think this mountain's cavin' in!"

John Henry said to his shaker, "Man,

That ain't nothin' but my hammer suckin' wind, Lord, Lord!

30   Nothin' but my hammer suckin' wind." E

D LITERARY FOCUS

What is the **tone** of this stanza? How does **repetition** affect the tone?

E LANGUAGE COACH

Hyperbole (HY PUR BUH LEE) is language that is exaggerated or overstated to make a strong point. What is an example of hyperbole from this page?

---

1. **shaker** (SHAY KUHR): worker who holds the drill.

The man that invented the steam drill

Thought he was mighty fine

But John Henry made fifteen feet

The steam drill only made nine, Lord, Lord!

35   The steam drill only made nine. **A**

John Henry hammered in the mountain

His hammer was striking fire

But he worked so hard, he broke his poor heart

He laid down his hammer and he died, Lord, Lord!

40   He laid down his hammer and he died.

John Henry had a little woman

Her name was Polly Ann

John Henry took sick and went to his bed

Polly Ann drove steel like a man, Lord, Lord!

45   Polly Ann drove steel like a man.

John Henry had a little baby

You could hold him in the palm of your hand

The last words I heard that poor boy say,

"My daddy was a steel-driving man, Lord, Lord!

50   My daddy was a steel-driving man." **B**

They took John Henry to the graveyard

And they buried him in the sand

And every locomotive comes a-roaring by

Says, "There lies a steel-driving man, Lord, Lord!

55   There lies a steel-driving man." **C**

Well, every Monday morning

When the bluebirds begin to sing

You can hear John Henry a mile or more

You can hear John Henry's hammer ring, Lord, Lord!

60   You can hear John Henry's hammer ring. **D**

Applying Your Skills

John Henry

LITERARY SKILLS FOCUS: REPETITION AND REFRAIN

DIRECTIONS: Write a short paragraph that answers the following questions: Did this song have a **refrain**? What was it? Was it worded the same or differently each time? What impact did the refrain have on the poem?

_____

_____

_____

_____

_____

_____

_____

READING SKILLS FOCUS: QUESTIONING

DIRECTIONS: Below are **questions** that you may have asked while reading "John Henry." Answer the questions to show that you understood the poem.

1. What does the "shaker" do in the poem?

   a. He holds the drill that John Henry hammers.

   b. He hammers for John Henry when he's tired.

2. How did John Henry die?

   a. He hammered steel so hard that the mountain caved in on him.

   b. He hammered steel so hard that his heart gave out.

3. What is John Henry's relationship to his "little woman," Polly Ann?

   a. He is her husband.

   b. He is her father.

Reading Standard 3.4 Define how tone or meaning is conveyed in poetry through word choice, figurative language, sentence structure, line length, punctuation, rhythm, repetition, and rhyme.

Ode to Mi Gato

by Gary Soto

LITERARY SKILLS FOCUS: FIGURATIVE LANGUAGE

When Gary Soto writes that his white cat leapt from a tree "Like a splash of/Milk," he's using **figurative language**—or more specifically, he's using a **simile** (a comparison that uses *like* or *as*). Figurative language describes one thing in terms of something else. Soto also uses **personification**, a type of figurative language that gives human qualities to non-humans, and **metaphors**, or direct comparisons without using *like* or *as*. Some poets use **extended metaphors**, which are metaphors that develop over the course of many lines, if not every line, of a poem. As you read "Ode to Mi Gato," watch for uses of figurative language and think about how they impact Soto's poem.

Tone refers to the way a speaker (the voice talking to you in the poem) is feeling. When you read, pay attention to the poet's word choice to help decide the poem's tone.

READING SKILLS FOCUS: RE-READING

The first step in reading a poem is to just read through it once and enjoy the language. Then, go back and **re-read** the poem to improve your understanding of it.

Gary Soto uses some Spanish words in this poem. If you don't speak Spanish, re-reading the poem may help you unlock the meanings of these words. For example, after reading the poem once, you should realize that "Mi Gato" (in the title) means "My Cat."

Use the Skill Create a chart like the one below. As you read the poem, keep track of words, lines, or sections to which you want to return, and why.

Lines to re-read	Why I want to re-read
Lines 17–22	
Line 27, "porque"	

Reading Standard 3.4 Define how tone or meaning is conveyed in poetry through word choice, figurative language, sentence structure, line length, punctuation, rhythm, repetition, and rhyme.

Vocabulary Development

Ode to Mi Gato

SELECTION VOCABULARY

dribble (DRIHB UHL) *n.:* irregular drops that flow slowly.

> *The cat loved to lick the dribble of milk that came out of old milk cartons.*

dangled (DANG GUHLD) *v.:* held something or swung it loosely.

> *The speaker dangled food in front of his cat.*

abandoned (UH BAN DUHND) *adj.:* not used or taken care of any longer.

> *The speaker of the poem found the cat on an abandoned car.*

WORD STUDY

DIRECTIONS: Write "Yes" after each sentence below if the vocabulary word is being used correctly. Write "No" if it is being used incorrectly and rewrite the sentence so that it uses the word correctly.

1. My mom and I rode the **dribble** to the store. _____

_____

2. The climber paused to rest and **dangled** from the ledge, deciding how to continue. _____

_____

3. Chris decided to adopt the **abandoned** dog; he couldn't believe that someone had just left it in the street. _____

_____

ODE TO MI GATO

by Gary Soto

He's white
As spilled milk,
My cat who sleeps
With his belly
5   Turned toward
The summer sky. **A**
He loves the sun,
Its warmth like a hand.
He loves tuna cans
10 And milk cartons
With their dribble
Of milk. **B** He loves
Mom when she rattles
The bag of cat food,
15 The brown nuggets
Raining into his bowl. **C**
And my cat loves
Me, because I saved
Him from a dog,
20 Because I dressed him
In a hat and a cape
For Halloween,
Because I dangled
A sock of chicken skin
25 As he stood on his
Hind legs. I love mi gato,
Porque I found
Him on the fender
Of an abandoned car. **D**
30 He was a kitten,

© Leana Alagia/Getty Images

"Ode to Mi Gato" from *Neighborhood Odes* by Gary Soto. Copyright © 1992 by Gary Soto. Reproduced by permission of **Harcourt, Inc.**

With a meow
Like the rusty latch
On a gate. I carried
Him home in the loop
35 Of my arms. **E**
I poured milk
Into him, let him
Lick chunks of
Cheese from my palms,
40 And cooked huevo
After huevo
Until his purring
Engine kicked in
And he cuddled
45 Up to my father's slippers. **F**
That was last year.
This spring,
He's excellent at sleeping
And no good
50 At hunting. At night
All the other cats
In the neighborhood
Can see him slink
Around the corner,
55 Or jump from the tree
Like a splash of
Milk. We lap up
His love and
He laps up his welcome. **G**

E LANGUAGE COACH

Loop has **multiple meanings**. It can be a noun that means "something formed in a circular shape," or it can be a verb that means "form into a loop." Which version of the word is being used here?

_____

_____

F READ AND DISCUSS

Comprehension
So far, what have you learned about the speaker and his cat?

G LITERARY FOCUS

How would you describe the **tone** of this poem?

_____

_____

_____

_____

_____

© SuperStock, Inc.

Skills Practice

Ode to Mi Gato

USE A COMPARISON TABLE

DIRECTIONS: Complete the table below by writing one example of each type of **figurative language** used in "Ode to Mi Gato." Write your examples in the right-hand column of the table.

Figurative language	Example
1. simile	
2. personification	

Applying Your Skills

Ode to Mi Gato

VOCABULARY DEVELOPMENT

DIRECTIONS: Select the correct vocabulary word from the Word Box to complete each sentence. Write your answers on the blanks.

Word Box

dribble

dangled

abandoned

1. One time my cat fell out of a tree, but he grabbed a branch and _____ there until I helped him down.

2. Sometimes my cat likes to explore an _____ house down the street where no one lives anymore.

3. I wiped up the water _____ with a towel.

LITERARY SKILLS FOCUS: FIGURATIVE LANGUAGE

DIRECTIONS: Decide whether each statement below about the **figurative language** or **tone** of "Ode to Mi Gato" is true or false. If a statement is true, write "True." If a statement is false, rewrite it on the line to make it true.

1. This is an example of a simile: "My cat was as white as a cloud."

_____

2. If the author wrote another poem after his cat ran away, its tone would probably be the same as the tone in "Ode to Mi Gato."

_____

3. This is an example of personification: "My mom rattles the bag of cat food to get my cat's attention."

_____

READING SKILLS FOCUS: RE-READING

DIRECTIONS: First, **re-read** "Ode to Mi Gato" to improve your understanding of the poem. Then, answer the questions below on a separate sheet of paper.

1. How was reading the poem the second time different than reading it the first time? What was helpful about re-reading?

2. Why do you think Soto chooses to use Spanish words such as *porque* and *huevo* instead of English words with the same meaning?

Reading Standard 3.4
Define how tone or meaning is conveyed in poetry through word choice, figurative language, sentence structure, line length, punctuation, rhythm, repetition, and rhyme.

Chapter 5

VOCABULARY REVIEW

DIRECTIONS: The sentences in the table below include academic and selection vocabulary words in italics. Some of the words are used correctly and some are used incorrectly. Put a checkmark in the proper columns to show whether each word is used correctly or incorrectly. If a word is used incorrectly, explain why and suggest a replacement.

	Correct	Incorrect
After working all day, he was too *keen* to have dinner and went straight to sleep.		Why?
The cat's behavior was very *peculiar* after its owner left for vacation.		Why?
The thief *dangled* completely motionless so the police officer would not see him.		Why?
I *abandoned* my dog, so she was always by my side.		Why?
I *appreciate* the support of my friends and family at this stressful time.		Why?
The mechanic said that his work on the car was *guaranteed*.		Why?
The movie wasn't very good, so we decided to *dribble* the theater.		Why?
I *detect* a hint of sarcasm in your voice.		Why?

Skills Review

Chapter 5

DIRECTIONS: Hyperbole is language that is overstated or exaggerated to make a strong point. Look at the examples of hyperbole below. Explain what point you think each example is making. Next, make up three of your own examples of hyperbole and explain what they mean.

1. **Hyperbole:** I just ate a mountain of food.

   Meaning: _____

2. **Hyperbole:** That backpack weighs a ton!

   Meaning: _____

3. **Hyperbole:** _____

   Meaning: _____

4. **Hyperbole:** _____

   Meaning: _____

5. **Hyperbole:** _____

   Meaning: _____

ORAL LANGUAGE ACTIVITY

DIRECTIONS: Choose one of the poems from Chapter 5—"The Sneetches," "Ode to Mi Gato," or "John Henry." Read the poem aloud to a partner. Pay attention to your pronunciation and emphasis on certain words. After you are done, ask your partner how you could adjust your reading to better capture the mood of the poem. Then listen to your partner's reading of a poem from Chapter 5.

Biography and
Autobiography

Walking to the Sky by Jonathan Borofsky/
© Stephen Chernin/Getty Images

Literary and Academic Vocabulary for Chapter 6

contribute (KUHN TRIHB YOOT) *v.:* give or add something, such as resources or ideas.

Doctors contribute to the community by helping people to stay healthy.

distinct (DIHS TIHNGKT) *adj.:* distinguishable; clearly different or of a different type.

Her distinct features made her stand out from the rest of the crowd.

perspective (PUHR SPEHK TIHV) *n.:* mental view or outlook; way of thinking.

My perspective about the Civil War changed after I read more about Abraham Lincoln.

uniform (YOO NUH FAWRM) *adj.:* having the same shape, size, quality or other characteristics.

All of the houses on the block were painted a uniform color.

biography (BY AH GRUH FEE) *n.:* story of a person's life, written by another person.

He wrote a biography about the princess.

autobiography (AW TOH BY AH GRUH FEE) *n.:* writer's account of his or her own life.

The President's autobiography revealed information about his time in office.

first-person point of view *n.:* an account in which the narrator tells his or her own story and uses the pronouns *I, me, we, us, our, my,* or *mine.*

Since the story was told from the first-person point of view, I knew exactly what the narrator thought and felt.

third-person point of view *n.:* a story that is not written from the "I" point of view and uses the pronouns *his, her, their, he, she, they,* or *them.*

Since the story was told from the third-person point of view, I wasn't sure exactly what the character thought and felt.

from The Land I Lost

by Huynh Quang Nhuong

LITERARY SKILLS FOCUS: NARRATORS: FIRST PERSON AND THIRD PERSON

Most of the stories you have read are probably narrated, or told, in either the first-person or third-person point of view. A **first-person narrator** tells about events that he or she has experienced personally, using pronouns like *I, me,* and *my.* First-person narrators are also used in autobiographies. **Autobiographies** are stories about a person's life as written by that person. In an autobiography, the writer talks about life from his or her own point of view. In a story told by a **third-person narrator**, the action is described as if by someone who is watching what is happening, using pronouns such as *he, she,* and *they.* In the story you are about to read, Nhuong uses both kinds of narrators at different points in the story.

- Example of first-person point of view: *I went to the store, but I left when I started feeling dizzy.*

- Example of third-person point of view: *Marie went to the store, but she left once she started feeling dizzy.*

Reading Standard 3.5 Identify the speaker and recognize the difference between first- and third-person narration (e.g., autobiography compared with biography).

READING SKILLS FOCUS: ANALYZING AUTHOR'S PURPOSE

An author typically writes with a **purpose**, or reason, to communicate different ideas to readers. For example, an author may entertain readers by using funny conversation. The author may also write to inform readers by, for example, including a description of his hometown. Authors also write to persuade their readers to agree with an idea or to express feelings.

Use the Skill As you read this selection, pay close attention to how the author's purpose changes. Make notes in the margin indicating when the author's purpose changes and why you think he does so.

Vocabulary Development

from The Land I Lost

SELECTION VOCABULARY

infested (IHN FEHST IHD) *v.*: inhabited in large numbers (said of something harmful).
> *The kitchen was infested with ants.*

wily (WY LEE) *adj.*: sly; clever in a sneaky way.
> *A crocodile becomes more wily with age.*

hallucination (HUH LOO SUH NAY SHUHN) *n.*: sight or sound of something that isn't really there.
> *The tired desert explorer thought he saw a city ahead of him, but it was a hallucination.*

desperate (DEHS PUHR IHT) *adj.*: having a great and urgent need.
> *I was desperate to get to the store before it closed.*

avenge (UH VEHNJ) *v.*: get even for; get revenge for.
> *In the movie, the hero vows to avenge the theft of the diamond.*

WORD STUDY

DIRECTIONS: Write the correct vocabulary words from the list above in the blanks to correctly complete the passage below. One word will not be used.

In *The Land I Lost*, author Huynh Quang Nhuong offers the readers a look at South Vietnam many decades ago. He describes one of the biggest fears of his youth, the (1) _____ crocodile, packs of which (2) _____ nearby rivers. As a(n) (3) _____ attempt to control these creatures, villagers would build barriers along riverbanks. In this excerpt from Nhuong's book, readers learn how one of Nhuong's neighbors struggles to (4) _____ a terrifying experience with a crocodile that breaks through a barrier.

from THE LAND I LOST

by Huynh Quang Nhuong

BACKGROUND

Today, much of South Vietnam is the same as Huynh Quang Nhuong describes it in *The Land I Lost*. Although war changed the country's landscape somewhat, much of South Vietnam remains rural and dependent on farming. Rice is grown along the rich plains of the Mekong River, and sweet potatoes, corn, beans, and fish are staples of the South Vietnamese lifestyle and economy.

A   READING FOCUS

What is the author's **purpose** for describing the "monkey bridge"?

_____

_____

_____

_____

_____

B   READ AND DISCUSS

Comprehension

Can you imagine living in this village? How do you think you would do in these conditions?

I was born on the central highlands of Vietnam in a small hamlet on a riverbank that had a deep jungle on one side and a chain of high mountains on the other. Across the river, rice fields stretched to the slopes of another chain of mountains.

There were fifty houses in our hamlet, scattered along the river or propped against the mountainsides. The houses were made of bamboo and covered with coconut leaves, and each was surrounded by a deep trench to protect it from wild animals or thieves. The only way to enter a house was to walk across
10   a "monkey bridge"—a single bamboo stick that spanned the trench. At night we pulled the bridges into our houses and were safe. **A**

There were no shops or marketplaces in our hamlet. If we needed supplies—medicine, cloth, soaps, or candles— we had to cross over the mountains and travel to a town nearby. We used the river mainly for traveling to distant
20   hamlets, but it also provided us with plenty of fish. **B**

© John William Banagan/Getty Images

During the six-month rainy season, nearly all of us helped plant and cultivate fields of rice, sweet potatoes, Indian mustard, eggplant, tomatoes, hot peppers, and corn. But during the dry season, we became hunters and turned to the jungle.

Wild animals played a very large part in our lives. There were four animals we feared the most: the tiger, the lone wild hog, the crocodile, and the horse snake. Tigers were always try-
30 ing to steal cattle. Sometimes, however, when a tiger became old and slow it became a man-eater. But a lone wild hog was even more dangerous than a tiger. It attacked every creature in sight, even when it had no need for food. Or it did crazy things, such as charging into the hamlet in broad daylight, ready to kill or to be killed.

The river had different dangers: crocodiles. But of all the animals, the most hated and feared was the huge horse snake. It was sneaky and attacked people and cattle just for the joy of killing. It would either crush its victim to death or poison it with a bite. **C**

40 Like all farmers' children in the hamlet, I started working at the age of six. My seven sisters helped by working in the kitchen, weeding the garden, gathering eggs, or taking water to the cattle. I looked after the family herd of water buffaloes. Someone always had to be with the herd because no matter how carefully a water buffalo was trained, it always was ready to nibble young rice plants when no one was looking. Sometimes, too, I fished for the family while I guarded the herd, for there were plenty of fish in the flooded rice fields during the rainy season. **D**

I was twelve years old when I made my first trip to the
50 jungle with my father. I learned how to track game, how to recognize useful roots, how to distinguish edible mushrooms from poisonous ones. **E** I learned that if birds, raccoons, squir-rels, or monkeys had eaten the fruits of certain trees, then those fruits were not poisonous. Often they were not delicious, but they could calm a man's hunger and thirst.

My father, like most of the villagers, was a farmer and a hunter, depending upon the season. But he also had a college

C READING FOCUS

Underline the places in this paragraph where the author's **purpose** is to express feelings.

D READ AND DISCUSS

Comprehension

What have you learned about the author and his life so far?

E LANGUAGE COACH

Synonyms are words that have the same or similar meanings. On the line below, write a synonym for the word *recognize*.

_____

education, so in the evenings he helped to teach other children
in our hamlet, for it was too small to afford a professional
60 schoolteacher.

My mother managed the house, but during the harvest
season she could be found in the fields, helping my father get the
crops home; and as the wife of a hunter, she knew how to dress
and nurse a wound and took good care of her husband and his
hunting dogs.

I went to the lowlands to study for a while because I wanted to
follow my father as a teacher when I grew up. I always planned to
return to my hamlet to live the rest of my life there. But war dis-
rupted my dreams. The land I love was lost to me forever. **A**

70 These stories are my memories. . . .

So Close

My grandmother was very fond of cookies made of banana, egg,
and coconut, so my mother and I always stopped at Mrs. Hong's
house to buy these cookies for her on our way back from the
marketplace. My mother also liked to see Mrs. Hong because
they had been very good friends since grade-school days. While
my mother talked with her friend, I talked with Mrs. Hong's
daughter, Lan. Most of the time Lan asked me about my older
sister, who was married to a teacher and lived in a nearby town.
Lan, too, was going to get married—to a young man living next
80 door, Trung. **B** **C**

Trung and Lan had been inseparable playmates until the
day tradition did not allow them to be alone together anymore.
Besides, I think they felt a little shy with each other after realizing
that they were man and woman.

Lan was a lively, pretty girl, who attracted the attention of
all the young men of our hamlet. Trung was a skillful fisherman
who successfully plied[1] his trade on the river in front of their
houses. Whenever Lan's mother found a big fish on the kitchen
windowsill, she would smile to herself. Finally, she decided that

---

1. **plied:** worked at.

90 Trung was a fine young man and would make a good husband for her daughter. 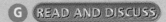 **D**

Trung's mother did not like the idea of her son giving good fish away, but she liked the cookies Lan brought her from time to time. Besides, the girl was very helpful; whenever she was not busy at her house, Lan would come over in the evening and help Trung's mother repair her son's fishing net. **E**

Trung was happiest when Lan was helping his mother. They did not talk to each other, but they could look at each other when his mother was busy with her work. Each time Lan went home,
100 Trung looked at the chair Lan had just left and secretly wished that nobody would move it. **F**

One day when Trung's mother heard her son call Lan's name in his sleep, she decided it was time to speak to the girl's mother about marriage. Lan's mother agreed they should be married and even waived[2] the custom whereby the bridegroom had to give the bride's family a fat hog, six chickens, six ducks, three bottles of wine, and thirty kilos[3] of fine rice, for the two families had known each other for a long time and were good neighbors.

The two widowed mothers quickly set the dates for the
110 engagement announcement and for the wedding ceremony. Since their decision was immediately made known to relatives and friends, Trung and Lan could now see each other often. . . . **G**

At last it was the day of their wedding. Friends and relatives arrived early in the morning to help them celebrate. They brought gifts of ducks, chickens, baskets filled with fruits, rice wine, and colorful fabrics. Even though the two houses were next to each other, the two mothers observed all the proper wedding day traditions.

First, Trung and his friends and relatives came to Lan's
120 house. Lan and he prayed at her ancestors' altars and asked for their blessing. Then they joined everyone for a luncheon.

After lunch there was a farewell ceremony for the bride. Lan stepped out of her house and joined the greeting party that was

---

2. **waived:** gave up voluntarily.
3. **kilos:** kilograms, about 2.2 pounds each.

D **READ AND DISCUSS**

Comprehension
What is Trung up to with the fish?

E **LANGUAGE COACH**

Synonyms are words that have similar meanings. For example, a synonym of *busy* is *occupied*. Name a synonym for *repair*.

F **READING FOCUS**

What do you think is the author's **purpose** in this paragraph: to persuade, to inform, to express feelings, or to entertain?

G **READ AND DISCUSS**

Comprehension
What are the two mothers thinking and planning?

A READ AND DISCUSS

Comprehension
What's good about the house's location?

B VOCABULARY

Selection Vocabulary
Based on the clues in this sentence, what might *infested* mean?

_____

_____

_____

_____

to accompany her to Trung's home. Tradition called for her to cry and to express her sorrow at leaving her parents behind and forever becoming the daughter of her husband's family. In some villages the bride was even supposed to cling so tightly to her mother that it would take several friends to pull her away from her home. But instead of crying, Lan smiled. She asked herself,

130   why should she cry? The two houses were separated by only a garden; she could run home and see her mother anytime she wanted to. So Lan willingly followed Trung and prayed at his ancestors' altars before joining everyone in the big welcome dinner at Trung's house that ended the day's celebrations. **A**

    Later in the evening of the wedding night, Lan went to the river to take a bath. Because crocodiles infested the river, people of our hamlet who lived along the riverbank chopped down trees and put them in the river to form barriers and protect places where they washed their clothes, did their dishes, or took a bath. **B**

140   This evening, a wily crocodile had avoided the barrier by crawling up the riverbank and sneaked up behind Lan. The crocodile

© Owen Franken/Getty Images

grabbed her and went back to the river by the same route that it had come.

Trung became worried when Lan did not return. He went to the place where she was supposed to bathe, only to find that her clothes were there, but she had disappeared. Panic-stricken, he yelled for his relatives. They all rushed to the riverbank with lighted torches. In the flickering light they found traces of water and crocodile claw-prints on the wet soil. Now they knew that a crocodile had grabbed the young bride and dragged her into the river. **C**

Since no one could do anything for the girl, all of Trung's relatives returned to the house, urging the bridegroom to do the same. But the young man refused to leave the place; he just stood there, crying and staring at the clothes of his bride.

Suddenly the wind brought him the sound of Lan calling his name. He was very frightened, for according to an old belief, a crocodile's victim must lure a new victim to his master; if not, the first victim's soul must stay with the beast forever.

Trung rushed back to the house and woke all his relatives. Nobody doubted he thought he had heard her call, but they all believed that he was the victim of a hallucination. Everyone pleaded with him and tried to convince him that nobody could survive when snapped up by a crocodile and dragged into the river to be drowned and eaten by the animal. **D**

The young man brushed aside all their arguments and rushed back to the river. Once again, he heard the voice of his bride in the wind, calling his name. Again he rushed back and woke his relatives. Again they tried to persuade him that it was a hallucination, although some of the old folks suggested that maybe the ghost of the young girl was having to dance and sing to placate[4] the angry crocodile because she failed to bring it a new victim. **E**

No one could persuade Trung to stay inside. His friends wanted to go back to the river with him, but he said no. He

4. **placate** (PLAY cayt): calm or soothe (someone who is angry).

150

160

170

Avenge looks similar to a closely related word, *revenge*. Although *revenge* is most often used as a noun, meaning "an act of getting even with someone or something," it can also be used as a verb. To *revenge* means exactly the same thing as *avenge*: "get even for." Use *avenge* in a sentence of your own. Then replace *avenge* with *revenge*. Does the sentence still mean the same thing?

_____

_____

_____

_____

_____

Comprehension

What is the narrator describing here?

Why would it not make sense for the author to describe Lan's experience using the **first-person** point of view?

_____

_____

_____

_____

_____

resented them for not believing him that there were desperate cries in the wind.

Trung stood in front of the deep river alone in the darkness. He listened to the sound of the wind and clutched the clothes Lan had left behind. The wind became stronger and stronger and often changed direction as the night progressed, but he did not hear any more calls. Still he had no doubt that the voice he had heard earlier was absolutely real. Then at dawn, when the wind died down, he again heard, very clearly, Lan call him for help.

Her voice came from an island about six hundred meters away. Trung wept and prayed: "You were a good girl when you were still alive, now be a good soul. Please protect me so that I can find a way to kill the beast in order to free you from its spell and avenge your tragic death." **A** Suddenly, while wiping away his tears, he saw a little tree moving on the island. The tree was jumping up and down. He squinted to see better. The tree had two hands that were waving at him. And it was calling his name. **B** **C**

Trung became hysterical and yelled for help. He woke all his relatives and they all rushed to his side again. At first they thought that Trung had become stark mad. They tried to lead him back to his house, but he fiercely resisted their attempt. He talked to them incoherently[5] and pointed his finger at the strange tree on the island. Finally his relatives saw the waving tree. They quickly put a small boat into the river, and Trung got into the boat along with two other men. They paddled to the island and discovered that the moving tree was, in fact, Lan. She had covered herself with leaves because she had no clothes on.

At first nobody knew what had really happened because Lan clung to Trung and cried and cried. Finally, when Lan could talk, they pieced together her story.

Lan had fainted when the crocodile snapped her up. Had she not fainted, the crocodile surely would have drowned her before carrying her off to the island. Lan did not know how many times the crocodile had tossed her in the air and

---

5. **incoherently** (EHN KO HEH REHNT LEE): not clearly.

smashed her against the ground, but at one point, while being tossed in the air and falling back onto the crocodile's jaw, she regained consciousness. The crocodile smashed her against the ground a few more times, but Lan played dead. Luckily the crocodile became thirsty and returned to the river to drink. At that moment Lan got up and ran to a nearby tree and climbed up it. The tree was very small.

Lan stayed very still for fear that the snorting, angry crocodile, roaming around trying to catch her again, would find her and shake her out of the tree. Lan stayed in this frozen position for a long time until the crocodile gave up searching for her and went back to the river. Then she started calling Trung to come rescue her. **D**

Lan's body was covered with bruises, for crocodiles soften up big prey before swallowing it. They will smash it against the ground or against a tree, or keep tossing it into the air. But fortunately Lan had no broken bones or serious cuts. It was possible that this crocodile was very old and had lost most of its teeth. Nevertheless, the older the crocodile, the more intelligent it usually was. That was how it knew to avoid the log barrier in the river and to snap up the girl from behind. **E**

Trung carried his exhausted bride into the boat and paddled home. Lan slept for hours and hours. At times she would sit up with a start and cry out for help, but within three days she was almost completely recovered.

Lan's mother and Trung's mother decided to celebrate their children's wedding a second time because Lan had come back from the dead. **F**

D READ AND DISCUSS

Comprehension
What is Lan explaining about her plan to get home?

E VOCABULARY

Word Study
The author uses a number of strong verbs like *snap* to emphasize the action taking place. Circle two other strong verbs in lines 204–218. Does the author's word choice make the story more or less interesting, and how?

_____

_____

_____

_____

_____

_____

_____

_____

F READ AND DISCUSS

Comprehension
How does the story conclude? **Follow-up:** How does the near tragedy contribute to the joy at the end?

from The Land I Lost

USE A VENN DIAGRAM

DIRECTIONS: The **first-person** and **third-person** points of view are very different, yet they share some things in common. For example, authors use both points of view to describe events, ideas, and feelings. Use the Venn diagram below to compare and contrast first-person and third-person points of view. List characteristics of the first-person point of view in the left circle, characteristics of the third-person point of view in the right circle, and characteristics shared by both in the part of the diagram where the circles overlap.

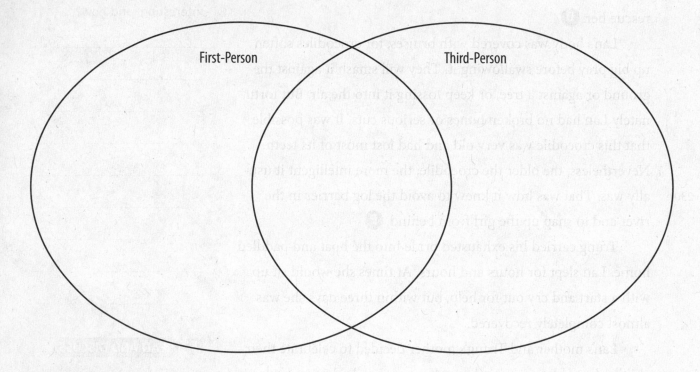

First-Person   Third-Person

Applying Your Skills

from The Land I Lost

VOCABULARY DEVELOPMENT

DIRECTIONS: Match the vocabulary words on the left with their synonyms on the right. Write the letter of the correct word in each blank.

_____ **1.** hallucination   **a.** sly

_____ **2.** avenge   **b.** overrun

_____ **3.** desperate   **c.** illusion

_____ **4.** wily   **d.** needy

_____ **5.** infested   **e.** revenge

LITERARY SKILLS FOCUS: NARRATORS: FIRST PERSON AND THIRD PERSON

DIRECTIONS: Choose a paragraph of at least three lines from the story that is written from the **first-person** point of view. On the lines below, rewrite the paragraph in the **third-person** point of view.

_____

_____

_____

_____

_____

_____

_____

_____

_____

_____

_____

_____

_____

READING SKILLS FOCUS: ANALYZING AUTHOR'S PURPOSE

DIRECTIONS: Skim the selection and find one example of each type of **purpose**. Write the line numbers of each example you choose in the spaces below.

1. The author *expresses feelings* in lines _____.

2. Nhuong tries to *persuade* the reader in lines _____.

3. Lines _____ *inform* the reader about something important.

4. The author *entertains* the reader in lines _____.

Reading Standard 3.5 Identify the speaker and recognize the difference between first- and third-person narration (e.g., autobiography compared with biography).

Storm

from Woodsong by Gary Paulsen

LITERARY SKILLS FOCUS: IMAGERY

Imagery is language that appeals to the senses. Writers use imagery to describe things in such a way that we can almost hear, see, smell, taste, or touch them. Imagery makes a story or poem more realistic for the reader, which is why imagery is especially useful in helping a nonfiction writer meet the goal of describing real-life people and situations.

READING SKILLS FOCUS: ANALYZING AUTHOR'S PURPOSE

An author might have one or more **purposes** for writing a story. For example, an author might write to **persuade** readers of an idea. The author might also write to **entertain** readers, **inform** them of something they should know to better understand the story, or **express feelings** that characters are experiencing.

Use the Skill As you read the following selection, monitor *why* the author writes the way he does. In which parts does he want to inform you of something? To persuade you? To entertain you? To express feelings? You can make a pie chart like the one below to record images and other details.

Reading Standard 3.7 Explain the effects of common literary devices (e.g., symbolism, imagery, metaphor) in a variety of fictional and nonfictional texts.

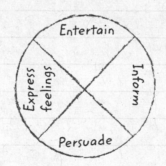

Vocabulary Development

Storm

SELECTION VOCABULARY

resembled (RIH ZEHM BUHLD) v.: was similar to.
Because of its shape and attitude, the dog resembled a bear.

WORD STUDY

DIRECTIONS: Each sentence below uses the word *resembled*. If *resembled* makes sense the way it is used in the sentence, write "Correct" on the blank. If *resembled* is not used properly, write "Incorrect" on the blank and explain why it is not used correctly.

1. My dirty room *resembled* a garbage dump. _____
   _____

2. As Dave grew older, he *resembled* his father more and more.
   _____
   _____

3. He brought out the glue and *resembled* his model airplane after it fell apart. _____
   _____

4. Every boy and girl in the class wore clothes that *resembled* one another; they all looked completely different! _____
   _____

5. We didn't buy anything from the store because all the clothes *resembled* what we had at home. _____
   _____

STORM

from Woodsong by Gary Paulsen

> **BACKGROUND**
>
> "Storm" is taken from *Woodsong*, the true account of
> Gary Paulsen's adventures with his sled dogs in northern
> Minnesota. Paulsen later ran the Iditarod (Y DIHT UH RAHD),
> a dog-sled race across Alaska.

It is always possible to learn from dogs, and in fact the longer
I'm with them, the more I understand how little I know. But
there was one dog who taught me the most. Just one dog. Storm.
First dog . . . .

Joy, loyalty, toughness, peacefulness—all of these were part
of Storm. Lessons about life and, finally, lessons about death
came from him. **A**

He had a bear's ears. He was brindle colored[1] and built like
a truck, and his ears were rounded when we got him, so that they
10 looked like bear cub ears. They gave him a comical look when
he was young that somehow hung on to him even when he grew
old. He had a sense of humor to match his ears, and when he
grew truly old, he somehow resembled George Burns.[2] **B**

At peak, he was a mighty dog. He pulled like a machine.
Until we retired him and used him only for training puppies,
until we let him loose to enjoy his age, he pulled, his back over in
the power curve, so that nothing could stop the sled.

---

1. **brindle colored:** gray or brown and streaked or spotted with a dark
color.
2. **George Burns** (1896–1996): American comedian and actor with large
ears.

In his fourth or fifth year as a puller, he started doing tricks. First he would play jokes on the dog pulling next to him. On long runs he would become bored, and when we least expected it, he would reach across the gang line and snort wind into the ear of the dog next to him. I ran him with many different dogs and he did it to all of them—chuckling when the dog jumped and shook his or her head—but I never saw a single dog get mad at him for it.  Oh, there was once a dog named Fonzie who nearly took his head off, but Fonzie wasn't really mad at him so much as surprised. Fonzie once nailed me through the wrist for waking him up too suddenly when he was sleeping. I'd reached down and touched him before whispering his name.

Small jokes. Gentle jokes, Storm played. He took to hiding things from me. At first I couldn't understand where things were going. I would put a bootie down while working on a dog, and it would disappear. I lost a small ladle[3] I used for watering each dog, a cloth glove liner I took off while working on a dog's feet, a roll of tape, and finally, a hat.

---

3. **ladle:** cup-shaped spoon with a long handle for dipping out liquids.

Courtesy of Scott Kennedy

C **READING FOCUS**

What is the author's **purpose** in sharing this information? Is he attempting to **entertain** or **inform** the reader? Explain your answer.

_____

_____

_____

_____

_____

_____

_____

_____

_____

D **READ AND DISCUSS**

Comprehension

What have you learned about Storm?

He was so clever. **A**

When I lost the hat, it was a hot day and I had taken the hat off while I worked on a dog's harness. The dog was just ahead of Storm, and when I knelt to work on the harness—he'd chewed almost through the side of it while running—I put the hat down on the snow near Storm.

Or thought I had. When I had changed the dog's harness, I turned and the hat was gone. I looked around, moved the dogs, looked under them, then shrugged. At first I was sure I'd put the hat down; then, when I couldn't find it, I became less sure, and at last I thought perhaps I had left it at home or dropped it somewhere on the run.

Storm sat quietly, looking ahead down the trail, not showing anything at all. **B**

I went back to the sled, reached down to disengage the hook, and when I did, the dogs exploded forward. **C** I was not quite on the sled when they took off, so I was knocked slightly off balance. I leaned over to the right to regain myself, and when I did, I accidentally dragged the hook through the snow.

And pulled up my hat.

It had been buried off to the side of the trail in the snow, buried neatly with the snow smoothed over the top, so that it was completely hidden. Had the snow hook not scraped down four or five inches, I never would have found it. **D**

I stopped the sled and set the hook once more. While knocking the snow out of the hat and putting it back on my head, I studied where it had happened.

Right next to Storm.

He had taken the hat, quickly dug a hole, buried the hat and smoothed the snow over it, then gone back to sitting, staring ahead, looking completely innocent.

When I stopped the sled and picked up the hat, he looked back, saw me put the hat on my head, and—I swear—smiled. Then he shook his head once and went back to work pulling.

A (READ AND DISCUSS)

Comprehension

How does this new information add to what we already know about Storm?

B (READ AND DISCUSS)

Comprehension

What new information about Storm has Paulsen given you?

C (LANGUAGE COACH)

A **prefix** is a word part added to the beginning of a word that changes the meaning of the word. *Disengage* begins with the prefix *dis-*. The word *engage* means "secure or hold fast." Based on other words you know that start with the prefix *dis-*, what do you think *disengage* means?

_____

_____

_____

_____

D (VOCABULARY)

Academic Vocabulary

How does smoothing out the snow *contribute*, or add, to the cleverness of Storm's prank?

_____

_____

_____

_____

_____

70　　　Along with the jokes, Storm had scale eyes. He watched as
the sled was loaded, carefully calculated the weight of each item,
and let his disapproval be known if it went too far. **E**

　　　One winter a friend gave us a parlor stove with nickel trim.
It was not an enormous stove, but it had some weight to it and
some bulk. This friend lived twelve miles away—twelve miles
over two fair hills followed by about eight miles on an old,
abandoned railroad grade.[4] We needed the stove badly (our old
barrel stove had started to burn through), so I took off with the
team to pick it up. I left early in the morning because I wanted to
80　get back that same day. It had snowed four or five inches, so the
dogs would have to break trail. By the time we had done the hills
and the railroad grade, pushing in new snow all the time, they
were ready for a rest. **F** I ran them the last two miles to where
the stove was and unhooked their tugs so they could rest while
I had coffee.

　　　We stopped for an hour at least, the dogs sleeping quietly.
When it was time to go, my friend and I carried the stove outside
and put it in the sled. The dogs didn't move.

　　　Except for Storm.

90　　　He raised his head, opened one eye, did a perfect double
take—both eyes opening wide—and sat up. He had been facing
the front. Now he turned around to face the sled—so he was
facing away from the direction we had to travel when we left—
and watched us load the sled. **G**

　　　It took some time, as the stove barely fit on the sled and had
to be jiggled and shuffled around to get it down between the side
rails.

　　　Through it all, Storm sat and watched us, his face a study
in interest. He did not get up but sat on his back end, and
100　when I was done and ready to go, I hooked all the dogs back in
harness—which involved hooking the tugs to the rear ties on
their harnesses. The dogs knew this meant we were going to
head home, so they got up and started slamming against the tugs,
trying to get the sled to move.

---

4. **railroad grade:** rise or elevation in a railroad track.

E READ AND DISCUSS

Comprehension

The author tells us that Storm has "scale eyes." What does he mean by that?

F VOCABULARY

Word Study

What do you think it means that the dogs will have to "break trail?" Read on, and circle the context clue that helps you figure out what it means to "break trail."

_____

_____

_____

_____

_____

_____

G READ AND DISCUSS

Comprehension

What is going on with Storm?

All of them, that is, but Storm.

Storm sat backward, the tug hooked up but hanging down. The other dogs were screaming to run, but Storm sat and stared at the stove. **A**

Not at me, not at the sled, but at the stove itself. Then he
110 raised his lips, bared his teeth, and growled at the stove.

When he was finished growling, he snorted twice, stood, turned away from the stove, and started to pull. But each time we stopped at the tops of the hills to let the dogs catch their breath after pulling the sled and stove up the steep incline, Storm turned and growled at the stove. **B**

The enemy.

The weight on the sled.

I do not know how many miles Storm and I ran together. Eight, ten, perhaps twelve thousand miles. He was one of the
120 first dogs and taught me the most, and as we worked together, he came to know me better than perhaps even my own family. He could look once at my shoulders and tell how I was feeling, tell how far we were to run, how fast we had to run—knew it all.

When I started to run long, moved from running a work team, a trap line team, to training for the Iditarod, Storm took it in stride, changed the pace down to the long trot, matched what was needed, and settled in for the long haul. **C**

He did get bored, however, and one day while we were running a long run, he started doing a thing that would stay
130 with him—with us—until the end. We had gone forty or fifty miles on a calm, even day with no bad wind. The temperature was a perfect ten below zero. The sun was bright, everything was moving well, and the dogs had settled into the rhythm that could take them a hundred or a thousand miles.

And Storm got bored.

At a curve in the trail, a small branch came out over the path we were running, and as Storm passed beneath the limb, he jumped up and grabbed it, broke a short piece off—about a foot long—and kept it in his mouth.

140   All day.

And into the night. He ran, carrying the stick like a toy, and when we stopped to feed or rest, he would put the stick down, eat, then pick it up again. He would put the stick down carefully in front of him, or across his paws, and sleep, and when he awakened, he would pick up the stick, and it soon became a thing between us, the stick.

He would show it to me, making a contact, a connection between us, each time we stopped. I would pet him on top of the head and take the stick from him—he would emit a low, gentle
150 growl when I took the stick. I'd "examine" it closely, nod and seem to approve of it, and hand it back to him.

Each day we ran, he would pick a different stick. And each time I would have to approve of it, and after a time, after weeks and months, I realized that he was using the sticks as a way to communicate with me, to tell me that everything was all right, that I was doing the right thing. **D**

Once, when I pushed them too hard during a pre-Iditarod race—when I thought it was important to compete and win (a feeling that didn't last long)—I walked up to Storm, and as I
160 came close to him, he pointedly dropped the stick. I picked it up and held it out, but he wouldn't take it. He turned his face away. I put the stick against his lips and tried to make him take it, but he let it fall to the ground. When I realized what he was doing, I stopped and fed and rested the team, sat on the sled, and thought about what I was doing wrong. After four hours or so of sitting—watching other teams pass me—I fed them another snack, got ready to go, and was gratified to see Storm pick up the stick. From that time forward I looked for the stick always, knew when I saw it out to the sides of his head that I was doing the
170 right thing. And it was always there. **E**

Through storms and cold weather, on the long runs, the long, long runs where there isn't an end to it, where only the sled and the winter around the sled and the wind are there, Storm had the stick to tell me it was right, all things were right. **F**

D **READ AND DISCUSS**

Comprehension

How does Storm solve his problem? **Follow-up:** What is the significance of this stick?

E **READ AND DISCUSS**

Comprehension

How does this information connect with what you've learned about the stick?

F **READING FOCUS**

What **feelings** do you think the author is trying to **express** in this story? What do you think he wants the reader to take away from the story?

_____

_____

_____

_____

_____

_____

_____

Skills Practice

Storm

USE AN IMAGERY TABLE

DIRECTIONS: Complete the chart below by writing at least two examples of **imagery** from "Storm" that appeals to each sense listed. Write the line numbers of the examples you use.

Sight	Hearing	Touch

Applying Your Skills

Storm

VOCABULARY DEVELOPMENT

DIRECTIONS: Write "Yes" after each sentence below if the vocabulary word *resembled* is being used correctly. Write "No" if it is not.

1. The narrator *resembled* to be kinder to his dogs. _____

2. Because of his round ears, Storm *resembled* a bear. _____

3. The heavy stove *resembled* an old-fashioned safe. _____

LITERARY SKILLS FOCUS: IMAGERY

DIRECTIONS: Write whether each example of **imagery** below appeals to the sense of sight, hearing, touch, taste, or smell.

1. The cool wind swept across my face. _____

2. A low-pitched hum filled the room. _____

3. I could tell without looking that there were dead fish in the box. _____

READING SKILLS FOCUS: ANALYZING AUTHORS' PURPOSE

DIRECTIONS: Complete the chart below by listing the **purpose** of each of the excerpts from "Storm" below. There may be more than one correct answer, so include a brief explanation of your answer.

Selection	Purpose and Explanation
Lines 19–25: "First he would play jokes..."	1.
Lines 70–72: "Along with the jokes..."	2.
Lines 118–121: "I do not know how many miles..."	3.

Reading Standard 3.7 Explain the effects of common literary devices (e.g., symbolism, imagery, metaphor) in a variety of fictional and nonfictional texts.

The Mysterious Mr. Lincoln

by Russell Freedman

LITERARY SKILLS FOCUS: FIGURATIVE LANGUAGE

Writers use **figurative language** to compare unlike objects.

A **metaphor** makes a comparison by saying something *is* something else.

A **simile** makes a comparison using *like* or *as*.

Personification makes something not human appear or act like a human. Figurative language can bring a text to life, strengthen a writer's point, or help us to see familiar things in new ways.

Figuring Out Figurative Language   First, read the examples of figurative language in the chart below. Then, create your own example of each kind of figurative language.

Example	Your Example
Metaphor: The moon is a wheel of cheese.	
Simile: The stars were like diamonds.	
Personification: The tree branches tapped us on the shoulders.	

READING SKILLS FOCUS: DISTINGUISHING BETWEEN FACT AND OPINION

Reading Standard 3.7
Explain the effects of common literary devices (e.g., symbolism, imagery, metaphor) in a variety of fictional and nonfictional texts.

In order to properly evaluate a work of nonfiction, you need to be able to determine what is fact and what is opinion. **Facts** can be proved. "Abraham Lincoln was 6 feet 4 inches tall" is a fact because it could have been observed or measured. There is enough evidence to prove that such a statement is true. **Opinions** are personal beliefs and attitudes that cannot be proved. "Apples taste better than oranges" is an example of an opinion. Someone will always disagree with this statement, and no amount of evidence can prove it to be true.

Use the Skill   As you read the following selection, determine what is fact and what is opinion. Be careful—if you see an opinion, check whether it is the author's opinion or someone else's opinion that the writer is stating.

The Mysterious Mr. Lincoln

SELECTION VOCABULARY

defy (DIH FY) *v.:* resist.
> Lincoln's beliefs defy easy explanations.

ambitious (AM BIHSH UHS) *adj.:* very much wanting success.
> Lincoln was ambitious and wanted to do great things.

cautious (KAW SHUHS) *adj.:* careful.
> Lincoln's approach to the war was cautious.

WORD STUDY

DIRECTIONS: Select the vocabulary word that best describes each of the people listed below.

1. a cartoonist who submits his comic strip to every newspaper he can find

_____

2. a girl who refuses to do anything her mother asks her to do

_____

3. a family with emergency food supplies in case of an earthquake

_____

THE MYSTERIOUS MR. LINCOLN

by Russell Freedman

The Mysterious Mr. Lincoln

Abraham Lincoln wasn't the sort of man who could lose himself in a crowd. After all, he stood six feet four inches tall, and to top it off, he wore a high silk hat.

His height was mostly in his long, bony legs. When he sat in a chair, he seemed no taller than anyone else. It was only when he stood up that he towered above other men. **A**

At first glance most people thought he was homely. Lincoln thought so too, referring once to his "poor, lean, lank face." As a young man he was sensitive about his gawky looks, but in time, he
10 learned to laugh at himself. When a rival called him "two-faced" during a political debate, Lincoln replied: "I leave it to my audience. If I had another face, do you think I'd wear this one?" **B**

© The Corcoran Gallery of Art/George Peter Alexander Healy/Corbis

According to those who knew him, Lincoln was a man of many faces. In repose he often seemed sad and gloomy. But when he began to speak, his expression changed. "The dull, listless features dropped like a mask," said a Chicago newspaperman. "The eyes began to sparkle, the mouth to smile; the whole countenance[1] was wreathed in animation, so that a stranger would have said, "Why, this man, so

20 angular and solemn a moment ago, is really handsome!"

Lincoln was the most photographed man of his time, but his friends insisted that no photo ever did him justice. It's no wonder. Back then, cameras required long exposures. The person being photographed had to "freeze" as the seconds ticked by. If he blinked an eye, the picture would be blurred. That's why Lincoln looks so stiff and formal in his photos. We never see him laughing or joking.

Artists and writers tried to capture the "real" Lincoln that the camera missed, but something about the man always

30 escaped them. His changeable features, his tones, gestures, and expressions, seemed to defy description. **C**

Today it's hard to imagine Lincoln as he really was. And he never cared to reveal much about himself. In company he was witty and talkative, but he rarely betrayed his inner feelings. According to William Herndon, his law partner, he was "the most secretive—reticent—shut-mouthed man that ever lived." **D**

In his own time, Lincoln was never fully understood even by his closest friends. Since then, his life story has been told and retold so many times he has become as much a legend as

40 a flesh-and-blood human being. While the legend is based on truth, it is only partly true. And it hides the man behind it like a disguise. **E**

The legendary Lincoln is known as Honest Abe, a humble man of the people who rose from a log cabin to the White House. There's no doubt that Lincoln was a poor boy who made good.

---

1. **countenance** (KOWN TUH NUHNS): face.

The Mysterious Mr. Lincoln **195**

C VOCABULARY

Selection Vocabulary

Artists and writers had trouble describing Lincoln's face. Considering this, what do you think *defy* means?

_____

_____

_____

D READ AND DISCUSS

Comprehension

From what you've read so far, what is your sense of Lincoln now?

E LITERARY FOCUS

Underline an example of **figurative language** in this paragraph. Is this figure of speech a **metaphor**, a **simile**, or an example of **personification**?

_____

Considering the description of Lincoln and his accomplishments in this paragraph, what do you think *ambitious* means?

_____

_____

_____

B **VOCABULARY**

Academic Vocabulary

What about Lincoln makes him *distinct*, or different, from many other United States Presidents?

_____

_____

_____

_____

C **LANGUAGE COACH**

Cool is a word with **multiple**, or many, meanings. Which of the following is the best meaning for *cool* in this sentence? Circle the letter of the best answer.
a. somewhat cold
b. calm
c. slow

And it's true that he carried his folksy manners and homespun speech to the White House with him. He said "howdy" to visitors and invited them to "stay a spell." He greeted diplomats while wearing carpet slippers, called his wife "mother" at receptions, and told bawdy[2] jokes at cabinet meetings.

Lincoln may have seemed like a common man, but he wasn't. His friends agreed that he was one of the most ambitious people they had ever known. Lincoln struggled hard to rise above his log-cabin origins, and he was proud of his achievements. By the time he ran for president he was a wealthy man, earning a large income from his law practice and his many investments. A As for the nickname Abe, he hated it. No one who knew him well ever called him Abe to his face. They addressed him as Lincoln or Mr. Lincoln.

Lincoln is often described as a sloppy dresser, careless about his appearance. In fact, he patronized the best tailor in Springfield, Illinois, buying two suits a year. That was at a time when many men lived, died, and were buried in the same suit.

It's true that Lincoln had little formal "eddication," as he would have pronounced it. Almost everything he "larned" he taught himself. All his life he said "thar" for *there*, "git" for *get*, "kin" for *can*. Even so, he became an eloquent public speaker who could hold a vast audience spellbound and a great writer whose finest phrases still ring in our ears. He was known to sit up late into the night, discussing Shakespeare's plays with White House visitors. B

He was certainly a humorous man, famous for his rollicking stories. But he was also moody and melancholy, tormented by long and frequent bouts of depression. Humor was his therapy. He relied on his yarns,[3] a friend observed, to "whistle down sadness."

He had a cool, logical mind, trained in the courtroom, and a practical, commonsense approach to problems. C Yet he was deeply superstitious, a believer in dreams, omens, and visions.

---

2. **bawdy** (BAW DEE): indecent or crude.
3. **yarns**: entertaining stories filled with exaggeration. Storytellers like Lincoln could be said to "spin" yarns.

80 We admire Lincoln today as an American folk hero. During the Civil War, however, he was the most unpopular president the nation had ever known. His critics called him a tyrant, a hick,[4] a stupid baboon who was unfit for his office. **D** As commander in chief of the armed forces, he was denounced as a bungling amateur who meddled in military affairs he knew nothing about. But he also had his supporters. They praised him as a farsighted statesman, a military mastermind who engineered the Union victory. **E**

90 Lincoln is best known as the Great Emancipator, the man who freed the slaves. Yet he did not enter the war with that idea in mind. "My paramount object in this struggle *is* to save the Union," he said in 1862, "and is *not* either to save or destroy slavery." As the war continued, Lincoln's attitude changed. Eventually he came to regard the conflict as a moral crusade to wipe out the sin of slavery. **F**

No black leader was more critical of Lincoln than the fiery abolitionist[5] writer and editor Frederick Douglass. Douglass had grown up as a slave. He had won his freedom by escaping to the North. Early in the war, impatient with Lincoln's cautious

100 leadership, Douglass called him "preeminently the white man's president, entirely devoted to the welfare of white men." Later, Douglass changed his mind and came to admire Lincoln. Several years after the war, he said this about the sixteenth president:

"His greatest mission was to accomplish two things: first, to save his country from dismemberment[6] and ruin; and second, to free his country from the great crime of slavery.... Taking him for all in all, measuring the tremendous magnitude of the work before him, considering the necessary means to ends, and surveying the end from the beginning, infinite wisdom has

110 seldom sent any man into the world better fitted for his mission than Abraham Lincoln." **G**

---

4. **hick:** awkward, inexperienced person from the country.
5. **abolitionist** (A BOH LI SHUN IST): person who supported abolishing, or ending, slavery in the United States.
6. **dismemberment:** separation into parts; division.

D **LITERARY FOCUS**

When Lincoln's critics called him a "stupid baboon," they didn't actually mean that he was a baboon. This criticism is an example of which kind of **figurative language**?

_____

E **READ AND DISCUSS**

Comprehension
What does all this say about Lincoln?

F **READING FOCUS**

Is this paragraph entirely made up of **facts**? What parts of this paragraph are or might be considered **opinions**? Explain.

_____
_____
_____
_____
_____
_____

G **READ AND DISCUSS**

Comprehension
How do Douglass's opinions of Lincoln mentioned in this part connect to the text as a whole?

Skills Practice

The Mysterious Mr. Lincoln

USE A FACT AND OPINION CHART

DIRECTIONS: Complete the chart below by listing three **facts** and three **opinions** expressed in "The Mysterious Mr. Lincoln."

Facts	Opinions
1. _____ _____ _____ _____ _____	1. _____ _____ _____ _____ _____
2. _____ _____ _____ _____ _____	2. _____ _____ _____ _____ _____
3. _____ _____ _____ _____ _____	3. _____ _____ _____ _____ _____

Applying Your Skills

The Mysterious Mr. Lincoln

VOCABULARY DEVELOPMENT

DIRECTIONS: Fill in the blanks with the vocabulary word that correctly completes each sentence.

Word Box

defy

ambitious

cautious

1. Lincoln was _____ upon entering the Civil War because he did not want to overextend Union forces.
2. _____ in both his personal and political life, Lincoln was determined to succeed.
3. While he came from humble beginnings, Lincoln managed to _____ the odds and achieve great success.

LITERARY SKILLS FOCUS: FIGURATIVE LANGUAGE

DIRECTIONS: Two **metaphors** from the text are listed below. Explain what each means in the space provided.

A rival called Lincoln "two-faced." (line 10)	1.
According to acquaintances, Lincoln "was a man of many faces." (lines 13–14)	2.

READING SKILLS FOCUS: DISTINGUISHING BETWEEN FACT AND OPINION

DIRECTIONS: On the lines below or on a separate sheet of paper, write a short paragraph that identifies the point the writer is trying to make in "The Mysterious Mr. Lincoln." Explain whether or not the use of **opinions** helped to make this point. What might this suggest about the use of opinions in nonfiction texts?

_____

_____

_____

_____

_____

_____

_____

Reading Standard 3.7
Explain the effects of common literary devices (e.g., symbolism, imagery, metaphor) in a variety of fictional and nonfictional texts.

What Do Fish Have to Do With Anything?

LITERARY SKILLS FOCUS: SYMBOLISM

Symbols are things that have meaning in themselves and also stand for something else. You've seen many symbols. For example, a skull and crossbones symbolizes danger. The use of symbols, or **symbolism**, adds another layer of meaning to literary works, movies, songs, and art. For example, the character Peter Pan is a symbol for everlasting childhood. In this story, the writer uses fish and a poundcake to mean what they are—and much more.

READING SKILLS FOCUS: SEQUENCING

The events of a story are often written in **chronological order**, or the order in which events actually happened. Writers show the **sequence**, or order, of events and how much time passes by using words such as *before*, *after*, *first*, *then*, and *later*. Keeping track of the sequence of events will help you understand a story's plot and how a writer develops symbols throughout a story.

Use the Skill   As you read, keep track of the sequence of events of the story in a chart like the one below.

Reading Standard 3.7 Explain the effects of common literary devices (e.g., symbolism, imagery, metaphor) in a variety of fictional and nonfictional texts.

Sequence of events
Page 202: Mrs. Markham and Willie walk home together.
Page 203:
Page 204:

Vocabulary Development

What Do Fish Have to Do With Anything?

SELECTION VOCABULARY

urgency (UR JUHN SEE) *n.:* pressure; insistence.
> *"Go!" shouted the boy with urgency.*

ashamed (UH SHAYMD) *adj.:* embarrassed.
> *She was ashamed of being alone.*

WORD STUDY

DIRECTIONS: Decide whether each sentence below describes a sense of *urgency* or someone who is *ashamed*. Write your answers on the blanks.

1. Charles had to quickly leave the burning building.

   _____

2. Jean got a terrible haircut and didn't want to be seen by anyone.

   _____

3. Everyone went outside to look for Kurt when he disappeared.

   _____

4. Emma was very sorry that she had said mean things to her friend.

   _____

WHAT DO FISH HAVE TO DO WITH ANYTHING?

by Avi

Every day Mrs. Markham waited for her son, Willie, to come out of school when it was over. They walked home together. If asked why, Mrs. Markham would say, "Parents need to protect their children."

One Monday afternoon as they approached their apartment building, she suddenly tugged at Willie. "Don't look that way," she said.

"Where?"

"At that man over there."

As they walked, Willie stole a look back over his shoulder. A man Willie had never seen before was sitting on a red plastic milk crate near the curb. His matted, streaky gray hair hung like a ragged curtain over a dirty face. His shoes were torn. Rough hands lay upon his knees. One hand was palm up. **A**

"What's the matter with him?" Willie asked.

Keeping her eyes straight ahead, Mrs. Markham said, "He's sick." She pulled Willie around. "Don't stare. It's rude." **B**

"What kind of sick?"

Mrs. Markham searched for an answer. "He's unhappy," she said.

"What's he doing?"

"Come on, Willie; you know. He's begging."

"Did anyone give him anything?"

"I don't know. Now come on, don't look."

© Mark Preston/HRW Photo

"Why don't you give him anything?"

30   "We have nothing to spare."

When they got home, Mrs. Markham removed a white cardboard box from the refrigerator. It contained poundcake. Using her thumb as a measure, she carefully cut a half-inch-thick piece of cake and gave it to Willie on a clean plate. The plate lay on a plastic mat decorated by images of roses with diamondlike dewdrops. She also gave him a glass of milk and a folded napkin. **C**

Willie said, "Can I have a bigger piece of cake?" **D**

Mrs. Markham picked up the cake box and ran a manicured pink fingernail along the nutrition information panel. "A

40   half-inch piece is a portion, and a portion contains the following nutrients. Do you want to hear them?"

"No."

"It's on the box, so you can accept what it says. Scientists study people and then write these things. If you're smart enough, you could become a scientist. Like this." Mrs. Markham tapped the box. "It pays well."

Willie ate his cake and drank the milk. When he was done, he took care to wipe the crumbs off his face as well as to blot the milk moustache with the napkin.

50   His mother said, "Now go on and do your homework. You're in fifth grade. It's important."

Willie gathered up his books that lay on the empty third chair. At the kitchen entrance he paused. "What *kind* of unhappiness does he have?"

© Mark Preston/HRW Photo

C READ AND DISCUSS

Comprehension

What is the author letting you know about Mrs. Markham and Willie?

D LITERARY FOCUS

What might a piece of cake (and wanting a bigger piece of cake) **symbolize**?

_____

_____

_____

_____

_____

_____

_____

_____

_____

_____

A **READING FOCUS**

Is the **sequence** of who is talking in this section clear to you? Explain your answer.

_____

_____

_____

_____

_____

_____

_____

"Who's that?"

"That man."

Mrs. Markham looked puzzled.

"The begging man. The one on the street."

"Could be anything," his mother said, vaguely. "A person can
60   be unhappy for many reasons."

"Like what?"

"Willie…"

"Is it a doctor kind of sickness? A sickness you can cure?"

"I wish you wouldn't ask such questions."

"Why?"

"Questions that have no answers shouldn't be asked."

"Can I go out?"

"Homework first." **A**

Willie turned to go.

70   "Money," Mrs. Markham suddenly said. "Money will cure a
lot of unhappiness. That's why that man was begging. A salesper-
son once said to me, 'Maybe you can't buy happiness, but you can
rent a lot of it.' You should remember that."

The apartment had three rooms. The walls were painted
mint green. Willie walked down the hallway to his room, which
was at the front of the building. By climbing up on the windowsill and pressing against the glass, he could see the sidewalk five
stories below. The man was still there.

It was almost five when he went to tell his mother he had
80   finished his school assignments. She was not there. He found her
in her bedroom, sleeping. Since she had begun working the night
shift at a convenience store—two weeks now—she took naps in
the late afternoon.

For a while Willie stood on the threshold,[1] hoping his
mother would wake up. When she didn't, he went to the front
room and looked down on the street again. The begging man
had not moved.

Willie returned to his mother's room.

---

1. **threshold** (THREHSH OHLD): doorway; entrance.

"I'm going out," he announced softly. **B**

90 Willie waited a decent interval[2] for his mother to waken. When she did not, Willie made sure his keys were in his pocket. Then he left the apartment.

Standing just outside his door, he could keep his eyes on the man. It appeared as if he had still not moved. Willie wondered how anyone could go on without moving for so long in the chilly October air. Was staying in one place part of the man's sickness?

During the twenty minutes that Willie watched, no one who passed looked in the beggar's direction. Willie wondered if they even saw the man. Certainly no one put any money into his 100 open hand.

A lady leading a dog by a leash went by. The dog strained in the direction of the man sitting on the crate. The dog's tail wagged. The lady pulled the dog away. "Heel!" she commanded.

The dog—tail between its legs—scampered to the lady's side. Even so, the dog twisted around to look back at the beggar.

Willie grinned. The dog had done exactly what he had done when his mother told him not to stare.

Pressing deep into his pocket, Willie found a nickel. It was warm and slippery. He wondered how much happiness you could 110 rent for a nickel. **C**

Squeezing the nickel between his fingers, Willie walked slowly toward the man. When he came before him, he stopped, suddenly nervous. The man, who appeared to be looking at the ground, did not move his eyes. He smelled bad. **D**

"Here." Willie stretched forward and dropped the coin into the man's open right hand.

"Bless you," the man said hoarsely, as he folded his fingers over the coin. His eyes, like high beams on a car, flashed up at Willie, then dropped.

120 Willie waited for a moment, then went back up to his room. From his front room he looked down on the street. He thought he saw the coin in the man's hand but was not sure.

---

2. **interval**: period of time between events.

B READ AND DISCUSS

Comprehension

Why does Willy softly tell his mother that he is going out?

C READ AND DISCUSS

Comprehension

What is Willie about to do?

D VOCABULARY

Academic Vocabulary

What facts *contribute*, or add, to Willie feeling nervous here?

LITERARY FOCUS

If the apartment is being compared to a cave, then who do you think is being compared to a fish? How might a cave fish be a **symbol** for this person?

_____

_____

_____

_____

_____

B **VOCABULARY**

Selection Vocabulary

Writers often put words in italics to show their importance, as seen here with the word *please*. Knowing this, what do you think is the meaning of the word *urgency*?

_____

_____

_____

C **READ AND DISCUSS**

Comprehension

What does it say about Willie that he keeps thinking about the homeless man?

After supper Mrs. Markham got ready to go to work. She kissed Willie good night. Then, as she did every night, she said, "If you have regular problems, call Mrs. Murphy downstairs. What's her number?"

"274–8676," Willie said.

"Extra bad problems, call Grandma."

"369–6754."

130   "Super-special problems, you can call me."

"962–6743."

"Emergency, the police."

"911."

"Don't let anyone in the door."

"I won't."

"No television past nine."

"I know."

"But you can read late."

"You're the one who's going to be late," Willie said.

140   "I'm leaving," Mrs. Markham said.

After she went, Willie stood for a long while in the hallway. The empty apartment felt like a cave that lay deep below the earth. That day in school Willie's teacher had told them about a kind of fish that lived in caves. These fish could not see. They had no eyes. The teacher had said it was living in the dark cave that made them like that. **A**

Before he went to bed, Willie took another look out the window. In the pool of light cast by the street lamp, Willie saw the man.

150   On Tuesday morning when Willie went to school, the man was gone. But when he came home from school with his mother, he was there again.

"*Please* don't look at him," his mother whispered with some urgency. **B**

During his snack Willie said, "Why shouldn't I look?"

"What are you talking about?"

"That man. On the street. Begging." **C**

"I told you. He's sick. It's better to act as if you never saw them. When people are that way, they don't wish to be looked at."

160   "Why not?"

Mrs. Markham thought for a while. "People are ashamed of being unhappy." **D**

"Are you sure he's unhappy?"

"You don't have to ask if people are unhappy. They tell you all the time."

"Is that part of the sickness?"

"Oh, Willie, I don't know. It's just the way they are."

Willie contemplated the half-inch slice of cake his mother had just given him. He said, "Ever since Dad left, you've been

170   unhappy. Are you ashamed?" **E**

Mrs. Markham closed her eyes. "I wish you wouldn't ask that."

Willie said, "Are you?"

"Willie…"

"Think he might come back?"

"It's more than likely," Mrs. Markham said, but Willie wondered if that was what she really thought. He did not think so. "Do you think Dad is unhappy?"

"Where do you get such questions?"

"They're in my mind."

180   "There's much in the mind that need not be paid attention to."

"Fish that live in caves have no eyes."

"What are you talking about?"

"My teacher said it's all that darkness. The fish forget to see. So they lose their eyes."

"I doubt she said that."

"She did."

"Willie, you have too much imagination." **F**

After his mother went to work, Willie gazed down onto the street. The man was there. Willie thought of going down, but he

190   knew he was not supposed to leave the building when his mother worked at night. He decided to speak to the man tomorrow.

Next afternoon—Wednesday—Willie said to the man, "I don't have any money. Can I still talk to you?"

D **(LANGUAGE COACH)**

A **word family** is a group of words that are related. *Thought, think,* and *thinking,* for example, are all part of the same word family. Which of the following words is not related to *ashamed*? Circle the letter of the correct answer.
a. assured
b. shameless
c. shame

E **(READING FOCUS)**

What is the **sequence** of events so far on this page?

_____

_____

_____

_____

_____

_____

_____

F **(READ AND DISCUSS)**

Comprehension

How do these conversations add to what we've already been thinking about Willie and his mother?

READING FOCUS

Explain in **chronological order** the **sequence** of events that leads Willie to talk to the man again.

_____

_____

_____

_____

_____

_____

_____

_____

_____

_____

B **LITERARY FOCUS**

Do you think the man is a **symbol** for unhappiness, or do you think he might be a symbol of something else? Explain your answer.

_____

_____

_____

_____

_____

_____

_____

_____

_____

The man's eyes focused on Willie. They were gray eyes with folds of dirty skin beneath them. He needed a shave.

"My mother said you were unhappy. Is that true?" **A**

"Could be," the man said.

"What are you unhappy about?"

The man's eyes narrowed as he studied Willie intently. He
200   said, "How come you want to know?"

Willie shrugged.

"I think you should go home, kid."

"I am home." Willie gestured toward the apartment. "I live right here. Fifth floor. Where do you live?"

"Around."

"*Are* you unhappy?" Willie persisted.

The man ran a tongue over his lips. His Adam's apple bobbed.

Willie said, "I'm trying to learn about unhappiness."

"Why?"

210   "I don't think I want to say."

"A man has the right to remain silent," the man said and closed his eyes.

Willie remained standing on the pavement for a while before walking back to his apartment. Once inside his own room, he looked down from the window. The man was still there. At one moment Willie was certain he was looking at the apartment building and the floor on which Willie lived.

The next day—Thursday—after dropping a nickel in the man's palm, Willie said, "I've decided to tell you why I want to
220   learn about unhappiness."

The man gave a grunt.

"See, I've never seen anyone look so unhappy as you do. So I figure you must know a lot about it."

The man took a deep breath. "Well, yeah, maybe." **B**

Willie said, "And I need to find a cure for it."

"A *what*?"

"A cure for unhappiness."

The man pursed his lips and blew a silent whistle. Then he said, "Why?"

230   "My mother is unhappy."

"Why's that?"

"My dad left."

"How come?"

"I don't know. But she's unhappy all the time. So if I found a cure for unhappiness, it would be a good thing, wouldn't it?"

"I suppose."

Willie said, "Would you like some cake?"

"What kind?"

"I don't know. Cake."

240   "Depends on the cake."

On Friday Willie said to the man, "I found out what kind of cake it is." C

"Yeah?"

"Poundcake. But I don't know why it's called that."

"Probably doesn't matter."

For a moment neither said anything. Then Willie said, "In school my teacher said there are fish that live in caves and the caves are dark, so the fish don't have eyes. What do you think? Do you believe that?"

250   "Sure."

"You do? How come?"

"Because you said so."

"You mean, just because someone *said* it you believe it?"

"Not someone. You."

Willie said, "But, well, maybe it *isn't* true."

The man grunted. "Hey, do you believe it?"

Willie nodded.

"Well, you're not just anyone. You got eyes. You see. You ain't no fish."

260   "Oh."

"What's your name?"

"Willie."

"That's a boy's name. What's your grownup name?"

Willie thought for a moment. "William, I guess."

"And that means another thing."

C **READ AND DISCUSS**

Comprehension
What is going on between Willie and the homeless man?

A **LANGUAGE COACH**

List two other words that are in the same **word family** as *proper*. How are these words related to *proper*?

_____

_____

_____

B **VOCABULARY**

Word Study

Use a dictionary to find the meaning of *bleary*. Then, write two synonyms, or words with similar meaning, for *bleary* on the lines below.

_____

_____

_____

_____

C **LITERARY FOCUS**

Compare the discussion of the cake on this page to the earlier conversation about cake between Willie and his mother on page 203. What do you think the cake is a **symbol** of, and why?

_____

_____

_____

_____

_____

"What?"

"I'll take some of that cake."

Willie smiled. "You will?"

"Just said it, didn't I?"

270   "I'll get it."

Willie ran to the apartment. He took the box from the refrigerator as well as a knife, then hurried back down to the street. "I'll cut you a piece," he said.

As the man looked on, Willie opened the box, then held his thumb against the cake to make sure the portion was the right size. With a poke of the knife he made a small mark for the proper width. A

Just as he was about to cut, the man said, "Hold it!"

Willie looked up. "What?"

280   "What were you doing with your thumb there?"

"I was measuring the right size. The right portion. One portion is what a person is supposed to get."

"Where'd you learn that?"

"It says so on the box. You can see for yourself." He held out the box.

The man studied the box, then handed it back to Willie. "That's just lies," he said.

"How do you know?"

"William, how can a box say how much a person needs?"

290   "But it does. The scientists say so. They measured, so they know. Then they put it there."

"Lies," the man repeated.

Willie studied the man. His eyes seemed bleary. B "Then how much should I cut?" he asked.

The man said, "You have to look at me, then at the cake, and then you're going to have to decide for yourself."

"Oh." Willie looked at the cake. The piece was about three inches wide. Willie looked up at the man. After a moment he cut the cake into two pieces, each an inch and a half wide. He gave

300   one piece to the man and kept the other. C

"Bless you," the man said, as he took the piece and laid it in his left hand. He began to break off pieces with his right hand and one by one put them into his mouth. Each piece was chewed thoughtfully. Willie watched him piece by piece. **D**

When the man was done, he dusted his hands of crumbs.

"Now I'll give you something," the man said.

"What?" Willie said, surprised.

"The cure for unhappiness."

"You know it?" Willie asked, eyes wide.

310 The man nodded.

"What is it?"

"It's this: What a person needs is always more than they say."

Willie thought for a while. "Who's *they*?" he asked.

The man pointed to the cake box. "The people on the box," he said.

Willie thought for a moment; then he gave the man the other piece of cake.

The man took it, saying, "Good man," and then ate it. **E**

The next day was Saturday. Willie did not go to school. All 320 morning he kept looking down from his window for the man, but it was raining and he did not appear. Willie wondered where he was but could not imagine it.

Willie's mother woke about noon. Willie sat with her while she ate the breakfast he had made. "I found the cure for unhappiness," he announced.

"Did you?" his mother said. She was reading a memo from the convenience store's owner.

"It's, 'What a person needs is always more than they say.'" **F**

His mother put her papers down. "That's nonsense. Where 330 did you hear that?"

"That man."

"What man?"

"On the street. The one who was begging. You said he was unhappy. So I asked him."

"Willie, I told you I didn't want you to even look at that man."

"He's a nice man . . . "

D READ AND DISCUSS

Comprehension
What just happened between Willie and the man?

E READ AND DISCUSS

Comprehension
What did you learn here?
Follow-up: How does Willie respond?

F READING FOCUS

Explain, in **chronological order**, what leads to Willie finding the cure for unhappiness.

_____
_____
_____
_____
_____
_____
_____
_____
_____
_____
_____
_____

© Dante Fenolio/Photo Researchers, Inc.

"How do you know?"

"I've talked to him."

"When? How much?"

340   Willie shrank down. "I did, that's all."

"Willie, I forbid you to talk to him. Do you understand me? Do you? Answer me!"

"Yes," Willie said, but in his mind he decided he would talk to the man one more time. He needed to explain why he could not talk to him anymore.

On Sunday, however, the man was not there. Nor was he there on Monday.

"That man is gone," Willie said to his mother as they walked home from school.

350   "I saw. I'm not blind."

"Where do you think he went?"

"I couldn't care less. And you might as well know, I arranged for him to be gone."

Willie stopped short. "What do you mean?"

"I called the police. We don't need a nuisance like that around here. Pestering kids." **A**

"He wasn't pestering me."

"Of course he was."

"How do you know?"

360   "Willie, I have eyes. I can see."

Willie stared at his mother. "No, you can't. You're a fish. You live in a cave."

"Willie, don't talk nonsense."

"My name isn't Willie. It's William." Turning, he walked back to the school playground. **B**

Mrs. Markham watched him go. "Fish," she wondered to herself; "what do fish have to do with anything?" **C**

Applying Your Skills

What Do Fish Have to Do With Anything?

VOCABULARY DEVELOPMENT

DIRECTIONS: Write two original sentences, each correctly using a different vocabulary word from the Word Box.

Word Box

ashamed

urgent

1. _____

_____

2. _____

_____

LITERARY SKILLS FOCUS: SYMBOLISM

DIRECTIONS: In the first column, list three **symbols** from the story. In the second column, explain what you think each symbol means.

Symbol	Meaning
1.	2.
3.	4.
5.	6.

READING SKILLS FOCUS: SEQUENCING

DIRECTIONS: Describe the most important events of this story in **chronological order** on the lines below.

_____

_____

_____

_____

_____

_____

_____

_____

_____

Reading Standard 3.7 Explain the effects of common literary devices (e.g., symbolism, imagery, metaphor) in a variety of fictional and nonfictional texts.

Preparing to Read

All Aboard with Thomas Garrett

by Alice P. Miller

INFORMATIONAL TEXT FOCUS: IDENTIFYING THE MAIN IDEA

When you are reading nonfiction selections with similar **topics**, you may notice that the pieces have main ideas in common. A **main idea** is the most important thing said about a topic. Being able to connect main ideas across texts lets you "see" a topic from different perspectives. It is also important to notice *how* related selections present their main ideas. You can do this by looking for the details (pieces of information) that support each idea.

SELECTION VOCABULARY

prudent (PROO DUHNT) *adj.*: wise; sensible.
   A prudent person prepares carefully for every situation.

hazardous (HAZ UHR DUHS) *adj.*: dangerous; risky.
   The mountain roads were hazardous in winter.

diligence (DIHL UH JUHNTS) *n.*: steady effort.
   He showed diligence by studying all week for the test.

jubilant (JOO BUH LUHNT) *adj.*: joyful.
   My jubilant parents held a big party to celebrate my graduation.

WORD STUDY

DIRECTIONS: Write words from the vocabulary above in the blanks to complete the passage.

   Traveling the Underground Railroad could be a very

(1) _____ journey for slaves, with danger at every turn.

The Railroad's success was largely due to the (2) _____

of people who worked hard to free slaves. Slaves had to make many

(3) _____ decisions along the journey in order to

make it to the North. Former slaves were often (4) _____

after they gained their freedom.

Reading Standard 2.3
Connect and clarify main ideas by identifying their relationships to other sources and related topics.

ALL ABOARD WITH THOMAS GARRETT

by Alice P. Miller

BACKGROUND

During the Civil War, many people in the North and South helped enslaved people to escape to the North, where they could be free. Most enslaved people traveled by way of the Underground Railroad, a system of secret routes along which they were given shelter and food. Both those who fled and those who helped them risked their lives to fight slavery. Thomas Garrett was one of these brave people.

The elderly couple walked sedately down the stairs of the red brick house, every detail of their costumes proclaiming their respectability. The small lady was wearing an ankle-length gray gown, a snowy-white lawn kerchief, and a pleated gray silk bonnet, draped with a veil. The tall white-haired gentleman wore the wide-brimmed beaver hat and the long black waistcoat that was customary among Quakers.

When they reached the sidewalk, he assisted her into the four-wheeled barouche[1] that stood at the curb. Then he climbed
10 into the barouche himself. The driver drove the horses away at a leisurely pace. Not until they were beyond the city limits did he allow the horses to prance along at a brisk pace across the few miles that separated Wilmington, Delaware, from the free state of Pennsylvania. **A**

That tall white-haired gentleman was Thomas Garrett, a white man who had for many years been breaking the law by sheltering runaway slaves. And the little lady at his side was

Thomas Garrett./Courtesy of the Historical Society of Delaware

A READING FOCUS

Based on the details in the first two paragraphs, do you think we have been introduced to the **main idea** of the article yet? Why?

_____

_____

_____

---

1. **barouche** (BUH ROOSH): type of horse-drawn carriage.

A VOCABULARY

Word Study

Secret is a noun that means "something that is hidden or concealed." Based on this, what do you think the verb *secreted* means?

_____

_____

_____

B READ AND DISCUSS

Comprehension

What is the author showing you with Harriet Tubman's and Thomas Garrett's actions?

C LANGUAGE COACH

Related words share the same root word, but may have different beginnings and endings, and may be different parts of speech. What related noun can you form by removing *-ous* from the adjective *hazardous*? What do you think this new word means?

_____

_____

_____

D READ AND DISCUSS

Comprehension

What does Thomas Garrett's life's work tell us about him?

runaway slave Harriet Tubman, clad in clothes donated by his wife. On the preceding night Harriet had slept in a small room
20 secreted behind one wall of Garrett's shoe store, a room that never remained unoccupied for very long. **A** It was Harriet's first visit to Garrett, but she would be returning many times in the future. **B**

Runaway slaves remained with Garrett for one night or two or three until such time as Garrett considered it prudent to send them along to the next station on the Underground Railroad. He provided them with clothing and outfitted them with new shoes from his shoe store. He fed them hearty meals and dressed their wounds. He also forged passes for them so that any slave stopped
30 by a slave catcher would have evidence that he or she was on a legitimate errand.

Some of the money he needed to cover the cost of his hospitality came out of his own pocket, but he was not a rich man. He could not have taken care of so many fugitives were it not for donations made by fellow abolitionists in the North as well as from supporters in foreign countries. There was never quite enough money, but no fugitive was ever turned away from his door. He would have gone without food himself before he would have refused food to a hungry slave.

40 Garrett, who was born in Upper Darby, Pennsylvania, in 1789, had been helping runaway slaves ever since 1822, when he rescued a young black woman who was trying to escape from her master. At that time he vowed to devote the rest of his life to helping fugitives, and he remained faithful to that vow.

Of all the stations on the Underground Railroad his was probably the most efficiently run and the one most frequently used. The fact that Wilmington was so close to Pennsylvania made it the most hazardous stop on the route. **C** Slave catchers prowled the streets of Wilmington, on the alert for any indication
50 that a black person might be a runaway. They kept a sharp eye on all roads leading north from Wilmington. **D**

For many years Garrett managed to get away with his illegal activities because he was a clever man and knew ways to avoid

Map of the Underground Railroad.

©The Granger Collection, New York

E READ AND DISCUSS

Comprehension
What do Garrett's different ways of helping the slaves show us?

F READING FOCUS

What **main idea** is presented in these two paragraphs?

_____

_____

_____

_____

detection by the slave catchers. Sometimes he disguised a slave, as he had done with Harriet. Sometimes he dressed a man in a woman's clothing or a woman in a man's clothing or showed a young person how to appear like one bent over with age.

60 Another reason for his success was that he had many friends who admired what he was doing and who could be trusted to help him. They might, for example, conceal slaves under a wagon-load of vegetables or in a secret compartment in a wagon. **E**

The slave catchers were aware of what he was doing, but they had a hard time finding the kind of evidence that would stand up in court. At last, in 1848, he was sued by two Maryland slave owners who hoped to bring a stop to his activities by ruining him financially.

The suit was brought into the federal circuit court of New Castle under a 1793 federal law that allowed slave owners to recover penalties from any person who harbored a runaway slave.
70 The case was heard by Willard Hall, United States District Judge, and by Roger B. Taney, Chief Justice of the United States Supreme Court. Bringing in a verdict in favor of the slave owners, the jurors decided that the slave owners were entitled to $5,400 in fines. **F**

Garrett didn't have anywhere near that much money, but he stood up and addressed the court and the spectators in these words:

A **READING FOCUS**

Does Garrett's speech in court introduce a new **main idea** or give more details about a main idea you have already discovered? Explain your answer.

_____

_____

_____

_____

_____

_____

_____

B **READ AND DISCUSS**

Comprehension

How do things turn out in court for Garrett? **Follow-up:** What does the juror's reaction to Garrett's speech demonstrate?

"I have assisted fourteen hundred slaves in the past twenty-five years on their way to the North. I now consider this penalty imposed upon me as a license for the remainder of my life. I am now past sixty and have not a dollar to my name, but be that as it may, if anyone knows of a poor slave who needs shelter and a breakfast, send him to me, as I now publicly pledge myself to double my diligence and never neglect an opportunity to assist a slave to obtain freedom, so help me God!" **A**

As he continued to speak for more than an hour, some of the spectators hissed while others cheered. When he finished, one juror leaped across the benches and pumped Garrett's hand. With tears in his eyes, he said, "I beg your forgiveness, Mr. Garrett." **B**

After the trial Garrett's furniture was auctioned off to help pay the heavy fine. But he managed to borrow money from friends and eventually repaid those loans, rebuilt his business, and became prosperous.

Meanwhile he went on sheltering slaves for many more years. By the time President Lincoln issued the Emancipation Proclamation[2] in 1863, Garrett's records showed that he had sheltered more than 2,700 runaways.

During those years he had many encounters with Harriet Tubman, as she kept returning to the South and coming back north with bands of slaves. Much of what we know about Harriet today is based on letters that he sent to her or wrote about her. A portion of one of those letters reads thus:

"I may begin by saying, living as I have in a slave State, and the laws being very severe where any proof could be made of anyone aiding slaves on their way to freedom, I have not felt at liberty to keep any written word of Harriet's labors as I otherwise could, and now would be glad to do; for in truth I never met with any person, of any color, who had more confidence in the voice of God, as spoken direct to her soul. . . . She felt no more fear of being arrested by her former master, or any other person, when

---

2. **Emancipation Proclamation:** presidential order abolishing slavery in the South.

©Louie Psihoyos/Corbis

C VOCABULARY

Selection Vocabulary

Jubilant means "joyful." Why were the people *jubilant*?

_____

_____

_____

_____

_____

D READ AND DISCUSS

Comprehension

What do Garrett's words about Tubman show? **Follow-up:** What does this celebration show you?

in his immediate neighborhood, than she did in the State of New York or Canada, for she said she ventured only where God sent her, and her faith in the Supreme Power truly was great."

In April, 1870, the black people of Wilmington held a huge celebration upon the passage of the fifteenth amendment to the Constitution of the United States. That amendment provided that the right of citizens to vote should not be denied or abridged by the United States or by any state on account of race, color, or previous condition of servitude.[3]

120 Jubilant blacks drew Garrett through the streets in an open carriage on one side of which were inscribed the words "Our Moses." **C** **D**

---

3. **servitude** (SUR VIH TOOD): condition of being under another person's control.

Skills Practice

All Aboard with Thomas Garrett

USE A MAIN IDEA CHART

DIRECTIONS: Fill in the chart below with four main ideas that are presented in "All Aboard with Thomas Garrett."

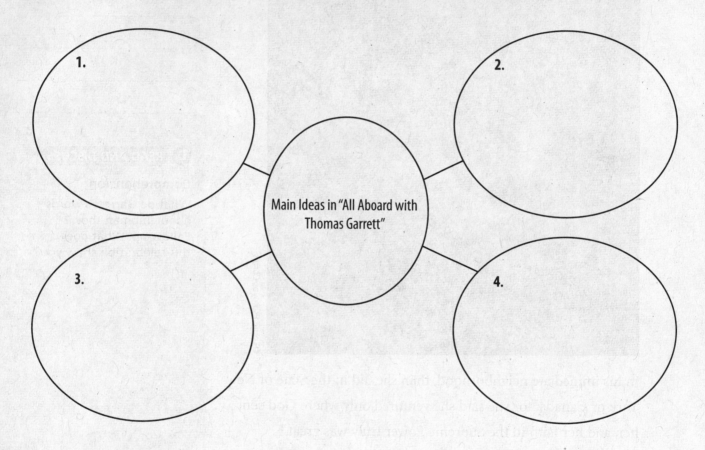

1.

2.

Main Ideas in "All Aboard with Thomas Garrett"

3.

4.

Applying Your Skills

All Aboard with Thomas Garrett

VOCABULARY DEVELOPMENT

DIRECTIONS: An analogy is a comparison between two things. The exercises below are word analogies. For each example, figure out the relationship between the first two words. Then, fill in the blank with the correct word from the Word Box that creates the same type of relationship. Here's how you read the first exercise: "*Plan* is to *strategy*, as *effort* is to _____." The relationship between *plan* and *strategy* is that they have similar meanings. Which word has a similar meaning to *effort*?

<table>
<tr><td>

Word Box

prudent

hazardous

diligence

jubilant

</td><td>

1. plan : strategy :: effort : _____

2. quiet : loud :: sad : _____

3. fruits : healthy :: chemicals : _____

</td></tr>
</table>

INFORMATIONAL TEXT FOCUS: IDENTIFYING THE MAIN IDEA

DIRECTIONS: The selection you just read has several **main ideas** and details to support those main ideas. Choose the idea you feel is the most important and briefly summarize it. Then, share your own opinions on that idea.

_____

_____

_____

_____

_____

_____

_____

_____

_____

Reading Standard 2.3
Connect and clarify main ideas by identifying their relationships to other sources and related topics.

Skills Review

Chapter 6

VOCABULARY REVIEW

DIRECTIONS: For each sentence, tell whether or not the boldfaced vocabulary word is a synonym or antonym for the underlined word in the sentence by circling either SYNONYM or ANTONYM. A synonym is a word that has the same or a similar meaning as another word. An antonym is a word that has the opposite meaning.

1. **wily:** Monica's practical joke was so <u>clever</u> that she tricked all of the other students.

   SYNONYM   ANTONYM

2. **cautious:** The <u>reckless</u> driver sped through the red light.

   SYNONYM   ANTONYM

3. **ashamed:** Mario was extremely <u>proud</u> of his accomplishment.

   SYNONYM   ANTONYM

4. **desperate:** The soothing music made him feel very <u>calm</u>.

   SYNONYM   ANTONYM

5. **prudent:** He made the <u>smart</u> decision to save money for college.

   SYNONYM   ANTONYM

6. **hazardous:** The <u>dangerous</u> chemicals were locked away for safety.

   SYNONYM   ANTONYM

7. **diligence:** His <u>perseverance</u> in his studying paid off when he passed the test.

   SYNONYM   ANTONYM

8. **jubilant:** She was <u>disappointed</u> about not getting the lead role in the play.

   SYNONYM   ANTONYM

Skills Review

Chapter 6

LANGUAGE COACH

Some **word families** have nouns that can be made into a related adjective by adding to or changing the ending of the noun.

For example:

poison (noun) + *-ous* = **poisonous** (adjective)

DIRECTIONS: Each exercise below shows a noun in boldface type. Complete each sentence with the adjective form of the boldfaced noun. Choose from the following endings to add to the boldfaced nouns to create adjectives: *-y, -en, -ic, -ous, -able*. The first one has been done for you.

1. **hair** (noun)

   The golden retriever was very <u>hairy</u>.

2. **wood** (noun)

   She bought _____ shoes on her trip to Holland.

3. **sweat** (noun)

   My hands were _____ because I was nervous.

4. **humor** (noun)

   The _____ story made him laugh.

5. **reason** (noun)

   Her request to replace her broken desk was _____.

ORAL LANGUAGE ACTIVITY

DIRECTIONS: With a partner, make up a story about a family going on vacation. One partner should tell the story using a **first-person narrator**. The other partner should tell the story using a **third-person narrator**. Take turns making up and telling parts of the story. Remember, a story with a first-person point of view uses pronouns such as *I, me, we, us, our, my,* and *mine*. A story with a third-person point of view uses pronouns such as *his, her, their, he, she, they,* and *them*.

Chapter

7

Expository Critique: Persuasive Texts and Media

© Todd Gipstein/CORBIS

Literary and Academic Vocabulary for Chapter 7

adequacy (AD ᴜʜ KWUH SEE) *n.*: quality of being enough to meet a need or requirement.

An argument's strength depends, in part, on the adequacy of the evidence.

authority (ᴜʜ THAWR ᴜʜ TEE) *n.*: someone who is respected because of his or her knowledge about a subject.

The writer quoted an authority on the subject for her article about climate changes.

conclude (KUHN KLOOD) *v.*: form an opinion or make a judgment after considering all the information you have.

You need to conclude whether or not the writer provides enough evidence to support his claim.

crucial (KROO SHUHL) *adj.*: very important.

It is crucial that you wake up by 7 A.M. so that you are not late for your test.

persuasion (PUHR SWAY ZHUN) *n.*: effort to make someone believe or do something.

The writer used persuasion to make the readers believe that they should buy a new car.

opinion (ᴜʜ PIHN YUHN) *n.*: belief or attitude.

It was his opinion that the movie was terrific.

reason (REE ZUHN) *n.*: why someone holds a particular opinion.

The reason he wrote the story was to honor his father's memory.

evidence (EHV ᴜʜ DEHNTS) *n.*: support or proof.

The writer provided enough evidence to support her final conclusion.

A Surprising Secret to a Long Life: Stay in School

INFORMATIONAL TEXT FOCUS: PERSUASION

Persuasion is the use of language or visual images to convince people to believe or do something. Persuasion is everywhere. Advertisements try to get us to buy products, and politicians ask people for their votes. Writers use persuasion, too, to get us to see things from their point of view.

READING SKILLS FOCUS: EVALUATING EVIDENCE

Many texts are written to present a conclusion, or a final opinion reached by reasoning. In order to persuade you to accept this conclusion, however, a writer needs to provide **evidence** (support or proof). As you read, use a chart like this one to track evidence and how it relates to the writer's conclusion:

Evidence	Conclusion
Statement by Michael Grossman, health economist	Education helps determine how long a person lives.

SELECTION VOCABULARY

dispute (DIHS PYOOT) *n.:* disagreement; argument.
  The dispute between the brothers continued for hours.

isolated (Y SUH LAY TIHD) *adj.:* apart from others; separate.
  Being isolated can lead to poor health.

declined (DIH KLYND) *v.:* dropped; went down.
  My weight declined after I began to exercise more.

WORD STUDY

DIRECTIONS: Write words from the vocabulary list above in the blanks to complete the passage below.

The writer of the following article states that education is very important to the length of a person's life. There are other factors to consider, though, such as how a person's income may have increased or (1) _____, or even how (2) _____ the person is. However, there is little (3) _____ about the importance of education.

Reading Standard 2.6
Determine the adequacy and appropriateness of the evidence for an author's conclusions.

A SURPRISING SECRET TO A LONG LIFE: STAY IN SCHOOL

by Gina Kolata

© Hans Neleman/Getty Images

James Smith, a health economist at RAND Corporation, has heard many ideas about what it takes to live a long life. The theories include money, lack of stress, a loving family, and lots of friends. But it has been Smith's job to question these beliefs. Clearly, some people live longer than others. The rich live longer than the poor in the United States, for instance. But what is cause and what is effect?

In every country, there is an average life span for the nation as a whole, and there are average life spans for groups within, based on race, geography, education, and even churchgoing. Smith and other researchers find that the one factor linked to longer lives in every country studied is education. In study after study, says Richard Hodes, director of the National Institute on Aging, education "keeps coming up."

Education is not the only factor, of course. There is smoking, which curtails life span. There is a connection between having a network of friends and family and living a long and healthy life. But there is little dispute about education's importance. Ⓐ Ⓑ

"If you were to ask me what affects health and longevity,"[1] says Michael Grossman, a health economist at the City University of New York, "I would put education at the top of my list."

---

1. **longevity** (LON JEHV UH TEE): length of life.

"A Surprising Secret to a Long Life: Stay in School," (adapted), by Gina Kolata from The New York Times, January 3, 2007. Copyright © 2007 by The New York Times Company. Reproduced by permission of the copyright holder.

Ⓐ **VOCABULARY**

Selection Vocabulary

Rewrite this sentence. Give the same information, but do not use the word *dispute*.

_____

_____

_____

Ⓑ **READING FOCUS**

The writer has stated a conclusion at the beginning of the article. What **evidence** does she need to persuade you that this conclusion is correct?

_____

_____

_____

_____

_____

Graduate Student Finds Answer

In 1999, Adriana Lleras-Muney was a graduate student at Columbia University. She found a 1969 research paper noting the correlation[2] between education and health. It concluded: to improve health, invest in education over investing in medical care. These findings could be true only if education caused good health, she thought. But there were other possibilities.

Maybe sick children did not go to school or dropped out early. Or maybe education was a part of wealth, and wealth led to

30 health. Perhaps richer parents provided better nutrition, medical care, and education—and their children lived longer.

How, she asked herself, could she sort out causes and effects? Then she read that, about 100 years ago, different states started forcing children to go to school for longer periods. She knew she had to study those results and see if she could find a difference in life spans.

When she finished, Lleras-Muney says, "I was surprised; I was really surprised." It turned out that life expectancy at age 35 was extended by as much as one and a half years simply by going

40 to school for one extra year. **A** **B**

Lessons Learned

Lleras-Muney has since become an assistant professor at Princeton,[3] and other papers on the subject have appeared in Sweden, Denmark, England, and Wales. In every country studied, forcing children to spend a longer time in school led to better health.

She and others pose this possible reason why education helps people live longer: As a group, less educated people are less able to plan for the future. They are not as able to delay gratification.[4]

---

2. **correlation** (KAWR UH LAY SHUHN): a relationship between two ideas, facts, etc., especially when one may be the cause of the other.
3. **Princeton:** a highly respected Ivy League college in New Jersey.
4. **gratification** (GRAT UH FUH KAY SHUHN): satisfaction or pleasure; a source of satisfaction and pleasure.

A **LANGUAGE COACH**

Groups of related words are called **word families**. The word *extend*, for example, is in the same word family as *extended* and *extending*; the words all have similar meanings but have different suffixes, or word endings. What are some words that are in the same word family as *expectancy*?

_____

_____

_____

_____

B **READING FOCUS**

What **evidence** has the author provided to support her conclusion?

_____

_____

_____

_____

_____

_____

_____

_____

_____

_____

_____

_____

How might that difference in outlook change life spans? 50 Consider smoking. Smokers are at least twice as likely to die as people who never smoked, says Samuel Preston, a researcher at the University of Pennsylvania. And poorly educated people are more likely to smoke, he says, even though "everybody [including the poorly educated] knows that smoking can be deadly."

In one large federal study of middle-aged people, Smith reports, those with less education were less able to think ahead. And living for the day, says Smith, can be "the worst thing for your health." **C**

Other Factors at Work

In the late 1970s, Lisa Berkman, a professor of public policy at 60 the Harvard School of Public Health, worked at a San Francisco health care center. And she noticed something. "In Chinatown and North Beach, there were these tightly bound social networks," Berkman recalls. "You saw old people with young people. In the Tenderloin[5] people were just sort of dumped. People were really isolated." **D**

The risks of being socially isolated proved to be "phenomenal,"[6] Berkman says. Isolation matched a twofold to fivefold increase in mortality rates. This effect emerges in study after study and in country after country.

70 She asked herself: Does social isolation shorten lives? **E** Or are people isolated when sick and frail? Berkman says, the more she investigated, the more she found that social isolation might lead to poor health and shorter lives. It can, for example, increase stress and make it harder to get assistance. **F**

Researchers at Dartmouth College also find the lowest death rates in the wealthiest places, leading to this possibility: that wealth buys health. Poorer people, at least in the United States, are less likely to have health insurance, after all. But the

---

5. **the Tenderloin:** a poor area in downtown San Francisco
6. **phenomenal** (FUH NOM IHN UHL) *adj.:* out of the ordinary; surprising; rare.

C READ AND DISCUSS

Comprehension

How does the federal study support Lleras-Muney's findings about education and planning for the future?

D VOCABULARY

Section Vocabulary

The word *isolated* means "separate or apart from others." What might cause a person to become *isolated*?

_____

_____

_____

E LANGUAGE COACH

The suffix *-ion* of the word *isolation* tells you that this word is a noun. You can also see that it is in the same **word family** as the word *isolated*, which you already know. Considering this, write a definition for *isolation*.

_____

_____

_____

F READ AND DISCUSS

Comprehension

What does Berkman's research show us?

_____

_____

_____

_____

_____

_____

Comprehension

What else did you learn about lengthening life?

©Tim Pannell/Corbis

differences between rich and poor do not shrink in countries
80 where everyone has health care. In fact, says Smith, it is not lower
incomes' leading to poor health so much as poor health's leading
to lower incomes.

The point, says Smith, is that sick people often are unable
to work or work full time. He analyzed data from a National
Institute on Aging sample of U.S. households with at least one
person aged 51 to 61. When someone developed cancer, heart
disease, or lung disease, his or her household income declined
an average of more than $37,000.

Smith asked whether getting richer made people healthier
90 and lengthened life. It did not, he concluded, after studying
increases in income during the stock market surge of the 1990s.
"I find almost no role of financial anything in the onset of
disease," Smith says. A

Clearly, factors other than education make a difference in
life span, yet even many of those factors point back to staying in
school: For the most part, genes have little effect on life spans.
But health and nutrition in early life can affect adult health and
longevity, researchers find. What also pays off is controlling
risk factors for heart disease, such as smoking, cholesterol,
100 blood pressure, and diabetes. And it seems increasingly likely
that education plays a major role in gaining that control—and
expanding life. B

Applying Your Skills

A Surprising Secret to a Long Life: Stay in School

VOCABULARY DEVELOPMENT

DIRECTIONS: In each exercise, circle the word that doesn't match the meaning of the boldfaced vocabulary word. Explain why you how the meaning of the word you circled is different on the line below.

1. accepted / **declined** / dropped

_____

2. crowded / alone / **isolated**

_____

3. **dispute** / agreement / argument

_____

INFORMATIONAL TEXT FOCUS: PERSUASION

DIRECTIONS: Explain whether or not you think the author's use of **persuasion** was successful. Were you convinced by her argument?

_____

_____

_____

READING SKILLS FOCUS: EVALUATING EVIDENCE

DIRECTIONS: The author presents her conclusion at the beginning *and* end of the article. Fill in the graphic organizer below to explain the **evidence** she uses in-between. If necessary, write your answers on a separate piece of paper.

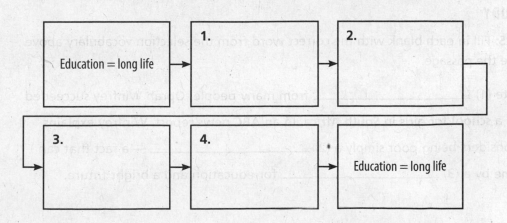

Reading Standard 2.6 Determine the adequacy and appropriateness of the evidence for an author's conclusions.

Oprah Talks About Her South African "Dreamgirls"

ABC News Report

INFORMATIONAL TEXT FOCUS: LOGICAL AND EMOTIONAL APPEALS

To persuade us, writers often use **logical appeals** that appeal to our sense of reason. Different types of logical appeals include facts and statistics. Writers also use **emotional appeals** to persuade us by affecting our feelings. Anecdotes (personal stories) and loaded words (words that suggest strong feelings) are two kinds of emotional appeals. As you read, ask yourself whether your opinion is being shaped by logical appeals, emotional appeals, or both.

READING SKILLS FOCUS: EVALUATING EVIDENCE

Before you accept people's opinions and conclusions, you need to make sure they are supported by good evidence. To **evaluate evidence**, ask yourself these questions: Have the writers presented *enough* evidence? Are they relying too much on emotional appeals? Does the evidence *directly support* the points? What other kinds of evidence could provide stronger support?

SELECTION VOCABULARY

criticism (KRIHT UH SIHZ UHM) *n.*: unfavorable remarks.
I agreed with my friend's criticism; I thought the movie was terrible.

circumstance (SUR KUHM STANS) *n.*: fact or condition that affects a situation, action, or event.
Finding my wallet was a fortunate circumstance.

yearning (YUR NIHNG) *n.*: feeling of wanting something badly.
John has had a yearning for a bicycle all year.

WORD STUDY

DIRECTIONS: Fill in each blank with the correct word from the selection vocabulary above to complete the passage.

Despite (1) _____ from many people, Oprah Winfrey succeeded in opening a school for girls in South Africa. In an ABC news report, Winfrey explains how she considers being poor simply a (2) _____ — a fact that can be overcome by a (3) _____ for education and a bright future.

Reading Standard 2.6
Determine the adequacy and appropriateness of the evidence for an author's conclusions.

OPRAH TALKS ABOUT HER SOUTH AFRICAN "DREAMGIRLS"

ABC News Report

© Fani Mahunts;/Images24

In South Africa on Tuesday, the curtain for the Oprah Winfrey Leadership Academy for Girls parted for 152 girls in ankle socks.

They bring a history of so much suffering and so much hope for the future.

"You want dream girls? Take a look at these," said Oprah Winfrey, who made good on her pledge six years ago to Nelson Mandela to build the school. **A**

Half the population of South Africa lives in poverty, a quarter of the people have HIV, and there is an epidemic of
10 violence among girls.

Still, for some in the country, Winfrey's school, with its amazing theater, beautiful library and African art everywhere, seems "too much."

Critics inside and outside the country have asked, in a land with this kind of poverty, how can you spend more than $40 million on one school? **B**

"I did love that the minister of education for this entire country stood up and said, 'I'm going to address the criticism.

A READ AND DISCUSS

Comprehension

What have you learned so far about the Oprah Winfrey Leadership Academy for Girls?

B READING FOCUS

At this point in the report, what kind of **logical appeals** have been presented to you?

_____

_____

_____

_____

_____

_____

_____

"Oprah Talks About Her South African 'Dreamgirls'" from *ABC News* Web site, accessed October 1, 2007, at http://abcnews.go.com/GMA/Story?id=2767103&page=1&CMP=OTC-RSSFeeds 0312. Copyright © 2007 by **ABC News**. Reproduced by permission of the copyright holder.

It is difficult to guess the meaning of the word *irrepressible* by only using context clues. Instead, think about **word families**, or related words. *Repress* is part of the word *irrepressible*. *Repress* means "keep down." The word part *ir*–usually means "not." Using these clues, write a definition for *irrepressible*. Check your answer using a dictionary.

_____

_____

_____

B **READ AND DISCUSS**

Comprehension

What is Losego thinking here?

Is it too much? No, it isn't,'" Winfrey said in an exclusive inter-
20 view with Diane Sawyer for "Good Morning America."

Winfrey said she got resistance from the very beginning,
even from the school's architects.

"The resistance was too much," Winfrey said. "'What are
you doing? What do they need all that room for? Why does a girl
need all that closet space when she has no clothes?' That's what
they first said to me."

"And my idea was to understand, yes, you come from
nothing, but oh, what a something you will become, if given the
opportunity," Winfrey said.

30 Most of the girls who were admitted to the school have
come from very little—no running water, no electricity, many of
them studying by candlelight.

They are still the best in their class.

At Tuesday's opening ceremony, one irrepressible girl named
Losego said, "I went to a lot of effort to come to this school." A

Diamonds and Dreams

Winfrey, who will stay very involved with the school and
even teach leadership classes, said she believed the future was
unimaginably bright for all of the girls.

"Somebody asked me, what do I think will happen or what
40 do I imagine for them. I don't. I don't imagine. . . . I can't imagine
what it's like to have a miracle like this. It's just a miracle,"
Winfrey said.

And the girls already have big dreams. Losego had a
suggested question for Winfrey: "What did you do with your
first million?" B

Winfrey dressed up for the school's opening ceremony,
diamonds and all. The girls had seen them in pictures, and
Winfrey said she had worn them as a signal that this was an
important celebration.

50 "One of the things that's very important for me is for the girls
to be proud of themselves and to be proud of the way they look

© Denis Farell/AP Photo

and where they come from, and a lot of them in the beginning were very embarrassed about being poor," Winfrey said.

When Winfrey asked some of the girls why they wanted to come to the school, many said they wanted to take care of their families.

"And some of them would say, 'I want to come to this school because I am a poor girl,' and then they would drop their heads," Winfrey said. "I was a poor girl, too. So there's no shame in being
60   a poor girl because being poor is just a circumstance. It's not who you are. It's not what can be possible for you." **C**

The school's curriculum and standards of behavior are high. This is a school for leaders, Winfrey says.

"I said to the girls, 'I'm going to take care of you. I'm going to do everything in my power to make sure you now have a good life and the best opportunity to go to the best schools in the world so when you leave this school you will choose universities all over the world,'" she said. **D**

A Responsibility to Her New Daughters

One question that has been asked of Winfrey is why not build
70   a school like this in the United States?

C READ AND DISCUSS

Comprehension
What did you find out about the girls attending the academy? **Follow-up:** What does Oprah think about the girls?

D READING FOCUS

In this section of the article, Oprah states that the girls at her school have a bright future. What **evidence** do Oprah and the writer provide to support this statement? Is the evidence persuasive?

_____

_____

_____

_____

_____

_____

_____

_____

_____

_____

_____

_____

_____

_____

_____

_____

B READING FOCUS

Why do you think the author chose to end the report with this quotation? Is this quotation an example of a **logical appeal** or an **emotional appeal**? Explain your answer.

_____

_____

_____

_____

_____

_____

_____

_____

_____

"What is different about this country is that there is this sort of desperate yearning to know better and do better that you just don't have in the United States," she said. **A** "You don't have it because the opportunity's always been there."

The parents of the South African girls are also grateful for the opportunity.

"And I don't know a South African mother or father who didn't understand what a value, what a gift, what an opportunity an education is," Winfrey said.

80   Winfrey admits that putting such a big stake into this school and these girls is a huge responsibility.

"It's not just about using your money wisely and making the best investment possible by investing in the future of young girls, but now I have a lot of responsibility," she said. "I feel it."

Winfrey has vowed to care for the new students at her school as if they were her own daughters.

"I said to the mothers, the family members, the aunts, the grannies—because most of these girls have lost their families, their parents—I said to them, 'Your daughters are now my

90   daughters and I promise you I'm going to take care of your daughters. I promise you.'" **B**

Applying Your Skills

Oprah Talks About Her South African "Dreamgirls"

VOCABULARY DEVELOPMENT

DIRECTIONS: Create flashcards like the ones below and write the definition for each vocabulary word on each card. Then, write a sentence that correctly uses each word.

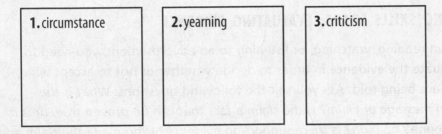

1. circumstance

2. yearning

3. criticism

INFORMATIONAL TEXT FOCUS: LOGICAL AND EMOTIONAL APPEALS

DIRECTIONS: On a separate sheet of paper, explain whether each of the following examples is a **logical appeal** or an **emotional appeal**.

1. "You want dreamgirls? Take a look at these."

2. Most of the girls . . . have come from very little—no running water, no electricity.

3. Half the population of South Africa lives in poverty.

READING SKILLS FOCUS: EVALUATING EVIDENCE

DIRECTIONS: Copy the chart below onto a separate sheet of paper. Fill in the blank boxes with **evidence** from the article that supports the statement below. Make sure the evidence you choose provides strong and direct support for the statement!

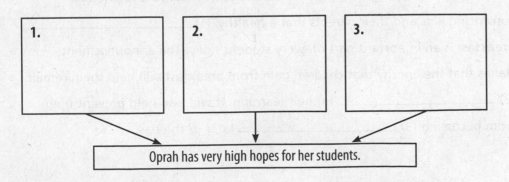

1.

2.

3.

Oprah has very high hopes for her students.

Reading Standard 2.6 Determine the adequacy and appropriateness of the evidence for an author's conclusions.

Oprah Talks About Her South African "Dreamgirls" **237**

Preparing to Read

Start the Day Right!

INFORMATIONAL TEXT FOCUS: PERSUASIVE TECHNIQUES

Persuasive techniques are the ways writers and marketers use language or images to get you to believe or do something. Persuasive techniques include **logical appeals**, which rely on hard evidence and reasons to support an opinion, and **emotional appeals**, which target the feelings of the audience. Many emotional appeals include **loaded words**—words with very positive or very negative connotations, or suggested meanings.

READING SKILLS FOCUS: EVALUATING EVIDENCE

When reading, watching, or listening to an advertisement, you need to **evaluate** the **evidence** in order to decide whether or not to accept what you are being told. Ask yourself the following questions: *What is the main message or claim? Is the claim a fact that can be proven true, or is it someone's opinion? Is there supporting evidence? Who made the claim and why? Who is the intended audience? Is the message using logical appeals or emotional appeals? What am I asked to do or believe?*

SELECTION VOCABULARY

engaged (EHN GAYJD) *adj.:* busy and interested; absorbed in something.
> *She was engaged in her lab experiment and didn't have time to talk.*

nutritious (NOO TRIHSH UHS) *adj.:* full of nourishment; healthful.
> *A piece of fruit is more nutritious than a cookie.*

irritable (IHR UH TUH BUHL) *adj.:* in a bad mood; short-tempered.
> *When I'm tired, I'm irritable and no fun to be around.*

WORD STUDY

DIRECTIONS: Fill in each blank with the correct term from the vocabulary list above to complete the passage.

"Start the Day Right" is a public service announcement focused on convincing kids and their parents that a healthy, (1) _____ breakfast is an important part of every student's day. The announcement claims that the energy that children gain from breakfast will help them remain (2) _____ in their learning. It will also help prevent them from becoming (3) _____ later in the day.

Reading Standard 2.6 Determine the adequacy and appropriateness of the evidence for an author's conclusions.

Reading Standard 2.8 Note instances of unsupported inferences, fallacious reasoning, persuasion, and propaganda in text.

BACKGROUND

A storyboard is a series of sketches and directions that show what scenes will be shown in an advertisement before the ad is actually filmed. The following storyboard describes a public service announcement that is promoting breakfast for kids.

STORYBOARD

CAMPAIGN: START THE DAY RIGHT!

FOR: Health For Kids and Other Important People

TV: 30-second spot

Read with a Purpose
Read this storyboard to decide if the televised public service announcement it represents would convince you that eating breakfast is important.

VIDEO
Camera opens on sunlit class-room with middle school students at desks. Most of them seem engaged, listening to a teacher at the front of the room, out of frame. The camera starts to focus on one boy, who looks like he is about to fall asleep. Ⓐ

AUDIO
Announcer: Every morning, in every classroom in America, students come to school without having eaten a nutritious breakfast. At most, they've eaten empty calories—sugary, fatty junk foods. Maybe they haven't eaten anything at all. The result? They're tired, irritable, unable to concentrate in class. Ⓑ

Ⓐ **VOCABULARY**

Selection Vocabulary
What are most of the children in the first sketch doing to look *engaged*? How is the boy in the middle showing that he is not *engaged* in what the teacher is saying?

_____

_____

_____

_____

_____

_____

_____

_____

_____

Ⓑ **READING FOCUS**

Circle all of the **loaded words** that you see in this audio introduction.

A (READ AND DISCUSS)

Comprehension

What is going on in this classroom?

B (LANGUAGE COACH)

Poor is an example of a word with **multiple,** or many, **meanings**. Think about the different definitions for *poor*. Which definition is used in this sentence?

_____

_____

_____

C (READING FOCUS)

Is this part of the advertisement a **logical appeal** or an **emotional appeal**? Explain your answer.

_____

_____

_____

_____

_____

_____

_____

_____

D (READ AND DISCUSS)

Comprehension

How does this new information add to what we know about eating a healthy breakfast?

VIDEO

Boy puts his head on his desk. His classmate looks over and pokes him in the arm. He looks up, a bit dazed, and realizes he is in class and should be taking notes. He shakes his head as if to wake himself, blinks his eyes a few times, and fights to stay awake. **A**

AUDIO

Announcer: Scientific studies show that the eating habits kids learn when they're young will affect them all their lives. Poor nutrition during the school years can lead to a variety of health problems in adulthood—everything from low energy and obesity to diabetes and heart disease. **B C**

VIDEO

Camera shows same boy at kitchen table the next morning with his parents and infant brother. The boy and his parents are eating cereal; a banana is on the table.

AUDIO

Announcer: You wouldn't let them go out the door without their homework—don't let them go out the door without a good breakfast. No matter how rushed you are, there's always a way to fit in a nutritious breakfast—for every member of the family. For some handy tips on how to create healthy on-the-go break-fasts, visit our Web site, Health for Kids and Other Important People, at www.hkoip.org. **D**

Read with a Purpose

How effective was this public service announcement in changing—or supporting—the way you think about eating breakfast in the morning?

_____

Preparing to Read

Shine-n-Grow: Hair Repair That Really Works!

INFORMATIONAL TEXT FOCUS: FALLACIOUS REASONING

It is important to look for **fallacious reasoning**, or faulty reasoning, when reading advertisements. Unlike **logical reasoning**, which supports an idea with facts and evidence (things that can be proved), fallacious reasoning uses no supporting facts.

READING SKILLS FOCUS: EVALUATING EVIDENCE

As you read a persuasive text, you need to evaluate or judge the evidence presented. Watch out for fallacious reasoning! There are three types of fallacious reasoning:

- **Hasty generalizations:** These are broad conclusions that are not backed up by much experience. They typically include words like *all*, *always*, *every*, and *never*. Example: "I ate a bad hamburger at a diner once. Hamburgers at all diners are horrible."

- **Circular reasoning:** This reasoning says the same thing over and over, in slightly different ways. Example: "This bicycle is the best because no other bikes are as good. It's better than any other bike."

- **Only-cause fallacies:** These present a situation as if it has only one cause, or the wrong cause. Example: "We played better after we got our new uniforms. Those uniforms are going to make us winners!"

SELECTION VOCABULARY

guarantee (GAR UHN TEE) *v.:* promise or assure.
We guarantee that you'll be satisfied with this product.

unique (YOO NEEK) *adj.:* one of a kind; rare or special.
Our hair formula is unique—no one else has it.

WORD STUDY

DIRECTIONS: Fill in each blank with the correct term from the vocabulary list above to complete the passage.

The following advertisement introduces the reader to what the manufacturer claims is a (1) _____ shampoo, one that does something no other shampoo can do. Want hair that is always long and shiny? The marketing professionals behind the advertisement (2) _____ that Shine-n-Grow is the best shampoo for you.

Reading Standard 2.8
Note instances of unsupported inferences, fallacious reasoning, persuasion, and propaganda in text.

A LANGUAGE COACH

Loaded words carry strong emotional connotations, or suggestions. Circle three loaded words in the first paragraph. Then write at least one synonym (word with a similar meaning) for each loaded word.

_____

_____

_____

B READ AND DISCUSS

Comprehension

What is the purpose of this advertisement?

C VOCABULARY

Selection Vocabulary

The word *unique* is used to describe Shine-n-Grow's "combination of vitamins, minerals and hair-growth ingredients." Why do you think it is important for some customers that their shampoo is *unique*?

_____

_____

_____

_____

_____

_____

_____

_____

_____

SHINE-N-GROW:
Hair Repair That Really Works!

Read with a Purpose

Read this newspaper advertisement to see if you believe the claims it makes.

Have you ever suffered at the hands of a barber or careless hair stylist who cut your hair much shorter than you wanted? Have you ever envied your friends who have long hair? Now you no longer have to wait for weeks, months, or even years for your hair to grow back the way you want it to. With SHINE-N-GROW shampoo, your hair can grow faster than you ever dreamed possible. We guarantee that in no time at all, you can achieve the look everyone wants: a full head of hair that's long, healthy, and shiny. **A B**

SHINE-N-GROW shampoo contains a unique combination of vitamins, minerals, and hair-growth ingredients that

- directly provide nutrients to each strand of hair to help it grow
- wash away dullness and replace it with shine
- bring life back to dry or damaged hair **C**

SHINE-N-GROW research scientists have discovered a combination of natural ingredients that helps hair grow faster. Studies have shown that the average person's hair

© Allana Wesley White/Corbis

Shine-n-Grow: Hair Repair That Really Works! **613**

D VOCABULARY

Academic Vocabulary

Does the photo on this page provide any facts or evidence that help to support the advertisement's claims? *Conclude*, or make a judgment about, why this photo is included.

_____

_____

_____

_____

_____

Describe one type of **fallacious reasoning** that is being used in this paragraph. What facts and evidence are missing?

_____

_____

_____

_____

_____

_____

_____

B READING FOCUS

What kind of **fallacious reasoning** is this customer using?

_____

_____

C READ AND DISCUSS

Comprehension

How do "secret" formulas and happy customers influence your thinking about this product?

---

grows at a rate of one-fourth to one-half inch or less per month. A study was conducted to determine the effects of using the SHINE-N-GROW formula. The results were amazing! Test subjects reported hair growth of up to **five inches in three months!** (See our Web site for results.)

Bacteria and dirty oils slow down hair growth. SHINE-N-GROW's natural ingredients kill bacteria, making it easier for hair to grow through the scalp. Thanks to our secret combination of ingredients, the cleansing value of the shampoo is far superior to that of any other products on the market. Customers who use SHINE-N-GROW just once never go back to their old brands. You'll love SHINE-N-GROW, too. **A**

People who use SHINE-N-GROW shampoo have reported that their hair has grown faster and has been cleaner, shinier, and easier to manage. Happy customers agree that their hair feels better after it's been washed. "I just feel more confident," one customer said, "and I've been getting more dates ever since I started using your shampoo." **B**

SHINE-N-GROW is the only shampoo that actually speeds up hair growth while it makes your hair smooth, shiny, and spectacular! Using SHINE-N-GROW guarantees what no other shampoo can: that you'll always have long, shiny hair.

"My hair has never been so long before in my life. I've tried everything, but nothing has worked as well as Shine-n-Grow to make my hair long and clean."
—Susan Steinberg, actress, Brooklyn, New York

"My boyfriend mentioned the shine in my hair the first time I used Shine-n-Grow. He really noticed how it helped my dry and damaged hair. "
—Christine Martinez, nurse, Tucson, Arizona

"My last haircut was way too short, so I tried Shine-n-Grow, and now my hair is long again—and clean! Finally my hair looks the way I like it."
—Roger Canter, accountant, Los Angeles, California

Learn more about SHINE-N-GROW on our Web site at www.shine-n-grow.com, and download a coupon for **15% off** your first purchase! SHINE-N-GROW is available now at better drugstores and supermarkets. **C**

Read with a Purpose Explain why you would—or would not—rush out to buy Shine-n-Grow for your hair.

Brain Breeze

INFORMATIONAL TEXT FOCUS: PROPAGANDA

Propaganda is an extreme type of persuasion that relies on appeals to an audience's emotions rather than logic.

READING SKILLS FOCUS: ANALYZING AN AUTHOR'S PURPOSE

Analyze the author's **purpose**, or reason, for using each technique. What feelings is the author trying to stir up in you? There are five common types of propaganda:

Type of Propaganda	How It Works	Example
Bandwagon appeal	tells you that everyone else is doing something	"Everyone is wearing GoGo jeans this year."
Stereotype	judges someone by a group they belong to	"Politicians can never be trusted."
Name-calling	uses loaded words to create negative feelings	"Silly tree-huggers want to protect the park."
Snob appeal	sends a message that only "special" people appreciate a product	"People with high standards, like you, drink Clear Water."
Testimonial	uses recommendations by celebrities who are not experts	"Grammy-winning singer Jag Smith loves Shiny toothpaste."

SELECTION VOCABULARY

concentration (KAHN SUHN TRAY SHUHN) *n.:* focused attention.
> *A good night's sleep helps improve my concentration.*

enhance (EHN HANS) *v.:* increase; improve.
> *Practicing helps to enhance my piano playing skills.*

complexity (KUHM PLEHK SUH TEE) *n.:* complication; difficulty.
> *The complexity of the rules made the game hard to learn.*

WORD STUDY

DIRECTIONS: Fill in each blank with the correct term from the vocabulary list above.

Identifying propaganda in an advertisement requires (1) _____.

Marketing professionals are aware of the (2) _____ of convincing

people to buy something, so they often (3) _____ an advertisement

with emotional appeals.

Reading Standard 2.8
Note instances of unsupported inferences, fallacious reasoning, persuasion, and propaganda in text.

ADVERTISEMENT

Read with a Purpose
Read this magazine ad to find out what "Brain Breeze" is and does—
and to see if you're influenced by this advertiser's techniques.

BRAIN BREEZE

The FIRST and ONLY Mental Power Booster that fits in the palm of your hand!

**Uses music and air movement to sharpen your
concentration and clear your clouded mind!**

- **Study with No Effort!**
- **Finish Big Projects While You Relax!**
- **Feel Smarter and Less Stressed!**

Do you have a big test coming up? a big project to complete? Are you so wound up with stress that you can't think straight? Time to open the windows of your mind and let *BRAIN BREEZE*® in!

Businesspeople, students, the guy next door—*everyone* is looking for that competitive mental edge. Now, getting that edge is easier than you ever thought possible with *BRAIN BREEZE*—the Mental Power Booster that uses scientifically researched music and the physics of airflow to make you more productive, less stressed—and smarter! A

BRAIN BREEZE is an amazing new technological breakthrough! It increases your concentration and keeps you at the top of your mental game while it soothes and relaxes you with a patented combination of moving air and music—all delivered from a device no larger than the palm of your hand! It's so easy to use that even the laziest couch potato can benefit.

BRAIN BREEZE, the Mental Power Booster, was developed by Professor Gary Fract of the University of Hadleyburg and was tested for effectiveness at Right Idea Labs, a scientific center for the advancement of learning. Researchers found that in a study of one hundred people aged sixteen to sixty-nine, scores were raised an average of five points overall on tests of memory and problem-solving ability among those who used *BRAIN BREEZE*. B

Brain Breeze **617**

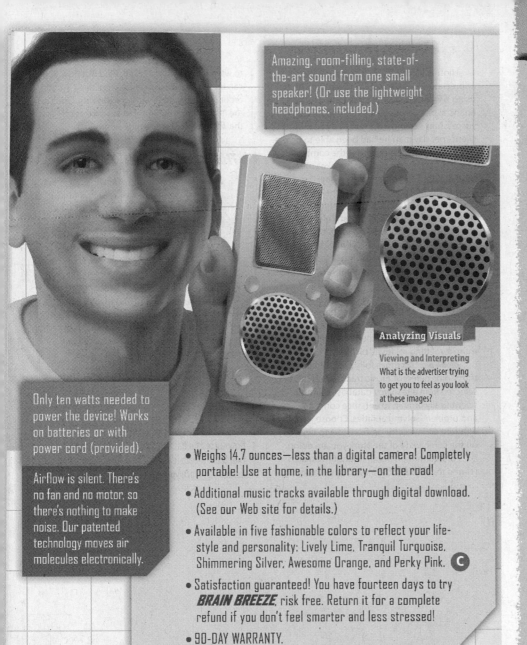

Amazing, room-filling, state-of-the-art sound from one small speaker! (Or use the lightweight headphones, included.)

Analyzing Visuals

Viewing and Interpreting
What is the advertiser trying to get you to feel as you look at these images?

Only ten watts needed to power the device! Works on batteries or with power cord (provided).

Airflow is silent. There's no fan and no motor, so there's nothing to make noise. Our patented technology moves air molecules electronically.

- Weighs 14.7 ounces—less than a digital camera! Completely portable! Use at home, in the library—on the road!
- Additional music tracks available through digital download. (See our Web site for details.)
- Available in five fashionable colors to reflect your life-style and personality: Lively Lime, Tranquil Turquoise, Shimmering Silver, Awesome Orange, and Perky Pink. **C**
- Satisfaction guaranteed! You have fourteen days to try **BRAIN BREEZE**, risk free. Return it for a complete refund if you don't feel smarter and less stressed!
- 90-DAY WARRANTY.

C (VOCABULARY)

Word Study

Lively, tranquil, shimmering, awesome, and *perky* are all descriptive adjectives. Why do you think these adjectives were added to the names of colors?

_____

_____

_____

_____

_____

_____

_____

High-achieving, high-income people appreciate the *BRAIN BREEZE* advantage. After using *BRAIN BREEZE* at his desk for two weeks, financial planner Tony Fine realized he was successfully dealing with two to three more clients per day than he had been able to before. "There's just something about the combination of the music and the airflow. It makes me feel more focused and organized," he says, "and I was already the most organized person I know." **A**

Emery Goodson, a medical student, had been using *BRAIN BREEZE* for just a week when she realized that studying no longer felt like a chore. "*BRAIN BREEZE* is like this little treat I give myself," she says. "Now studying is something I look forward to. It's like a mental vacation, except I'm working!" **B**

Even elderly people can enjoy the benefits of *BRAIN BREEZE.* Studies have shown that using *BRAIN BREEZE* at least once a week can vastly improve people's memories. Imagine—no more forgetting relatives' birthdays!

BRAIN BREEZE comes fully programmed with thirty-nine different music tracks, each carefully selected from a research database of music scientifically proven to enhance concentration and problem-solving abilities. Choose from five different airflow settings, from low to high, based on the complexity of the work you are doing.

For information about scientific research related to *BRAIN BREEZE,* all you have to do is go to www.gobrainbreeze.com. Find out how you can try *BRAIN BREEZE* on a free trial basis—and order one today for overnight delivery. Don't be the last person you know to act on this offer. Get the *BRAIN BREEZE* advantage now! **C**

THE DEVELOPMENT TEAM

Professor Gary Fract, *specialist in cognitive advancement, is author of* The Effect of Music on Developing Thought, *a major study of the cognitive changes that individuals undergo when listening to certain types of music. Right Idea Labs pioneered important studies in the effects of indoor airflow on mental focus by testing thousands of participants in the Idea Room, a model controlled environment.*

Find out more about *BRAIN BREEZE* at www.gobrainbreeze.com.

Read with a Purpose
How successful has this ad been in convincing you that Brain Breeze is worth a try? What details in the ad helped you reach your conclusion?

Applying Your Skills

Start the Day Right, Shine-n-Grow, *and* Brain Breeze

VOCABULARY DEVELOPMENT

DIRECTIONS: Write four sentences that could be used in an advertisement, each correctly using a different vocabulary word from the Word Box.

Word Box

engaged

nutritious

irritable

guarantee

unique

concentration

enhance

complexity

1. _____

_____

2. _____

_____

3. _____

_____

4. _____

_____

INFORMATIONAL TEXT FOCUS: PERSUASIVE TECHNIQUES, FALLACIOUS REASONING, AND PROPAGANDA

DIRECTIONS: In the table, answer each question for all three advertisements.

Question	Start the Day Right	Shine-n-Grow	Brain Breeze
1. What is the main message, or claim?			
2. Is the claim a fact with evidence, or an opinion?			
3. Who made the message and who is the intended audience?			
4. Are logical or emotional appeals used?			
5. What is the audience asked to do or believe?			

Reading Standard 2.6 Determine the adequacy and appropriateness of the evidence for an author's conclusions.

Reading Standard 2.8 Note instances of unsupported inferences, fallacious reasoning, persuasion, and propaganda in text.

Skills Review

Chapter 7

VOCABULARY REVIEW

DIRECTIONS: Match each selection and academic vocabulary word in the left column with its definition in the right column. Write the letter of the correct definition on the blank.

_____ 1. yearning

_____ 2. guarantee

_____ 3. enhance

_____ 4. isolated

_____ 5. criticism

_____ 6. conclude

_____ 7. irritable

_____ 8. circumstance

_____ 9. authority

_____ 10. unique

_____ 11. dispute

_____ 12. complexity

_____ 13. nutritious

_____ 14. declined

_____ 15. crucial

_____ 16. concentration

_____ 17. engaged

a. very important

b. argument

c. condition that affects a situation

d. like no other

e. judgment

f. absorbed in something

g. focused attention

h. promise

i. went down

j. feeling of wanting

k. improve

l. complication

m. alone

n. healthful

o. decide or determine

p. short-tempered

q. respected, knowledgeable person

Skills Review

Chapter 7

LANGUAGE COACH

Advertisements often use **loaded words**—words that carry strong emotional connotations, or suggestions. For example, the word *guarantee* makes us feel a degree of trust. A guarantee suggests that we will get what we have been promised.

DIRECTIONS: Explain the **connotations** of each of the words in the table below, and then identify the kind of advertisement in which you might find the words. The first row of the table has been filled in for you.

Loaded Word	Connotations	Advertisement
eternal	lasting, will always be around	advertisement for wedding rings
1. unique		
2. satisfaction		
3. gorgeous		
4. delicious		

WRITING ACTIVITY

DIRECTIONS: Suppose that you have been hired to write a persuasive advertisement about the importance of exercise. Write a paragraph-long advertisement that uses both **logical appeals** and **emotional appeals**. Remember to include reasons and evidence for the logical appeals, and loaded words for the emotional appeals.

_____

_____

_____

_____

_____

Chapter

8

Literary Criticism

Object (Le Dejeuner en fourrure) (1936) by
Meret Oppenheim. Fur-covered cup, saucer and spoon/
Digital Image © The Museum of Modern Art/Licensed by
SCALA/Art Resource, NY. The Museum of Modern Art,
New York, NY, U.S.A. © 2008 Artists Rights Society (ARS),
New York/ProLitteris, Zürich, Switzerland.

Literary and Academic Vocabulary for Chapter 8

_____

contrived (KUHN TRYVD) *adj.:* unnatural; artificial.

A story with a contrived plot has too many unrealistic events to be believable.

correspond (KAWR UH SPOND) *v.:* be similar to.

In believable stories, characters' reactions correspond to those of real people.

insight (IHN SYT) *n.:* clear understanding of the true nature of something.

Stories can give you insight into many parts of life.

perceive (PUHR SEEV) *v.:* grasp mentally; understand.

You might perceive a character through his or her actions.

credibility (KREHD IH BIHL IH TEE) *n.:* believability.

The speaker lost all credibility after we discovered that he had been using a fake accent.

The Dog of Pompeii

by Louis Untermeyer

LITERARY SKILLS FOCUS: CREDIBILITY AND HISTORICAL FICTION

"The Dog of Pompeii" is **historical fiction**. In historical fiction, the author mixes fantasy—fictional characters and events—with facts about actual historical events. Writers of historical fiction face a great challenge. The fictional parts of their stories must seem as real and **credible**, or believable, as the historical events.

READING SKILLS FOCUS: READING FOR DETAILS

Writers use **details**, or specific information about characters, places, and events, to turn their ideas into stories. The details in a story are mainly responsible for making the characters and plot seem credible and realistic. As you read "The Dog of Pompeii," decide whether the details in the story are credible, based on what you know. Make notes on a chart like the one below. One example is given.

Detail about plot or character	Credible or not credible?	Why? (based on my own knowledge)
Bimbo takes total care of Tito.	Credible	Dogs can assist blind people.

Reading Standard 3.8
Critique the credibility of characterization and the degree to which a plot is contrived or realistic (e.g., compare use of fact and fantasy in historical fiction).

Vocabulary Development

The Dog of Pompeii

SELECTION VOCABULARY

ambitious (AM BIHSH UHS) *adj.:* eager to succeed or to achieve something.
    The ambitious citizens of Pompeii hoped to make their city famous.

proverb (PRAHV UHRB) *n.:* short traditional saying that expresses a truth.
    "Haste makes waste" is a proverb.

revived (RIH VYVD) *v.:* awakened; brought back to life.
    The splash of water revived him, and he opened his eyes.

WORD STUDY

DIRECTIONS: Determine if the italicized vocabulary words are being used correctly in the sentences below. Write "Yes" if the vocabulary word is used correctly in the sentence. If the vocabulary word is used incorrectly, write "No" and rewrite the sentence in order to make it correct.

1. An *ambitious* student never studies for tests or does any homework.

_____

_____

2. "Where there's a will, there's a way" is my favorite *proverb.* _____

_____

_____

3. Fred felt sleepy until his morning walk *revived* him. _____

_____

_____

THE DOG OF POMPEII

by Louis Untermeyer

> **BACKGROUND**
>
> "The Dog of Pompeii" is historical fiction. Louis Untermeyer weaves together a fictional story and actual historical events. The story's setting is Pompeii, an ancient Roman city that was buried by a volcanic eruption in A.D. 79.

A **LITERARY FOCUS**

What facts about Pompeii are included in this paragraph? Do you think these facts help make the setting for this story **credible**? Why or why not?

_____

_____

_____

_____

_____

_____

_____

_____

_____

_____

_____

Tito and his dog Bimbo lived (if you could call it living) under the wall where it joined the inner gate. They really didn't live there; they just slept there. They lived anywhere. Pompeii was one of the gayest of the old Latin towns, but although Tito was never an unhappy boy, he was not exactly a merry one. The streets were always lively with shining chariots and bright red trappings; the open-air theaters rocked with laughing crowds; sham[1] battles and athletic sports were free for the asking in the great stadium. Once a year the

10 Caesar[2] visited the pleasure city and the fireworks lasted for days; the sacrifices[3] in the forum were better than a show. **A**

But Tito saw none of these things. He was blind—had been blind from birth. He was known to everyone in the poorer quarters. But no one could say how old he was, no one remembered his parents, no one could tell where he came from. Bimbo was another mystery. As long as people could remember seeing Tito—about twelve or thirteen

---

1. **sham:** make-believe.
2. **Caesar** (SEE ZUHR): Roman emperor. The word *Caesar* comes from the family name of Julius Caesar, a great general who ruled Rome as dictator from 49 to 44 B.C.
3. **sacrifices:** offerings (especially of slaughtered animals) to the gods.

---

years—they had seen Bimbo. Bimbo had never left his side.
He was not only dog but nurse, pillow, playmate, mother, and
20 father to Tito. **B**

Did I say Bimbo never left his master? (Perhaps I had
better say comrade, for if anyone was the master, it was
Bimbo.) **C** I was wrong. Bimbo did trust Tito alone exactly
three times a day. It was a fixed routine, a custom understood
between boy and dog since the beginning of their friendship,
and the way it worked was this: Early in the morning, shortly
after dawn, while Tito was still dreaming, Bimbo would
disappear. When Tito awoke, Bimbo would be sitting quietly
at his side, his ears cocked, his stump of a tail tapping the
30 ground, and a fresh-baked bread—more like a large round
roll—at his feet. Tito would stretch himself; Bimbo would
yawn; then they would breakfast. At noon, no matter where
they happened to be, Bimbo would put his paw on Tito's knee
and the two of them would return to the inner gate. Tito would

B READ AND DISCUSS

Comprehension
What is the author telling you
in these opening paragraphs?

C READING FOCUS

What **details** tell you about
the relationship between
Tito and Bimbo?

_____

_____

_____

_____

_____

_____

_____

How does this add to what
we already know about Tito
and Bimbo?

Is the routine that Tito and
Bimbo follow every day an
example of historical facts
or fantasy? Does it seem
credible? Explain.

_____

_____

_____

_____

_____

_____

_____

_____

_____

_____

_____

_____

_____

_____

_____

_____

curl up in the corner (almost like a dog) and go to sleep, while
Bimbo, looking quite important (almost like a boy), would
disappear again. In half an hour he'd be back with their lunch.
Sometimes it would be a piece of fruit or a scrap of meat, often
it was nothing but a dry crust. But sometimes there would be
40   one of those flat rich cakes, sprinkled with raisins and sugar,
that Tito liked so much. At suppertime the same thing happened, although there was a little less of everything, for things
were hard to snatch in the evening, with the streets full of
people. Besides, Bimbo didn't approve of too much food before
going to sleep. A heavy supper made boys too restless and dogs
too stodgy[4]—and it was the business of a dog to sleep lightly
with one ear open and muscles ready for action. A B

But, whether there was much or little, hot or cold, fresh
or dry, food was always there. Tito never asked where it came
50   from and Bimbo never told him. There was plenty of rainwater
in the hollows of soft stones; the old egg woman at the corner
sometimes gave him a cupful of strong goat's milk; in the grape
season the fat winemaker let him have drippings of the mild
juice. So there was no danger of going hungry or thirsty. There
was plenty of everything in Pompeii—if you knew where to find
it—and if you had a dog like Bimbo.

As I said before, Tito was not the merriest boy in Pompeii.
He could not romp with the other youngsters and play "hare
and hounds" and "I spy" and "follow your master" and "ball
60   against the building" and "jackstones" and "kings and robbers"
with them. But that did not make him sorry for himself. If he
could not see the sights that delighted the lads of Pompeii, he
could hear and smell things they never noticed. He could really
see more with his ears and nose than they could with their eyes.
When he and Bimbo went out walking, he knew just where they
were going and exactly what was happening.

"Ah," he'd sniff and say, as they passed a handsome villa,[5]
"Glaucus Pansa is giving a grand dinner tonight. They're going

---

4. **stodgy** (STAH JEE): heavy and slow in movement.
5. **villa**: large house.

to have three kinds of bread, and roast pigling, and stuffed goose,
70 and a great stew—I think bear stew—and a fig pie." And Bimbo
would note that this would be a good place to visit tomorrow. **C**

Or, "H'm," Tito would murmur, half through his lips, half
through his nostrils. "The wife of Marcus Lucretius is expecting
her mother. She's shaking out every piece of goods in the house;
she's going to use the best clothes—the ones she's been keeping
in pine needles and camphor[6]—and there's an extra girl in the
kitchen. Come, Bimbo, let's get out of the dust!"

Or, as they passed a small but elegant dwelling opposite the
public baths, "Too bad! The tragic poet is ill again. It must be
80 a bad fever this time, for they're trying smoke fumes instead of
medicine. Whew! I'm glad I'm not a tragic poet!" **D**

Or, as they neared the forum, "Mm-m! What good things
they have in the macellum[7] today!" (It really was a sort of
butcher-grocer-marketplace, but Tito didn't know any better.
He called it the macellum.) "Dates from Africa, and salt oysters
from sea caves, and cuttlefish, and new honey, and sweet onions,
and—ugh!—water-buffalo steaks. Come, let's see what's what in
the forum." And Bimbo, just as curious as his comrade, hurried
on. Being a dog, he trusted his ears and nose (like Tito) more
90 than his eyes. And so the two of them entered the center of
Pompeii. **E**

The forum was the part of the town to which everybody
came at least once during the day. It was the central square, and
everything happened here. There were no private houses; all
was public—the chief temples, the gold and red bazaars, the silk
shops, the town hall, the booths belonging to the weavers and
jewel merchants, the wealthy woolen market, the shrine of the
household gods. Everything glittered here. The buildings looked
as if they were new—which, in a sense, they were. The earth-
100 quake of twelve years ago had brought down all the old structures
and, since the citizens of Pompeii were ambitious to rival Naples

---

6. **camphor** (KAM FUHR): strong-smelling substance used to keep moths
away from clothing. Camphor is still used for this purpose.
7. **macellum** (MUH SEH LUHM): market, especially a meat market.

C READ AND DISCUSS

Comprehension

Why does Bimbo think this
villa would be a good place
to visit tomorrow?

D VOCABULARY

Academic Vocabulary

What *insight,* or clear
understanding, do you gain
about Tito in lines 57–81?

_____

_____

_____

_____

_____

_____

E READING FOCUS

Underline the **details** in this
paragraph that help make
Tito a credible, or realistic,
character.

_____

_____

_____

_____

_____

_____

and even Rome, they had seized the opportunity to rebuild the whole town. **A** And they had done it all within a dozen years. There was scarcely a building that was older than Tito. **B**

Tito had heard a great deal about the earthquake, though being about a year old at the time, he could scarcely remember it. This particular quake had been a light one—as earthquakes go. The weaker houses had been shaken down, parts of the outworn wall had been wrecked; but there was little loss of life, and the brilliant new Pompeii had taken the place of the old. No one knew what caused these earthquakes. Records showed they had happened in the neighborhood since the beginning of time. Sailors said that it was to teach the lazy city folk a lesson and make them appreciate those who risked the dangers of the sea to bring them luxuries and protect their town from invaders. The priests said that the gods took this way of showing their anger to those who refused to worship properly and who failed to bring enough sacrifices to the altars and (though they didn't say it in so many words) presents to the priests. The tradesmen said that the foreign merchants had corrupted the ground and it was no longer safe to traffic in imported goods that came from strange places and carried a curse with them. Everyone had a different explanation and everyone's explanation was louder and sillier than his neighbor's. **C**

They were talking about it this afternoon as Tito and Bimbo came out of the side street into the public square. The forum was the favorite promenade[8] for rich and poor. What with the priests arguing with the politicians, servants doing the day's shopping, tradesmen crying their wares, women displaying the latest fashions from Greece and Egypt, children playing hide-and-seek among the marble columns, knots of soldiers, sailors, peasants from the provinces[9]—to say nothing of those who merely came to lounge and look on—the square was crowded to its last inch. His ears even more than his nose guided Tito to the place where the talk was loudest. It was in

---

8. **promenade** (PRAHM UH NAYD): public place where people stroll.
9. **provinces** (PRAH VINS EHZH): places far from the capital, under Roman control.

front of the shrine of the household gods that, naturally enough, the householders were arguing.

"I tell you," rumbled a voice which Tito recognized as bath master Rufus's, "there won't be another earthquake in my lifetime or yours. There may be a tremble or two, but earthquakes, like lightnings, never strike twice in the same place." **D**

"Do they not?" asked a thin voice Tito had never heard. It had a high, sharp ring to it and Tito knew it as the accent of a stranger. "How about the two towns of Sicily that have been ruined three times within fifteen years by the eruptions of Mount Etna? And were they not warned? And does that column of smoke above Vesuvius mean nothing?"

"That?" Tito could hear the grunt with which one question answered another. "That's always there. We use it for our weather guide. When the smoke stands up straight, we know we'll have fair weather; when it flattens out, it's sure to be foggy; when it drifts to the east—"

"Yes, yes," cut in the edged voice. "I've heard about your mountain barometer.[10] But the column of smoke seems hundreds of feet higher than usual and it's thickening and spreading like a shadowy tree. They say in Naples—"

"Oh, Naples!" Tito knew this voice by the little squeak that went with it. It was Attilio the cameo cutter.[11] "They talk while we suffer. Little help we got from them last time. Naples commits the crimes and Pompeii pays the price. It's become a proverb with us. **E** Let them mind their own business."

"Yes," grumbled Rufus, "and others', too."

"Very well, my confident friends," responded the thin voice, which now sounded curiously flat. "We also have a proverb—and it is this: *Those who will not listen to men must be taught by the gods.*

---

10. **barometer** (BUH RAHM UH TUHR): instrument for measuring atmospheric pressure. Barometers are used in forecasting changes in the weather.
11. **cameo cutter:** artist who carves small, delicate pictures on gems or shells.

D READ AND DISCUSS

Comprehension

What is going on at the forum? What didn't people at this time understand about earthquakes?

E VOCABULARY

Selection Vocabulary

A *proverb* is a short traditional saying that expresses a truth. Underline the proverb that the people of Pompeii use to describe their relationship with Naples. What do you think this proverb means?

Do you think the story's plot is **credible**, or believable, so far? If so, why? If not, what parts are unbelievable?

_____
_____
_____
_____
_____
_____
_____

What **details** do you notice about the celebrations of ancient Pompeii? How are they similar to or different from your culture's celebrations?

_____
_____
_____
_____
_____
_____
_____
_____
_____
_____

I say no more. But I leave a last warning. Remember the holy ones. Look to your temples. And when the smoke tree above Vesuvius grows to the shape of an umbrella pine, look to your lives."

Tito could hear the air whistle as the speaker drew his toga about him, and the quick shuffle of feet told him the stranger had gone. **A**

"Now what," said the cameo cutter, "did he mean by that?"

"I wonder," grunted Rufus. "I wonder."

Tito wondered, too. And Bimbo, his head at a thoughtful angle, looked as if he had been doing a heavy piece of pondering. By nightfall the argument had been forgotten. If the smoke had increased, no one saw it in the dark. Besides, it was Caesar's birthday and the town was in a holiday mood. Tito and Bimbo were among the merrymakers, dodging the charioteers who shouted at them. A dozen times they almost upset baskets of sweets and jars of Vesuvian wine, said to be as fiery as the streams inside the volcano, and a dozen times they were cursed and cuffed. But Tito never missed his footing. He was thankful for his keen ears and quick instinct—most thankful of all for Bimbo.

They visited the uncovered theater, and though Tito could not see the faces of the actors, he could follow the play better than most of the audience, for their attention wandered—they were distracted by the scenery, the costumes, the byplay,[12] even by themselves—while Tito's whole attention was centered in what he heard. Then to the city walls, where the people of Pompeii watched a mock naval battle in which the city was attacked by the sea and saved after thousands of flaming arrows had been exchanged and countless colored torches had been burned. Though the thrill of flaring ships and lighted skies was lost to Tito, the shouts and cheers excited him as much as any, and he cried out with the loudest of them. **B**

The next morning there were two of the beloved raisin-and-sugar cakes for his breakfast. Bimbo was unusually active and

---

12. **byplay:** action taking place outside the main action of a play.

thumped his bit of a tail until Tito was afraid he would wear it out. The boy could not imagine whether Bimbo was urging him to some sort of game or was trying to tell him something. After a while, he ceased to notice Bimbo. He felt drowsy. Last night's late hours had tired him. Besides, there was a heavy mist in the air—no, a thick fog rather than a mist—a fog that got into his throat and scraped it and made him cough. He walked as far as the marine gate[13] to get a breath of the sea. But the blanket

210 of haze had spread all over the bay and even the salt air seemed smoky.

He went to bed before dusk and slept. But he did not sleep well. He had too many dreams—dreams of ships lurching in the forum, of losing his way in a screaming crowd, of armies marching across his chest, of being pulled over every rough pavement of Pompeii.

He woke early. Or, rather, he was pulled awake. Bimbo was doing the pulling. The dog had dragged Tito to his feet and was urging the boy along. Somewhere. Where, Tito did not know. His

220 feet stumbled uncertainly; he was still half asleep. For a while he noticed nothing except the fact that it was hard to breathe. The air was hot. And heavy. So heavy that he could taste it. The air, it seemed, had turned to powder—a warm powder that stung his nostrils and burned his sightless eyes.

Then he began to hear sounds. Peculiar sounds. Like animals under the earth. Hissings and groanings and muffled cries that a dying creature might make dislodging the stones of his underground cave. There was no doubt of it now. The noises came from underneath. He not only heard them—he could feel

230 them. The earth twitched; the twitching changed to an uneven shrugging of the soil. Then, as Bimbo half pulled, half coaxed him across, the ground jerked away from his feet and he was thrown against a stone fountain. **C**

The water—hot water—splashing in his face revived him. **D** He got to his feet, Bimbo steadying him, helping him

---

13. **marine gate:** gate in a city wall leading to the sea.

C (READ AND DISCUSS)

Comprehension
What is causing these peculiar sounds? **Follow-up:** Why is Bimbo reacting like this?

D (LANGUAGE COACH)

The word *revived* comes from the Latin prefix *re-*, which means "again," and the Latin root word *vivere*, which means "to live." Based on this origin, it is clear that revived means "brought back to life." People aren't the only ones that can be revived, however. Look up other meanings of the word *revive*. Then, name one nonliving thing that might be revived. Explain how the term makes sense in such a context.

on again. The noises grew louder; they came closer. The cries were even more animal-like than before, but now they came from human throats. A few people, quicker of foot and more hurried by fear, began to rush by. A family or two—then a section—then, it seemed, an army broken out of bounds. Tito, bewildered though he was, could recognize Rufus as he bellowed past him, like a water buffalo gone mad. Time was lost in a nightmare.

It was then the crashing began. First a sharp crackling, like a monstrous snapping of twigs; then a roar like the fall of a whole forest of trees; then an explosion that tore earth and sky. The heavens, though Tito could not see them, were shot through with continual flickerings of fire. Lightnings above were answered by thunders beneath. A house fell. Then another. By a miracle the two companions had escaped the dangerous side streets and were in a more open space. It was the forum. They rested here awhile—how long, he did not know. **A**

Tito had no idea of the time of day. He could feel it was black—an unnatural blackness. Something inside—perhaps the lack of breakfast and lunch—told him it was past noon. But it didn't matter. Nothing seemed to matter. He was getting drowsy, too drowsy to walk. But walk he must. He knew it. And Bimbo knew it; the sharp tugs told him so. Nor was it a moment too soon. The sacred ground of the forum was safe no longer. It was beginning to rock, then to pitch, then to split. As they stumbled out of the square, the earth wriggled like a caught snake and all the columns of the temple of Jupiter[14] came down. It was the end of the world—or so it seemed. To walk was not enough now. They must run. Tito was too frightened to know what to do or where to go. He had lost all sense of direction. He started to go back to the inner gate; but Bimbo, straining his back to the last inch, almost pulled his clothes from him. What did the creature want? Had the dog gone mad? **B**

Then suddenly he understood. Bimbo was telling him the way out—urging him there. The sea gate, of course. The

---

14. **Jupiter:** the supreme god in the religion of the Romans.

sea gate—and then the sea. Far from falling buildings, heaving ground. He turned, Bimbo guiding him across open pits and dangerous pools of bubbling mud, away from buildings that had caught fire and were dropping their burning beams. Tito could no longer tell whether the noises were made by the shrieking sky or the agonized people. He and Bimbo ran on—the only silent beings in a howling world.

New dangers threatened. All Pompeii seemed to be thronging toward the marine gate and, squeezing among the crowds,
280 there was the chance of being trampled to death. **C** But the chance had to be taken. It was growing harder and harder to breathe. What air there was choked him. It was all dust now—dust and pebbles, pebbles as large as beans. They fell on his head, his hands—pumice stones from the black heart of Vesuvius. The mountain was turning itself inside out. Tito remembered a phrase that the stranger had said in the forum two days ago: "Those who will not listen to men must be taught by the gods." The people of Pompeii had refused to heed the warnings; they were being taught now—if it was not too late. **D**

290 Suddenly it seemed too late for Tito. The red-hot ashes blistered his skin, the stinging vapors tore his throat. He could not go on. He staggered toward a small tree at the side of the road and fell. In a moment Bimbo was beside him. He coaxed. But there was no answer. He licked Tito's hands, his feet, his face. The boy did not stir. Then Bimbo did the last thing he could—the last thing he wanted to do. He bit his comrade, bit him deep in the arm. With a cry of pain, Tito jumped to his feet, Bimbo after him. Tito was in despair, but Bimbo was determined. He drove the boy on, snapping at his heels, worrying his way through
300 the crowd, barking, baring his teeth, heedless of kicks or falling stones. Sick with hunger, half dead with fear and sulfur fumes, Tito pounded on, pursued by Bimbo. How long, he never knew. At last he staggered through the marine gate and felt soft sand under him. Then Tito fainted . . . . **E**

C READING FOCUS

What **details** does the author use to show what it was like in Pompeii at the time the volcano erupted? How do these details make the story more credible?

_____

_____

_____

_____

D READ AND DISCUSS

Comprehension
What are you picturing from the words in the last few paragraphs?

E READ AND DISCUSS

Comprehension
What is Bimbo up to?

Some people rescue Tito after he faints, but Bimbo is left behind. Does this seem **credible** to you? Why or why not?

_____

_____

_____

_____

_____

_____

_____

_____

_____

_____

B READ AND DISCUSS

Comprehension

If Tito was saved, why does it say, "he could not be comforted"?

Someone was dashing seawater over him. Someone was carrying him toward a boat.

"Bimbo," he called. And then louder, "Bimbo!" But Bimbo had disappeared.

Voices jarred against each other. "Hurry—hurry!" "To the
310 boats!" "Can't you see the child's frightened and starving!" "He keeps calling for someone!" "Poor boy, he's out of his mind." "Here, child—take this!"

They tucked him in among them. The oarlocks creaked; the oars splashed; the boat rode over toppling waves. Tito was safe. But he wept continually. **A**

"Bimbo!" he wailed. "Bimbo! Bimbo!"

He could not be comforted. **B**

Eighteen hundred years passed. Scientists were restoring the ancient city; excavators[15] were working their way through
320 the stones and trash that had buried the entire town. Much had already been brought to light—statues, bronze instruments, bright mosaics,[16] household articles; even delicate paintings had

---

15. **excavators** (EHKS KUH VAYT UHRZ): diggers; here, archaeologists.
16. **mosaics** (MO ZAY IHKS): pictures or designs made by inlaying small bits of stone, glass, tile, or other materials in mortar.

© Scala/Art Resource

C READ AND DISCUSS

Comprehension
What solution can you offer to the mystery of why the dog would want a raisin cake at such a dangerous time?

been preserved by the fall of ashes that had taken over two thousand lives. Columns were dug up, and the forum was beginning to emerge.

It was at a place where the ruins lay deepest that the director paused.

"Come here," he called to his assistant. "I think we've discovered the remains of a building in good shape. Here are four huge
330   millstones that were most likely turned by slaves or mules—and here is a whole wall standing with shelves inside it. Why! It must have been a bakery. And here's a curious thing. What do you think I found under this heap where the ashes were thickest? The skeleton of a dog!"

"Amazing!" gasped his assistant. "You'd think a dog would have had sense enough to run away at the time. And what is that flat thing he's holding between his teeth? It can't be a stone."

"No. It must have come from this bakery. You know it looks to me like some sort of cake hardened with the years. And, bless
340   me, if those little black pebbles aren't raisins. A raisin cake almost two thousand years old! I wonder what made him want it at such a moment."

"I wonder," murmured the assistant.

The Dog of Pompeii

USE A CHARACTER EVALUATION CHART

DIRECTIONS: In the chart below, answer the questions about Tito's character to determine if he is a **credible** character. Give examples from the story to support your answers. Finally, discuss with a partner whether or not you each found Tito's character to be credible.

Tito	
Question	**Answers with examples from the story**
Does the character have both strengths and weaknesses? Explain.	1.
Does the character talk and act as a real person would? Explain.	2.
Does the character grow and change as a result of story events? Explain.	3.

Applying Your Skills

The Dog of Pompeii

VOCABULARY DEVELOPMENT

DIRECTIONS: Complete the exercise below by deciding if the pairs of words are synonyms (words with similar definitions) or antonyms (words with opposite definitions). Write your answers on the blank lines.

1. ambitious and unmotivated: _____

2. proverb and saying: _____

3. revived and killed: _____

LITERARY SKILLS FOCUS: CREDIBILITY AND HISTORICAL FICTION

DIRECTIONS: Answer the questions below about this **historical fiction**.

1. In the story, Mount Vesuvius erupted shortly after the warnings of the man from Naples. How does the author mix fact and fantasy in this scene?

_____

_____

2. Did you find it believable that Mount Vesuvius erupted shortly after these warnings, or was it a little too far-fetched?

_____

_____

READING SKILLS FOCUS: READING FOR DETAILS

DIRECTIONS: Complete the chart below with **details** from the text that support each statement.

Statement	Details
Tito depends on Bimbo's help to survive.	1.
Bimbo saves Tito's life when Mount Vesuvius erupts.	2.

Reading Standard 3.8
Critique the credibility of characterization and the degree to which a plot is contrived or realistic (e.g., compare use of fact and fantasy in historical fiction).

Skills Review

Chapter 8

VOCABULARY REVIEW

DIRECTIONS: Choose the correct selection or academic vocabulary word from the Word Box to complete each sentence below.

Word Box

- ambitious
- contrived
- correspond
- insight
- perceive
- proverb
- revived

1. Aisha is a very _____ young girl with a strong desire to be a great success.

2. The copy of the painting was made so well that Darren was unable to _____ any differences between the copy and the original.

3. Omar's excuse was so _____ that no one believed him.

4. Professor Nara likes to give us a little wisdom at the end of each class, so he shares with us a _____ before we leave.

5. The bicycle parts I have don't seem to _____ with the very different ones shown in the instruction manual.

6. After ten years, someone finally _____ Ivanna's favorite Broadway musical.

7. Cassandra's great _____ about history always makes her essays interesting to read.

Chapter 8

LANGUAGE COACH

DIRECTIONS: Many states in the United States were named after people or words from other languages. Sometimes the exact **origins** of their names are unclear, so occasionally people disagree on where state names actually came from. Below is a list of actual and possible origins for the names of five different states. Write the states named after these origins on the blanks. If you have trouble, look carefully at the spelling of the italicized words and try to say them out loud to hear how they are pronounced.

1. from the Spanish word *montaña*, meaning "mountain"

   _____

2. named for King *Louis* XIV of France _____

3. named after a river whose name came from the Dakota word *minisota*, which has to do with white water _____

4. named after a river whose name came from the Iroquois word *oheo*, meaning "beautiful" _____

5. named after a French mountain range called *Verts Monts*

   _____

ORAL LANGUAGE ACTIVITY

DIRECTIONS: With a partner, have a discussion about "The Dog of Pompeii." Are the characters in the story **credible**? Even though they are from another time period, can you relate to the characters in the story? What details about the characters make you feel the way you do?

Index of Authors and Titles

All Aboard With Thomas Garrett 215
All Summer in a Day. 4
Avi 202

Bakowski, Barbara. 131
Blanca Flor. 42
Bradbury, Ray. 4
Brain Breeze 246

CAVE Online 137
Day, Nancy 13
Dog of Pompeii, The. 256

Freedman, Russell. 194

Gold Cadillac, The. 110

Iraqi Treasures Hunted 131

John Henry. 156

King of Mazy May, The. 28
Kolata, Gina 227
Kroll, Jennifer 127

La Bamba. 98
Land I Lost, from The 172
London, Jack 28

Making It Up As We Go:
    The History Of Storytelling. 127
Miller, Alice P 215
Mysterious Mr. Lincoln, The 194

Ode to Mi Gato. 162

Olympic Glory: Victories in History 65
Oprah Talks About Her South
    African "Dreamgirls" 233
Paulsen, Gary 184
Pet Adoption Application. 89

Quang Nhuong, Huynh 172

Seuss, Dr. (Theodor Geisel) 148
Shine-n-Grow: Hair Repair
    That Really Works! 242
Sneetches, The 148
Soto, Gary 98, 162
Start the Day Right. 239
Storm 184
Surprising Secret to a Long Life:
    Stay in School, A 227

Ta-Na-E-Ka 76
Taylor, Mildred D. 110

Untermeyer, Louis 256

Vigil, Angel 42

Wartime Mistakes, Peacetime
    Apologies 13
What a Character: Iwao
    Takamoto and His Toons 17
What Do Fish Have to Do
    With Anything?. 202
Whitebird, Mary. 76